Flavors of Tuscany

Lunigiana

Apennine Mountains

Garfagnana

Carrara

Pistoia

Prato

Mugello

Lucca

Montecatini
Terme

Florence

Tiber River

Pisa

Arno River

Casentino

Montevarchi

Livorno

Ligurian

San Gimignano

Chianti

Arezzo
val di
Chiana

Cortona

Cecina

Siena

Camucia

Bolgheri

Murlo

Montefollonico

Lake
Trasimeno

Pienza

Montepulciano

Montalcino

Chiusi

Sea

Monte
Amiata

Grosseto

Scansano

Pitigliano

Tuscany

ITALY

Tuscany

Rome

Martie Holmer 1997

Flavors of Tuscany

TRADITIONAL RECIPES FROM
THE TUSCAN COUNTRYSIDE

Nancy Harmon Jenkins

BROADWAY BOOKS
New York

FOR SARA AND NICHOLAS

In celebration of smoky fires,

olive oil for breakfast,

porcini from the gold mine,

and long, long lunches

under the chestnut tree

LIBRARY OF CONGRESS CATALOGING-IN-PUBLICATION DATA
Jenkins, Nancy Harmon.
Flavors of Tuscany : traditional recipes from the Tuscan countryside / Nancy Harmon Jenkins.
p.   cm.
Includes bibliographical references (p. 275) and index.
ISBN 0-7679-0144-4
1. Cookery, Italian—Tuscan style.   I. Title.
TX723.2.T86J46   1998
641.5945′5—dc21   97-2215   CIP

FIRST EDITION

Designed by Vertigo Design

98 99 00 01 02 10 9 8 7 6 5 4 3 2 1

Contents

Introduction
my tuscany

A little more than a quarter of a century ago, I found a home for my young family in the Tuscan countryside, on a high spur of land in the steep mountains east of Cortona where the watershed divides the upper Tiber valley from the Val di Chiana to the west. We called this place "the farm," though for years nothing at all had been cultivated on our stony twenty-five acres. The farmhouse, built of local rock and mortared with mud, was, to put it kindly, tumbling down, its tiled roof pocked with holes that let rain into the attic, and its walls, in places a meter thick, veering decisively away from true. Stinging nettles and bramble bushes smothered a pergola of half-wild grapevines along the entrance wall, and the owner, a veterinarian from Rome best known for tending Elizabeth Taylor's pet dogs, swiped the brush with a stout stick to frighten away vipers as he led us up to the door. It would take years to make the place habitable.

This is a book about Tuscan country cooking, not about how I bought a crumbling wreck and, with money, luck, time, and the aid of colorful locals, turned it into something of which Martha Stewart herself would be proud. Nonetheless, it helps, I think, to know something of my viewpoint, and that viewpoint is firmly centered in the prospect from this hilltop, which looks up and down a broad valley of terraced fields and open tracts, pasture and steep woodland, liberally scattered with farmsteads, some of which belong to rusticating foreigners like ourselves who come for a time and leave again, but most still the abodes of people whose parents and grandparents dwelt on the same or similar demesnes.

Superficially at least, the landscape of the valley looks much the same as it must have in the grandparents' day, but there have been monumental changes in recent years, not least of which was the arrival of electricity, which brought with it television, and of the telephone, which ended forever the enforced isolation of country people. What we called the "valley telegraph" used to operate by calling out from farm to farm, and certain people were renowned for the strength of their voices. Nowadays they shout into telephones instead.

If the land looks the same, the agriculture has changed utterly with the introduction of cash crops, mainly tobacco and sunflowers, in place of the more traditional wheat, vines, and olives. Many of the old walled terraces, built with great care and maintained over centuries, have been ploughed into broad fields, while farm ponds have been excavated to provide water for thirsty tobacco. Now, my neighbors tell me, we are beginning to see a dearth of groundwater, the inevitable result of too great a demand. In the end, new forms of communication and new modes of production to service distant markets mean that what had been small, isolated, but almost entirely self-sufficient communities of farming families, living much as did their ancestors going back many generations, have in the last quarter of the century become drawn irrevocably into a voracious world economy and a world culture that has no roots here in this countryside and no need or desire to comprehend this way of life.

In no way is our valley unique. All over the world, traditional societies are changing, mostly in ways that thoughtful people consider harmful and even pernicious. In Italy it's an old story by now. Rapid industrialization after World War II sucked people off the farms and into urban factories. At the same time, land reform broke up large estates and, in a curious consequence, made it difficult for individual families to survive on reduced holdings. It was one reason why we were able to buy Pian d'Arcello so cheaply—no Italian wanted it, least of all the veterinarian from Rome whose family had owned the small and unproductive estate of great house and four or five minifarms for generations but who could no longer find the *mano d'opera,* the manpower, to work the land. (Most certainly he was not going to do it himself.)

Of course human life is not static. Change occurs. But in the past, change took place slowly, over generations, with time to absorb new products, ideas, processes, and make them part of a culture. It's the rapidity of change today that's most striking, and the fact that nothing seems to stick for long. Everything is ephemeral. One minute they're all dancing the lambada, the next minute it's the macarena instead. And they're no different from their fellow dancers all over the world, following the beat of a distant band.

Food habits, fortunately, die hardest of all, especially in a culture like Italy's where food is taken seriously as an important—no, *the* important—factor in family and community life. Many of the dishes and the ways of preparing them described in this book are old and honored traditions, especially foods associated with feasts, seasons of the year, or regional identities—like buccellato, the sweet bread from Lucca, or the rice fritters made for San Giuseppe (St. Joseph), the mid-Lenten feast on March 19, or castagnaccio, the chestnut flour cake made in the fall after the chestnuts *(castagne)* have been harvested and dried.

Others, however, are new, or new twists on old preparations. My neighbor Maura Antolini, a splendid cook, makes bomboloni, a sort of fried cream puff, for martedì grasso (Shrove Tuesday), the last day of Carnival before Lent begins. But instead of filling the puffs with a tricky Tuscan version of crema inglese, Maura uses Nutella, the commercial chocolate spread that comes in a jar.

Maura also makes tiramisù, a sweet that has become as popular in Italy as it has in America. Why tiramisù, a dessert unknown to her mother or her mother-in-law? It is, explains Arezzo food historian Pier Francesco Greci, a simpler version of Tuscan zuppa inglese, made with mascarpone instead of old-fashioned homemade crema inglese. With mascarpone, a soft cow's milk cheese once obtainable only around Milano but now widely available all over Italy, it's possible not just for Maura but for cooks throughout the country to have their tiramisù and eat it too. And a little bit of Tuscan tradition dies, while a pan-Italian tradition comes into being.

Last Easter I had lunch, as I often do, at the Antolinis' farm. We were twenty-four in number, including cousins, aunts, uncles, in-laws, and grandparents, and at our end of the long table we had been talking about organic ("biological") farming when the salad came around. As usual at that time of the year, it was a true insalata del bosco, an immense and tasty collection of wild greens that had been patiently harvested by Maura's mother-in-law Mita, who combed the still wintry fields and terraces, accompanied by her three-year-old granddaughter, for an assortment of delicacies that would have brought a fortune in a fancy Florentine *fruttivendolo*.

"Now *that's* what you call biological," said Arnaldo, Maura's husband and Mita's son, who remains forever skeptical about my plans to turn the whole valley into a vast organic vegetable garden. "Are you crazy?" said his older sister sharply. "With all the crap you put on your tobacco fields, you think there's anything biological left around here?" Meanwhile, I caught a glimpse of something deep blue purple amid the greens—violets, shy little blossoms sprinkled liberally throughout the salad. In all my years in Tuscany, I'd never seen flowers served in a salad—in fact I'd never seen flowers at all except in vases, or deep-fried zucchini blossoms. I thought I was at Chez Panisse. "Violets?"

"Oh," said Mita cheerfully, "I saw it last week on the television. It seemed like a good idea."

This book is not about violet blossoms in salads or tiramisù. Rather, it's a look at what I think of and what has been presented to me as traditional Tuscan country food. In that sense, it's not eternal, not fixed in time, and in fact if I had been able to write this book in 1950 or 1900, it would have been quite different. But not entirely, because while some things change (violets become part of an insalata del bosco and Nutella fills the bombolone at Carnival), certain things persist, most of all the basic tastes of the Tuscans themselves, the underlying themes, of which there are so many variations, both seasonal and geographical.

The food of Tuscany is (like the people) simple, direct, honest, and straightforward. This is a masculine cuisine, not subtle or elusive but full of flavors that declare themselves at the first taste: rich green olive oil, pungent herbs like rosemary and sage, the full-bodied flavors of sheep's milk cheeses, of game and wild mushrooms roasted over the embers of a hardwood fire. Food like this is good all year round, but for me it has a special appeal in autumn and winter when white mists slide up from the river valleys, drift across bare, rolling wheat fields, and wrap around steep hillsides where vines and olive trees stand dormant in the cold. It's the time for gather-round-the-fire food, robust and full of country tastes, perfect for cold winter nights.

Blessed with one of Italy's most agreeable climates, Tuscany is best known as a summer haven, but to many of us who know and love this ancient region, there is a special quality to winter. The land itself, subdued and tranquil, lies at rest, and little country hill towns like Cortona and Gaiole, so exuberant in summer, are still and peaceful, the fragrance of woodsmoke permeating the air and the low winter light barely reaching their cobbled streets.

Perhaps I love winter so much here because it's the most Tuscan of seasons. The great number of foreigners has departed, leaving only us diehards and the Tuscans themselves to brave what can be truly hideous weather, especially in a stone farmhouse without central heating. But summer, I'd be the first to admit, has its admirable qualities too, even when the season is devoted to hard but productive work as farm families labor to grow, harvest, and preserve the fruits of fields and gardens, orchards, and vineyards in ways not too different from those their forebears used, going back over generations. It's true that harvest combines have taken the place of old-fashioned scythes for cutting grain, and much of the grain itself has been replaced over the years by more lucrative tobacco, even in my isolated mountain community, which cherishes an ironic affection for the most labor-intensive farming. Instead of hand-chopping, Mita purées the gorgeous big red tomatoes from her garden in an electric machine, but she still bottles and preserves them the old way, in a boiling water bath over an open fire, then stores the jars for winter sauces. And the country people hereabouts still search the steep hillsides after late summer showers, gathering wild porcini mushrooms to slice and dry in the sun; farm children still wait like little birds, mouths wide, beneath the fig trees for the rich purple fruit to crack and drop, heavy with sweet ripeness; and farmers like Arnaldo still hover with increasing anxiety over fat grape clusters as they swell and start to color on overarching vines.

For all its labors, summer brings considerable rewards, not least to farmhouse tables. The season is liberally sprinkled with events that demand festive recognition, whether it's the successful completion of a harvest (wheat, tobacco, grapes, olives, each in due course, stretching from midsummer nearly to Christmas); a wedding scheduled for the few weeks of freedom between the *trebbiatura* (threshing) of the wheat and the *vendemmia* (harvesting) of the grapes, or the grand August 15 festival, the Feast of the Assumption, when all of Italy closes down for a month's vacation.

Except of course for farmers, the Antolinis like to remind me: Who could take a holiday when there are pigs and chickens, ducks and rabbits, always to be fed?

Even farmers have their festive celebrations, however, entire days given over to the pleasures of eating and drinking, when huge extended families, up to second cousins twice removed and including anyone who lent a hand or the use of a hammer during the course of the previous year, gather together at long tables set under a pergola of grapevines or along the shady wall of the house. Often Sunday alone is enough to justify a festa at the Antolinis' big stone farmhouse with its sweeping view of the upper Tiber valley and the distant chain of the Appenines.

Hospitality on such a Homeric scale is what continues to bind together Tuscan villages like Teverina, where family pride is displayed in the simple abundance of a table on which almost all the dishes represent the fruits of the family's own labor. My neighbors' wheat provides the flour for their bread and pasta, the brilliance of their own tomatoes colors the red pasta sauce, their chickens and rabbits, fragrant with rosemary and sage that grow outside the farmhouse door and roasted in the wood-fired bread oven, grace the center of the table, while green beans, zucchini, salad greens, and scarlet and gold peppers, gathered that morning from the *orto,* the family vegetable garden, provide the colorful trimmings, the contorni, of the meal.

There's an elemental joy in these occasions that comes as much from their special nature as it does from the quality of the food and the company. And there's a studied ease that derives from the predictable nature of the feast—the crostini, the pasta, the roasted meats, prepared and served just as they've always been, and the dry cake at the end to dip in vin santo, the Tuscan countryman's prized dessert wine. Admittedly, women like Mita, her daughters Fernanda and Anna, and her daughter-in-law Maura, do most of the work, but familiar work like this is not difficult. Moreover, it's work done with pleasure and pride—pleasure from the company and the quick, gossipy exchange with other women, pride when a young bride, perhaps, wins instant acclaim with a new take on a favorite tradition.

Meanwhile the menfolk relax in the shade of the ancient chestnut tree, smoking and sampling wine, talking of crops and weather, tobacco prices, and the state of the government, as if what they said could make any difference at all. The feasting goes on for hours, from the first platter of crostini, when everyone crowds around the long tables, to the final crumbs of *ciambella,* a ring-shaped sponge cake, and tiramisù, the dessert that has conquered old-fashioned zuppa inglese.

Late in the day, after the last chicken bone has been tossed to the dogs, the last bit of sauce scraped from the plate with a crust of bread, someone, usually Arnaldo, a talented musician, pushes back from the table and brings out a fisarmonica or piano accordion. Then the old songs and the dancing begin, as homemade grappa and vin santo flow into outstretched glasses, children fall asleep in their mothers' arms, and the moon rises over the mountains.

The agricultural calendar here doesn't vary much from a medieval Book of Hours. Technology may be state-of-the-art, machinery may be hot off the tractor line, but the moon still rules planting and harvest as well as the time to cut fenceposts and rack the wine. Grapevines are still pruned in March and potatoes planted shortly thereafter, olives are still the last harvest of the agricultural year, and hog-butchering and sausage-making are end-of-the-year tasks as they have been ever since Etruscan farmers, forebears of modern-day Tuscans, used that quiet time to age their prosciuttos. Products like these, wine, fresh olive oil, hams, pancetta (unsmoked bacon), and sausages, play starring roles in year-round menus, along with an abundance of other food from farmhouse larders—tomato conserva put up in jars during the summer, plum and fig marmalades, dried chestnuts, white and speckled beans, chick-peas and dried wild funghi porcini, the boletus mushroom so prized by Tuscan cooks.

I think of the plainspoken Tuscans as the Yankees of Italy, which may be one reason why Tuscany appeals so much to rock-ribbed Yankees like me. A Tuscan's highest praise for any comestible, be it food or drink, is to call it *genuino.* The word means genuine, not so much in the sense of real as in the sense of pure and unadulterated. Tuscans, like Yankees, are thrifty in their approach to food (truth is, one of their *favorite* foods is leftovers), and they share a similar passion for beans: Other Italians call them *mangiafagioli,* bean-eaters.

Rosemary and sage are favored seasonings, used in braising or roasting chickens, rabbits, or fresh pork from the slaughtered pig. Wild fennel goes into sausages and dried fennel pollen into pasta sauces, while the crumbled leaves of a wild mint called *nepitella,* similar to pennyroyal, add fragrance to field mushrooms braised in an earthenware tegame. Good green Tuscan extra virgin olive oil is not just a cooking medium but a flavoring or condiment, drizzled over soups and stews, spooned on grilled T-bone steaks (a Tuscan specialty), or poured straight from the bottle onto crusts of toasted bread that have been rubbed with a cut clove of garlic. This is the original, the only (as far as Tuscans are concerned) true bruschetta and it's made only during late autumn and winter when the oil is fresh and new from the *frantoio* or olive mill and still has that raw, peppery, back-of-the-throat kick to it that's truly addictive.

Tuscan bread, crusty, rough-textured, and unsalted, baked in a wood-fired oven, plays the kind of supporting role that is delegated to pasta or rice in other parts of Italy. Bread even becomes an important ingredient in other dishes—as in panzanella, a great summertime salad of tomatoes, basil, onions, and stale bread, or ribollita, Tuscany's world-class way to deal with leftover soup. Ribollita is so simple it's almost banal: The previous day's minestrone is warmed up and stewed with chunks of stale bread to absorb the herbal aromas of this basic, beany, vegetable soup. Then it's served, with a healthy drizzle of aromatic green olive oil, some cracked black pepper, a good sprinkling of crunchy salt, sliced onions, and perhaps *una manciata di pecorino,* a handful of well aged but freshly grated sheep's milk cheese sprinkled over the top. Country bread from a wood-fired oven also makes a sturdy foundation for crostini, slices of stale or toasted bread spread with a paste of chicken livers flavored with capers and anchovies.

Throughout the region, there has been a tremendous and heartwarming revival in recent years of this traditional, rural, farmhouse cuisine. In restaurants like Osteria di Rendola near Montevarchi, Fattoria La Chiusa in Montefollonico south of Siena, Cibrèo in Florence, and La Mora at Ponte a Moriano outside Lucca, talented cooks are turning to the old dishes and the old ways of doing things. In other places, many of them not so well known as those I've mentioned, cooks have never forgotten, never really known another way to cook. The support of traditional cuisine from chefs and restaurateurs like these has also had a profound influence on small, regional producers of high-quality ingredients.

It's not enough, these cooks find, to bring back a splendid dish like zuppa di farro, a zesty soup based on an old-fashioned strain of wheat called farro, or *sugo d'anatra,* a savory duck sauce, traditionally served with pappardelle in Arezzo, or panforte, a Christmas cake from Siena that, like many Tuscan sweets, dates from a time when honey was a luxury, like nuts and candied sweets, available only in monasteries and for the monks' aristocratic patrons.

Cooks with revivalist fervor for dishes like these, and many others, also have to find and develop and work with the farmer who still grows that strain of wheat (Tuscan tradition says it was farro that led the armies of Imperial Rome) and the country woman who raises fat, free-range ducks in her farmyard, along with shepherds who fabricate traditional cheeses, vintners who make wines by traditional methods, and olive growers who harvest and press the olives at precisely the moment for the best and truest flavor in the oil. Out of a movement like this, it's easy to see, a whole nation's cuisine can be reborn.

There are also parts of Tuscany where the old ways never died out. In our mountain valley, many country families still bake bread once a week in masonry ovens built into the walls of old stone farmhouses, and the oil on the table, the wine in the glass, the slice of sweet and salty prosciutto served with a rough carving of bread for a midmorning snack, all come from the family's own production. Their olive groves, their vineyards, their pigs, and their gardens all contribute to the goodness of their table.

You may notice a lot of "on the one hand, on the other hand" in this book. That's because there is precious little agreement from one area to the next, almost from one hearth to the next, about precisely what goes into any particular dish, precisely what a particular ingredient should be like. Some say underripe tomatoes are best for the luscious bread salad called panzanella; others insist that only dead-ripe tomatoes, practically on the verge of spoiling, will do. I was told that the word *zenzero*, meaning ginger, when used in the Chianti district, refers to peperoncini, the little hot red chile peppers that add zing to certain sauces—"This," said my source, "is because ginger was the seasoning used before the introduction of American chiles." Sounds indisputable, yet another equally impeccable authority, from a village south of Greve in the very heart of Chianti, had never heard of such a thing. "Here," the source said, meaning in his own village and its most immediate surroundings, "zenzero means what you call ginger." Yet in my local supermercato, a place for amazing discoveries, little dried hot red chile peppers come in a packet indisputably labeled "zenzeri essiccati," dried gingers.

Italians have a word for this. It's called *campanilismo*, referring to the campanile, the bell tower of the parish church round which everyone collects in times of danger as much as in celebration, whether of a marriage, a christening, or the annual mid-summer *perdono* in the Valdarno, when, along with indulgence for malfeasance in the previous year, thanks are offered for harvest abundance and blessings sought for the year ahead. Nowhere is campanilismo carried to greater lengths than in Siena, where the town itself is divided into seventeen campaniles or contradas, each one racing against the others twice a year in the Palio, a horse race of ritualistic drama and almost unbearable excitement. (In this race, coming in second is more shameful than coming in last, because it signifies that if you were a little more resourceful, you might have been first.) Marrying outside the contrada to which one is born is still something of a disgrace in Siena—better a Florentine than a member of the Aquila (Eagle), say those who were born under the sign of the Worm.

Even the landscape of Tuscany evokes campanilismo, changing dramatically in brief spaces. From the rolling hills of Chianti, deeply forested in parts and interspersed with flourishing vineyards and olive groves, it's but two steps, it seems, to the stark and undulating dunes of the Crete Senese, where, especially after the autumn ploughing when the soil is barren and bleached, the great farmhouses stand like abandoned fortresses amid the arid fields. The *macchia*, a dense and tangled forest of scrub oak, brambles, and broom, fragrant with yellow blossoms in late spring, with the resinous odors of pine and wild herbs at summer's height, exists side-by-side with trim and orderly fields that look as if they flowed from a Perugino canvas. Hill towns like Volterra and Cortona, with forbidding Etruscan walls looking over terraces of olives, seem worlds away from amiable Lucca, its rose red brick walls never broached by enemy fire, or elegant Bolgheri with its receiving line of cypresses leaning like dowagers over the long approach to the town—somewhat dowdy dowagers at that, though celebrated by Giosuè Carducci, the nineteenth-century poet, in a poem every Italian schoolchild is forced to memorize.

The valleys too encourage campanilismo—high, often narrow, and guarded by steep mountains, these are places that may be unfamiliar even to other Tuscans, yet they seem to ring with the events of Tuscan history, with legends, and, a seldom discussed topic, with Tuscan mysticism and superstition: the Mugello, the valley of the Sieve river north and east of Florence, home to artists like Giotto and Fra Angelico, as well as the wellspring of the Medici; the Casentino, along the Upper Arno, dominated by three great medieval monasteries, Vallombrosa, Camaldoli, and La Verna, the last founded by St. Francis and deeply venerated as the site where he received the stigmata; the Garfagnana and Lunigiana, twin valleys north of Lucca and the Ligurian coast, that have been from time immemorial important trade and pilgrimage routes between Rome and the Gallo-Celtic territories beyond the Alps.

People often ask me how old our house is. I can't answer that. I know somewhere there's a stone in the house wall that reads 1784, but I suspect there's been a dwelling place on this spot for as long as humans have inhabited this valley. It's a natural position, after all, easily defensible, with a good source of water nearby, plenty of light for a high mountain valley, and a broad, sunny meadow, good for all kinds of crops, stretching back behind the house. Once, when I had been working in the garden a long time, I looked up and thought I saw an Etruscan crossing at the end of the terrace, heading down toward the stream below the house that eventually flows into the Tiber. But I could have been wrong.

Still, it's not unlikely that all sorts of shades inhabit these spaces—Etruscans, ancient Umbrians, Romans, Lombards, Germans (one of whom was shot out of the sky in 1943 right above our house). Even today when most of the fields are planted to tobacco and sunflowers, no longer the wheat, vines, and olives of tradition, to read this landscape is to learn something of Tuscan history, a history that in its broad outlines is familiar to Americans, possibly better known than that of any other part of Italy except Rome. (Don't we all know the Renaissance, aren't Leonardo and Michelangelo part of our cultural baggage, wouldn't most of us recognize a picture postcard of Pisa's leaning tower?) Yet, the particulars of this history, of time, place, character, the very smell of it, are mysteries only partly elucidated by the landscape.

"La cucina si fa nella storia; non si fa nella geografia," says my friend Roberto, who runs a fine little restaurant called La Solita Zuppa ("the usual soup") in his hometown of Chiusi. "Cuisine is created by history, not by geography." But I don't agree. Cuisine is made of both history *and* geography, and the traditional cuisine of Tuscany, for me at least, is unassailable proof.

The Farmhouse Kitchen

I keep speaking of the Tuscan kitchen as if it were a discrete room, set apart from the rest of the house, as kitchens are in North America even when they're the heart of the home. In the Tuscan farmhouses I know, the kitchen is not just the heart, it *is* the home, almost in its entirety, one large room that extends end to end across the front of the farmhouse. In this room all family activities take place, except for sleeping, giving birth, and dying, and sometimes even those have taken place in the kitchen. Here food is prepared and consumed, both the food of the day and that to be stored for winter; here the family enjoys its social life, guests are received, largesse is dispensed. Even the most casual visitor, a neighbor at midmorning, say, on his way down to the stream to fish, is offered, in an ancient gesture of civility, a sweet biscuit and a glass of wine to dip it in. Here, too, the family television is kept—and kept on, constantly, a flickering background of silly stuff that no one ever seems actually to watch except in the evening.

The kitchen *is* the casa, and to say that a person is *in casa* is to say that he is, yes, in the house, but more specifically in the kitchen and not in one of the adjacent bedrooms or storerooms.

This great room is always on what Europeans call the first floor, meaning the floor above the ground floor, where the animals are stabled, the theory being that the warmth of the animals rises from the stalls to help warm the house in winter. ("Yes," says Mita, who no longer keeps pigs and a mule below the house, "and when the animals shit, the smell rises up too.") Even today, when Tuscans build new houses, they stable their cars on the ground floor and live on the floor above, where they can have a more elevated view of what's going on around them.

On one long wall of the great room, the fireplace provides heat to warm the house and cook the food. Until recently, most of the cooking was done on the hearth, except for when the outside bake oven was fired. Often there might be a little two- or three-burner gas cooktop, and sometimes a *cucina economica,* a wood-fired range with a tiny oven, used as auxiliary heat and to prepare the *pomarola* (tomato sauce) and other canning chores, making blackberry or fig jam, for instance, or cooking down pig parts for *testina,* a head cheese made when the pig was slaughtered.

Hearths are built deep, partly for cooking space but also to allow for benches along either side where the old people sit to keep warm. You can judge a person's age and status in the family by the distance from the fire. Close up and huddled over the embers are the most ancient ones, treated with dignity and given tasks like shelling beans and keeping small children out of the flames. Then come the more active family members, those who keep the fire going, and the farmwife herself who, with the bustle of her life, has no need for a fire to warm her. At night in winter, when the chores were done, the animals bedded down, the supper dishes cleared away, the whole family would settle around the fire for a bit of evening fun called the *veglia,* story-telling, reminiscing, riddle-making, game-playing. Neighbors might come calling, especially on moonlit nights, chestnuts would be roasted in a long-handled pan over the fire, and a jug of wine would be passed around. Nowadays, people watch television instead, and there's less socializing as each person's attention is focussed not on the others but on a distant studio in Rome.

On the opposite wall from the fireplace is the *madia,* an austerely handsome piece of furniture that was as much a focus of family life as the hearth because it was here that the staple food, bread, was prepared. The madia, a chest of considerable size, is handed down over generations, a thing of great beauty, with a design similar to Shaker artifacts in its simplicity. Like Shaker things, too, these are greatly sought after by modern dealers to add a touch of tradition to modern flats in Milano, London, or New York. The bottom of the chest is a double cupboard with all the paraphernalia of bread and pasta making, bowls, big spoons, cheese graters, and so forth; in the top of the madia, under a lid that can be lifted, is the flour bin wherein sits the flour and a lump of dough from the previous baking, concealed under a clean cloth and waiting to be reawakened with more flour and water and kneaded into new life.

It is hard to know whether to speak of these things in the present tense or in the past. Twenty-five years ago, every Tuscan country home could be fit into the description above, but fifteen years ago, even traditional and conservative families like my neighbors were closing off one end of the great room to make a separate kitchen and installing gas ranges and Formica-clad cabinetry in the most up-to-date color combinations.

Part of this was the result of electrification, which made possible a whole range of functions from washing machines to television sets that changed the use of the space. Part of it came about because of the propaganda television itself offered to educate its viewers and train them to be modern consumers. But part of it has to do with deep changes in the nature of families and communities, not just in Tuscan mountain villages but all over the globe. Anthropologists call this a secondary privatization, within the privacy of the family, of certain family functions; sociologists link it to the esteem for the individual that is such a feature of modern life. Nowadays it's hard to find a house with a great room like the one I've described, unless it's in the homes of foreigners (Germans, the British) or Italians from distant cities, trying to re-create in vacation residences something of the style of the traditional Tuscan farmhouse.

Tuscan Ingredients

BREAD

Saltless Tuscan bread is a very special ingredient in many dishes and not easily obtainable unless you make your own. There is a recipe for *pane sciocco,* as it's called, in this book, but if you don't care to make your own, look for a good artisanal bread (fortunately, there are more and more of them in this country), with a dense crumb and a thick, chewy crust, with no added flavors beyond wheat flour, water, and yeast. Even so, I urge you to make pane sciocco if only once to see exactly what Tuscan cooks are dealing with.

FLOUR

Tuscan bakers and pasta-makers use a soft wheat flour that is considerably lower in protein than American all-purpose flour. The King Arthur flour company has an Italian-style flour that is about 9 percent protein, as opposed to the 11.5 percent protein of their unbleached all-purpose flour. When I don't have King Arthur's Italian-style flour, however, I use their unbleached pastry flour, which is also low in protein, blended in a ratio of about 1:3 with their unbleached all-purpose flour.

PASTA

The traditional pasta made in Tuscan farmhouse kitchens is almost always made with a dough of soft wheat flour and eggs—as many eggs as the dough will absorb. The only exception is *pici,* hand-rolled eggless pasta, made only with soft wheat flour and water, from southern Tuscany. But many modern cooks, in Tuscany and through-out Italy, use the excellent commercial brands of eggless durum-wheat pasta available. Among my favorites, to be found in specialty food stores in America, are Martelli, which is made in Tuscany; Rustichella d'Abruzzo; Latini pasta from the Marche; and Benedetto Cavalieri pasta from Puglia. Barilla, the largest-selling Italian pasta, and De Cecco, another good national brand, are also widely available in this country.

CHEESES

Aged Tuscan pecorino cheeses are unaccountably difficult to find in the United States. Even when I do find Pecorino Toscano or Caciotta Toscana (a name used in the United States but rarely found in Tuscany) being sold, it's usually a young, rubbery cheese without a great deal of flavor. In cooking, I substitute Pecorino Sardo, from Sardinia, or Parmigiano-Reggiano; Pecorino Romano is a very different cheese, with a strong, acid flavor that is unacceptable in Tuscan cooking. For eating, your best bet, really, is to go to Tuscany and bring it back yourself.

There are many cheeses called parmesan but only one Parmigiano-Reggiano. It comes in big sixty- to eighty-pound wheels but even when it has been cut into wedges for sale, you'll recognize the distinctive lettering stamped into the hard golden rind. Although it's not Tuscan at all, Parmigiano-Reggiano is used throughout

Italy, one of the few but growing number of food products that are truly national. There is just no substitute for this superb cheese; fortunately, it is widely available in America, from specialty food shops to well-stocked supermarkets.

Most of the ricotta used in Tuscan kitchens is freshly made from the whey left over from making sheep's milk cheeses. Sheep's milk ricotta is difficult to find in this country, but goat's milk ricotta, available by mail order from Paula Lambert's Mozzarella Company, and occasionally from local goat's milk cheese producers, is a fine substitute. Commercially available ricotta is made from cow's milk, and it should be drained in a sieve for thirty minutes or more to rid it of excess liquid.

TOMATOES

The best tomatoes, it goes without saying, come from your own or a neighbor's garden, picked when they're full of ripe, sunny flavors and used immediately or converted into home-canned jars of *pomarola* (see recipe, page 120). Surprisingly, however, when local tomatoes are not in season, a good brand of canned tomatoes, whether whole, crushed, pureed, or in concentrate, makes a fine substitute. Muir Glen organic canned tomatoes from California are my first choice, but Hunt's tomatoes are also very good. Read the list of ingredients—canned tomatoes in any form are best when they're nothing but ripe fruit and a little salt, with no added garlic or other flavors.

To prepare fresh tomatoes for cooking, you'll want to peel and seed them. Simply dip each tomato in rapidly boiling water for about fifteen seconds, after which the skin slips off easily. Slice the tomato in half and gently press the seeds and excess juice out of each half.

PEPERONCINI ROSSI: ZENZERI

Small, dried hot red chile peppers are used in many Tuscan preparations, but discretion is the rule. Mouth-filling hot flavors are not part of the Tuscan repertoire. When in doubt, use less rather than more—you can always add a bit later. Peperoncini rossi is proper Italian for these peppers, but in Tuscany they are often called *zenzeri,* or "gingers," indicating that the flavoring agent once upon a time was probably dried powdered ginger.

ANCHOVIES

Whole salted anchovies can be found in shops in Italian neighborhoods and are much to be preferred over oil-packed anchovy fillets. Buy them in big tins and, after opening, transfer the anchovies to a plastic container. Refrigerated, they'll keep—forever, it seems.

To use salted anchovies, rinse the salt off thoroughly under running water, then strip each fillet away from the central bones. Don't worry if you can't get all the bones out—they'll disintegrate while cooking and in any case provide valuable calcium.

CAPERS

As with anchovies, I much prefer salt-packed capers to the ones packed in brine. Rinse the capers thoroughly in a narrow-mesh strainer to rid them of salt before using.

PANCETTA AND RIGATINO

Two types of salted but unsmoked bacon, well-streaked with lean, *pancetta* (the name most commonly used in the United States) is usually sliced from a roll like a jelly roll; in Tuscany *rigatino* (the name most commonly used there) more often comes in a chunk, like slab bacon. Slab bacon, if it's first blanched briefly in boiling water to rid it of its smoky flavor, makes an acceptable substitute. I've tried substituting salt pork but find most of it too fatty and with a very different flavor.

ODORI (FRESH AND DRIED AROMATICS)

Odori are the aromatics that flavor soups, stews, and sauces, usually incorporated into a dish with the *battuto* or *soffritto,* the finely chopped mixture of herbs and vegetables that is sautéed in oil at the start of the preparation. Carrots, onion, garlic, and celery (especially the dark-green tough but flavorful Tuscan celery) are part of the battuto, but so too is parsley (*prezzemolo*—and it's always Italian flat-leaf parsley), sage *(salvia),* and rosemary *(rosmarino)*—always used fresh, never dried. *Nepitella* or *mentuccia,* a kind of wild mint closely related to pennyroyal, is also used fresh, but I've found that, in the absence of pennyroyal, a very small pinch of dried mint can be used in place of nepitella. (Fresh garden mint, on the other hand, has too spirited a flavor for this.) Wild fennel *(finocchio),* which grows in abundance throughout the Tuscan countryside, is also an important flavoring, especially for pork dishes. Cooks who live in California will find wild fennel growing by roadsides. The topmost fronds are used fresh, but the best finocchio comes in the form of powdered fennel flowers, harvested just after they've opened—it has an extraordinary flavor, and I can only hope that some enterprising Californian will latch onto this idea and provide it for American cooks. In the absence of powdered fennel flowers, use fennel seeds and pound them in a mortar just before using. Bay leaves or laurel *(lauro)* is another aromatic, used fresh or dried, to flavor grilled meat dishes.

POLENTA (CORNMEAL)

Polenta is nothing more or less than cornmeal. Stone-ground cornmeal is available in specialty and health-food stores and is usually preferable to polenta imported from Italy, which is often stale. I especially like coarsely ground meal (called *bramata* in Tuscany) from Gray's Grist Mill in Adamsville, Rhode Island, or Morgan's Mills in East Union, Maine.

DRIED BEANS

You'll find several different kinds of dried beans mentioned in the recipes in this book, but don't worry if the particular variety called for is unavailable. I've made these bean recipes with everything from Tuscan cannellini beans (most of which are imported these days in any case) to Maine yellow-eye and soldier beans. Don't, however, use dark-red kidney beans or black beans in Tuscan recipes if you want to create a truly Tuscan-looking dish.

Tuscan cooks always soak beans for several hours or overnight, then drain and simmer them very slowly in fresh water until the beans are tender. Although some food writers dispute the need to soak beans, I prefer to follow the advice of Tuscans who've been doing this for a lot longer than most of us.

DRIED MUSHROOMS

In late summer and early fall when the porcini mushrooms poke through the forest floor, Tuscans gather them in abundance. Those that are not consumed immediately are sliced and dried outdoors in the sunshine, then stored for winter uses.

To reconstitute dried mushrooms: Place the mushrooms in a bowl and cover them with very warm water to a depth of about half an inch. Set aside to soak for at least thirty minutes. When ready to use, drain the soaking water through a fine sieve to strain out any dust, then set aside to add to the soup or sauce later on. Rinse the refreshed mushrooms under running water to rid them of any bits of forest still clinging to them. Then use as directed in the recipe.

SALT

Sea salt, most of it from Sicily, is the only salt used in Italian cooking. If you don't think salt matters, try a taste test using sea salt from France or Britain (Italian sea salt seems not to be exported), kosher salt, and a standard commercial salt like Morton's. I think you'll be surprised at the results. Fine sea salt is best when you want the salt to dissolve into the dish, but a little coarse sea salt, sprinkled on top, makes an elegantly sparkling garnish.

Bread
pane

In the old days every Tuscan farmstead grew its own wheat, a soft white winter wheat that was harvested in July, threshed with great ceremony, and ground monthly as needed into flour to make the family bread. And just about every farmhouse had its own bread oven, built into the house wall near the outside staircase that led up to the living quarters over the stables. Once every ten days or so the oven would be lit with thick faggots of dried heather and broom. When the inside oven walls were powdery dry and white with heat, the coals were raked out and the pale, lumpish loaves, which had been set to rise the night before with a bit of dough left over from the previous week, were distributed over the oven floor to bake to a dull, toasty brown.

Traditionally, Tuscan bread is made with flour, leavening, and water, nothing else. It's called *pane sciocco,* insipid bread, because it has no salt and it takes getting used to. Why does it have no salt? visitors ask. There are many reasons offered, none satisfactory. "Because Tuscan food is very salty, very highly seasoned, so the bread goes well with that." "Because salt was taxed by the government—leaving salt out was a way of getting around the government, and besides it was cheaper." But other parts of Italy have even more highly seasoned food, other parts of Italy are just as adept at getting around the government, other parts of Italy make bread *with* salt, so why . . . ? "Because it is."

Salt-free bread lasts longer because it doesn't attract moisture; it dries but doesn't go moldy, and this may be the major reason why even town bakers leave out the salt. Bread that lasts can be the frugal foundation of many other dishes, and frugality is a virtue widely recognized in Tuscany. *"Pane raffermo,"* firmed-up bread, as it's called in Italian, is a nicer designation than our "stale bread" with its connotation of something no longer any good. You eat it fresh for a couple of days and then it becomes the basis for soups, salads, crostini, or it's grated, maybe toasted, and turned into bread crumbs. The last bits of crust, the ones no one has teeth strong enough to chew, are thrown to the chickens in the farmyard.

Bread is fundamental in the Tuscan country diet, far more so than pasta, a recent addition and often still considered something for the Sunday or festive table, not for every day. Bread, on the other hand, is always on the table (but never upside down, which is serious bad luck), a part of every meal, sometimes the whole meal all by itself. You might rub it with a cut clove of garlic and dribble a little olive oil over the top, or eat it with an onion and some salt, spread it with thick, jammy tomato concentrate, or add a few fragments of dried cheese or a bit of finocchiona, the Tuscan fennel-flavored sausage. Up by the Carrara marble quarries a favorite *companatico* (literally, that-which-goes-with-bread) is a slice of creamy colored, pink-streaked *lardo,* pork belly that's been brine-cured in a carved marble box.

Most country towns and villages still have a baker (or two, or more) to serve local needs, but the old habit of carrying the family's weekly bread to the oven is dying out, as are the wood-fired ovens that create bread with such crisp crust, such matchless flavor. If you go to Tuscany, you'd do well to seek these bakers out, for they won't be around much longer, at least in part because of the need to conform to sanitary codes drawn up in Brussels by engineers of the European Community who have no interest in tradition and even less in flavor.

One such old-fashioned bread bakery *(panificio)* is in the picturesque hamlet of Gòrgiti, way up the winding mountain road that climbs along the steep banks of the Ciuffenna river above San Giovanni Valdarno and the village of Loro Ciuffenna. Just don't go on Mondays, when the baker and his wife go down to Loro for the weekly market, and be sure to go early, because by 10:00 A.M., the baker's wife has sold all the bread.

Another is the bakery run by a sweet, handsome old man named Marino Cecarelli in Castel San Niccolò, a town in the Casentino, the long valley that embraces the Arno north of Arezzo. The Cecarelli bakery is especially interesting because the flour used is grown right in the Casentino and ground at one of the few water-powered grist mills left anywhere in Italy, Molino Grifoni on the Sorana River, just a few kilometers upstream from the town.

The Grifoni mill recently celebrated its 300th anniversary—that's 300 years in the Grifoni family, who bought the mill in 1696. But there's been a mill here at this spot on the Sorana at least since the 1400s, when it was called Mulino di San Pancrazio and was owned by the little *comune* of the same name. Young Andrea Grifoni now runs the mill with his brother Fabrizio, and he's pleased and proud to show visitors around.

The ancient, archaic sounds of a water-driven grist mill are soothing: the whirr of the grindstones, the rhythmic clicketyclack, like miniature locomotive wheels, of the bolter that sifts the different grades of flour, the gurgling rush of water beneath the mill turning the wheels that turn the stones that grind the flour. There are three stones turning at any one time in the scrupulously whitewashed milling room. On one, the Grifonis grind wheat flour for several Tuscan bakeries—you can buy bread made with their flour, for instance, at the Panificio Cortonese in Cortona, although, unlike Cecarelli's, it's not baked in a wood-fired oven. Still it's good bread, with the fresh flavor of wheat in it.

The other two stones in the mill are used to grind corn, *granturco,* for the polenta that's a staple in Tuscan country diets, and chestnuts, to make *farina di castagne,* sometimes called *farina dolce,* sweet flour. In the Casentino and a few other parts of Tuscany chestnuts are dried slowly in special sheds over smoky fires. It gives farina dolce casentinese a special depth of flavor.

Chestnuts and chestnut flour were once even more of a staple than Indian corn, and the chestnut tree was called the *albero del pane,* the bread tree. The original polenta, before maize corn arrived from America, was frequently made from chestnut flour, and that flour was also added to bread dough when wheat flour was scarce (when chestnuts were scarce, flour made from ground acorns was used) but those were tough times indeed. Chestnuts have no gluten, of course, so the bread was pretty dense and chewy, not something you'd want to eat often. Still, it helped get poor mountain families through the winter. Today chestnut flour is used almost exclusively to make castagnaccio (see page 230), an old-fashioned cake flavored with rosemary and olive oil.

But this is getting us a long way from bread.

The best flour for bread should be freshly ground, with a creamy color, still lightly tinged with the carotene in the wheat. (Professional bakers often age their flour for several weeks, but this seems unnecessary with home baking.) Humidity content of the flour is important and varies, obviously, from one place to another all around the world. Tuscan bakers test the humidity of their flour by sticking a finger in: If a light coating of flour adheres to your finger when it's withdrawn, or if you take up a handful and squeeze it gently and it remains together for a moment when released, then the humidity is in harmony. (If the flour doesn't do this, there's not much you can do about it, but it's a factor to bear in mind when adding water to make dough.)

Most Tuscan bakers, but not the best, use a very ordinary, industrially produced Tipo 00, a finely ground, highly refined flour with a low ash content, most often ground from imported wheat; some bakers make whole-wheat bread, *pane di farina integrale* or *pane scuro,* but it isn't really traditional. The best flour is stone-ground *(farina macinata a pietra),* but it's also hardest to find, in Tuscany and in America.

To my mind, the Tipo 00 flour that's most commonly available in Italy represents the very worst of modern hyperindustrial flour milling—bleached, lifeless, inert. It lacks the seductively creamy color, the fragrance and flavor, that good flour should have. For that reason, it never seemed to me worth the effort to make bread in Tuscany, even though I had the use of my neighbor's wood-fired bake oven whenever I wanted. All that changed when Fabrizia Fabbroni introduced me to the Molino Grifoni's extraordinary Tipo 00 flour, creamy, lightly flecked with bran, and with the warm, nutty aroma that good wheat freshly ground is supposed to have. Extraordinary indeed, but a hundred years ago it was probably considered pretty normal, and most likely four or five such mills turned out flour like this on every rushing Tuscan stream.

Tuscan Bread *(Master Recipe)*
pane sciocco

This recipe makes bread that recalls traditional Tuscan country-style loaves without imitating them exactly, impossible to do without a wood-fired oven. It's always seemed to me an exercise in futility to try to imitate traditional, old-fashioned European-style breads in modern American home kitchens, especially if one uses instant yeasts and bread machines. But we are lucky in this country to have a growing movement of artisan bakers who, in fact, are producing breads that, in many cases, are far superior to what's currently available in Italy and France. Most of them are experimenting with natural leavenings and slow-rising dough to give plenty of flavor and texture to their breads, and many are able to bake in wood-fired masonry ovens.

Even if you can get good bread from an artisan baker, however, I urge you to make this bread just once to get a sense of what Tuscan bread is like. Then, when you don't feel like baking, seek out a baker who understands the true meaning of a slow rise, because only long, slow fermentation develops good flavor in bread.

If you decide in the end that you just don't care for unsalted bread, you can use the same directions and mix a tablespoon or more of salt, to taste, with the whole-wheat flour.

The ratio of flour to water is something professional bakers refer to as hydration. The Bread Bakers Guild of America, a wonderful organization that supports good bread and artisan bakers, says that underhydration, or not enough water, is a common error made both by professionals and home bakers. American flours can absorb between 60 percent and 70 percent water (that is, 60 percent of the total quantity of flour *by weight,* not by cups). The quantities listed below should give you the proper hydration rate, although that will vary with ambient temperature and humidity as well as with the freshness of the wheat and flour you're using—the fresher the wheat, the fresher the flour, the more humidity it will contain. Novice bakers may find it takes a little practice to get the feel of bread dough, but fortunately bread is a very forgiving product. Most people are so deeply grateful even for the smell of baking bread that you can give them almost anything and they'll be happy.

At first glance, this recipe may appear long and difficult, but it really isn't. The process is drawn out over several days, but the actual time spent working on the dough is very brief—probably not more than half an hour all told. And the results are worth it.

I recommend using King Arthur Italian-style flour, available through The Baker's Catalogue (see the Source Guide, page 276), which is actually a U.S.-grown soft red winter wheat ground very fine to simulate an Italian Tipo 00. With a protein content of 9.7 to 9.8 percent, this is a good deal softer than King Arthur Unbleached All-Purpose Flour, which is 11.7 percent, but Europeans tend, probably for historic reasons, to use flours with a lower protein content than we do here. Nonetheless, despite its high protein content, I use King Arthur Unbleached All-Purpose Flour, which is widely available at least in the northeast, if I can't get their Italian-style.

If you don't have access to King Arthur flours, use an unbleached, unbromated all-purpose flour, preferably organically grown, and you'll have good success with this recipe.

I believe that the best bread, like the best coffee, is made with untreated natural spring water from as local a source as possible. In Maine, that's Poland Spring.

> 1 teaspoon active dry yeast
> Warm or very warm water as necessary, preferably spring water
> 9 cups unbleached all-purpose flour
> 1 cup whole-wheat flour

Dissolve the yeast in ½ cup very warm water in a small bowl. Set aside until the yeast turns creamy.

Put 2 cups of the flour in a bowl, make a well in the middle, and pour in the yeast mixture. Pull in a little flour from the sides to be absorbed in the liquid, then gradually mix in another cup of very warm water. Using a wooden spoon, mix the flour and water together to a thick slurry. Sprinkle another cup of flour over the top, cover with plastic wrap, and set aside in a cool place to rise for 6 to 8 hours, or overnight.

Next day add 1 cup whole-wheat flour, 1 cup very warm water, and 1 cup white flour. Mix, kneading slightly in the bowl with your hands—the dough will be quite sticky—just enough to combine the liquid and flours thoroughly. Set aside again, covered, to rise for 6 to 8 hours or overnight.

Next day, stir in 1½ cups water. Work in the remaining flour, leaving a little flour unmixed to spread on a board or work surface. Turn the dough onto the floured board and knead for 10 to 15 minutes, or until the dough is silky, springy, and has lost its stickiness.

Turn the well-kneaded dough into a clean bowl (you may rub a very little olive oil around the bowl if you wish to keep the dough from sticking to the sides), cover again with plastic wrap, and this time set in a warm place, near the stove or on top of the refrigerator, to rise and more than double—about 2 to 3 hours.

If you are using a baking stone, set it in the oven and turn the oven on to 450°F. Turn the fully risen dough out of its bowl onto a lightly floured board, punch it down, knead briefly, and form the dough into two loaves. (Or use half the dough for a loaf of bread and the other half for Focaccia—page 24.) Set the loaves on a board dusted with semolina or cornmeal to rise for about 45 minutes while the oven heats. Cover lightly with a sheet of plastic wrap or a slightly dampened kitchen towel.

When ready to bake, transfer a loaf to a wooden peel sprinkled with semolina or cornmeal. Using a very sharp knife, slash the loaf with either two longitudinal slashes or 3 shorter diagonal slashes. Open the oven door and quickly shift the loaf to the baking stone, leaving room for both loaves. Repeat with the second loaf. If you are not using a baking stone, set your loaves for their final rising on a baking sheet lightly strewn with semolina or cornmeal. Cover as above and let rise. Slash as above just before sliding the baking sheet into the oven.

Bake for 10 minutes, then lower the temperature to 350°F. and continue baking another 40 to 45 minutes, or until the bread is nicely browned and feels a little hollow when you knock it with your fist. Remove the bread to cool on a rack before slicing.

The bread may be served as is, or it may be used in any bread-based recipe or as a foundation for many of the soups in Chapter 3.

Plain Flatbread
schiacciata or focaccia (sometimes called 'ciaccia)

THE MASTER RECIPE (page 21) WILL MAKE TWO ROUGHLY 14-X-17-INCH SCHIACCIATE; or, if you wish, use half that recipe to make one schiacciata and the rest to make a loaf of bread.

Schiacciata (the name means flattened or squashed) or focaccia (the name derives from the hearth, the focus or *focolare*) is a homey, domesticated version of that wild man of the bake ovens, pizza. Like pizza, it's eaten when hot and fresh from the oven. You could put all sorts of things on top of a schiacciata—fresh tomatoes, sun-dried tomatoes, bits of mozzarella and black olives, and it would be delicious . . . but it wouldn't be Tuscan schiacciata, which is either garnished simply with olive oil, rosemary, and a sprinkle of salt, or split open while warm and fragrant and stuffed with a thick slice of home-cured prosciutto or Pecorino. Most focacce made by bakers in this country are far too thick to be Tuscan—the ideal should be not much more than about 3/4 inch thick after baking.

> For each schiacciata:
> 2 to 3 tablespoons extra virgin olive oil
> Half the master recipe for Tuscan Bread (page 21), or 2 to 2½ pounds bread dough
> 1 tablespoon salt
> 1 tablespoon coarsely chopped fresh rosemary

Use a rectangular, low-sided baking pan or a baking sheet and oil it lightly with a little of the olive oil.

After the second rising (page 22 in the master recipe), turn the risen dough out of its bowl onto a lightly floured board, punch it down, knead briefly, and smooth the dough out with your hands into a rough rectangular shape, stretching the edges gently. If your dough is very elastic, you may find a rolling pin helpful, but most of the stretching should be done by hand. Transfer the dough to the oiled pan, stretching it if necessary to meet the edges of the pan. The shape should not be precise.

Using your fingers or a wooden spoon, dimple the dough all over in an irregular pattern. Drizzle the remaining oil over the dough, letting it run over the top and pool in the dimples. Then sprinkle with salt and rosemary leaves. Cover lightly with plastic wrap and set aside to rise while you preheat the oven.

Set the oven at 425°F. Let preheat for about 30 minutes, even if the oven thermostat light goes out. Slide the pan into the oven and bake for 45 minutes, or until the top is golden brown and crisp.

Remove from the oven, cut in squares, and serve immediately.

Flatbread for the Grape Harvest
schiacciata coll'uva

8 TO 10 PORTIONS

During the golden days of autumn when the vendemmia, the grape harvest, is in full swing, country bakers take advantage of the abundance of wine grapes to make *schiacciata coll'uva,* an old-fashioned treat that's sometimes called *'ciaccia coll'uva*. If you live in wine country, you're in luck, because this schiacciata is best made with the small, tartly sweet, dark purple grapes used for red wine. In Tuscany, canaiolo or sangiovese grapes, the ones that go into the Chianti blend, are used, but merlot or cabernet grapes will do just fine. If you can't find these, you can still make an acceptable 'ciaccia coll'uva with purple or red table grapes, but use half the amount of sugar to counteract their sweetness.

You may wonder if the grape seeds should be removed. Not in Tuscany, where the seeds give a bit of crunch to the finished product.

1 teaspoon active dry yeast
3½ cups unbleached all-purpose flour, plus a little more for the board
¼ cup plus 3 tablespoons extra virgin olive oil
¼ cup plus 3 tablespoons sugar
Salt to taste
1½ pounds fresh grapes, preferably small, tart wine grapes

Dissolve the yeast in ½ cup warm water, preferably spring water. Put the flour in a mixing bowl, make a well in the center, and pour in the dissolved yeast and water. Gradually stir in the flour, adding up to 1 cup more warm water to get a very soft dough. Mix in ¼ cup of olive oil, ¼ cup of the sugar, and a fat pinch of salt. Turn the dough out on a lightly floured board and knead for about 5 minutes, or until the dough is soft and elastic, with a good spring. Return to the cleaned bowl, cover with plastic wrap, and set aside in a warm place to rise for 1 hour.

Remove the stems from the grapes and rinse the fruit well. Set aside to dry while the dough is rising.

When the dough has risen, lightly grease a shallow rectangular cake pan about 8 × 10 inches, using ½ teaspoon of the remaining oil. Divide the dough into two pieces, one slightly larger than the other. On the lightly floured board roll out the larger piece in a rectangle to fit the bottom and sides of the cake pan. Distribute about ⅔ of the grapes over the bottom and sprinkle with 2 tablespoons of the oil and 2 tablespoons of sugar.

Roll out the second piece of bread dough in a rectangle and cover the grapes, folding the bottom and top pieces of dough together all around the edges of the pan to seal. Distribute the remaining grapes over the top and sprinkle with remaining oil and sugar. Set aside to rise again for about 30 minutes. Meanwhile, preheat the oven to 375°F.

Bake the risen schiacciata for about 1 hour, or until the top is golden and crisp, with the juices from the grapes running over it. Remove from the oven and let cool slightly before cutting in squares and serving.

Rosemary Buns
pan di ramerino

8 ROLLS

These aromatic favorites are made throughout Lent, but especially for Giovedì Santo, the Thursday before Easter. Be careful not to overdo the rosemary: It should be a subtle perfume that suffuses the dough rather than a piney, resiny presence.

> Half the quantity of bread dough for the Tuscan Bread master recipe (page 21)
> 3 tablespoons extra virgin olive oil
> 1 tablespoon fresh rosemary
> 2 tablespoons sugar, if desired
> $1/2$ cup golden sultana raisins, soaked in warm water
> 1 large egg beaten with 1 tablespoon cool water

Use half the recipe for the bread, following it through the second rising; or make the whole recipe and divide the dough in half after the second rising, using half the dough to make a loaf of bread and the other half to make these buns.

Place the oil and rosemary in a small saucepan and set over low heat until the oil is very hot; don't let the rosemary fry. Remove from the heat and set aside for 15 minutes or longer to infuse the oil with the rosemary fragrance.

After the second rising in the master recipe, turn the risen dough out on a lightly floured board, punch it down, and stretch it on the board, leaving a slight indentation in the middle of the dough. Strain the rosemary-infused oil over the dough and, if you wish, sprinkle with the sugar. Drain the plumped raisins well, drying with a paper towel, and add to the dough. Work the dough well, kneading to mix in the oil, sugar, and raisins. Then set the dough aside, lightly covered, to rise for 1 hour or until doubled in bulk.

Preheat the oven to 375°F.

Divide the dough into 8 portions. Lightly oil a baking sheet and use a little of the oil to grease your hands. Shape the dough portions into small, round, lightly oiled buns and place on the sheet. Cover lightly with a towel and set aside to rise for about 30 minutes while the oven heats.

When ready to bake, brush the beaten egg lightly over the top of each bun, slash the tops with a cross if desired, and bake for about 10 minutes or until the buns are golden brown and cooked through.

Saintly Bread with Nuts and Dried Fruits
pan co' santi

6 BUNS, OR BREAD TO SERVE 8

Pan co' santi is always associated with new wine, hence with St. Martin's day on November 11 when the *vino novello*, the newly fermented wine, is tasted for the first time. (*"San Martino, ogni mosto diventa vino*—every must becomes wine," Tuscan wine makers say.) It's a delicious bread for any occasion but if in late November you can get a good Tuscan vino novello with a fresh, grapey flavor, this spirited bread is an ideal accompaniment.

Honey and raisins may stick to a baking stone, so I bake these on a sheet pan instead.

1½ cups very warm water

½ teaspoon active dry yeast

2 tablespoons honey

5 to 6 cups unbleached all-purpose flour

2 teaspoons extra virgin olive oil, or 1 teaspoon oil and 1 teaspoon pure lard,
    plus additional oil to coat the breads

3 tablespoons coarsely chopped walnuts

3 tablespoons golden sultana raisins, plumped in warm water

Grated zest of 1 lemon

1 teaspoon salt

Freshly ground black pepper to taste

In a large mixing bowl combine ½ cup of the water with the yeast and 1 tablespoon of the honey. Stir to mix well and set aside until the yeast has dissolved. Add the remaining water and 4 cups of the flour and mix, first with a wooden spoon and then with your hands. Spread 1 cup of flour on a wooden or marble surface and knead the dough, gradually incorporating most of the flour on the board, for about 5 minutes or until the dough is soft and supple. Set aside in a clean bowl, covered with a damp cloth, to rise for at least 1 hour, or until doubled in bulk.

While the dough is rising, put the oil, or the oil and lard, in a small saucepan and set over medium-high heat. When the fat is hot, add the walnuts and toast them in the fat, watching carefully to keep them from burning, until they turn golden. Remove from the heat immediately and set aside to cool in their fat.

Drain the raisins and pat dry with paper towels.

When the bread dough has doubled in bulk, punch it down and press it out on the board, scattering a little more flour if necessary to keep it from sticking. Toss the raisins in a little flour to dry them. Spread the remaining tablespoon of honey over the dough, sprinkle with the raisins, the nuts and their oil, and the lemon zest. Add the salt and several grinds of black pepper and roll the dough up, jelly-roll fashion, then knead briefly to distribute the extra ingredients thoroughly throughout the dough.

Shape the dough into an oval loaf or divide it into 6 little breads or buns—a single loaf will take longer to bake, obviously. Place the bread or buns on a baking sheet dusted with cornmeal or semolina and set aside, covered with a damp towel, to rise in a warm place for 30 minutes. Meanwhile, preheat the oven to 425°F.

When the breads are risen, rub about a tablespoon of olive oil in the palms of your hands and brush over their surfaces. Bake for 20 to 25 minutes for small breads, 45 minutes for a single large loaf.

Using Leftover Bread
PANE RAFFERMO

In the countryside, where there were no public ovens, the home oven was fired for baking every week or ten days, and bread had to keep until the next baking. Tuscan bread is high in natural acids from the use of a leavening of old dough that's saved from one baking to the next and from the long, slow fermentation. A bread like this keeps better than a sweeter, more fragile bread made with fresh yeast and a more rapid fermentation. Bread made this way also retains its shape better when liquids are poured over it, as in most of the traditional soups from the Tuscan country kitchen. A bread raised quickly, with commercial or, even worse, instant yeast, will fall apart if it's used for soups or crostini. If you were simply trying to thicken an everyday kind of soup, you might in fact want the bread to fall apart and dissolve into the liquid, but for these Tuscan soups, only Tuscan bread—properly made, with a long, slow fermentation—will do. In fact, a recipe for Tuscan soup really begins with a recipe for Tuscan bread.

The same is true for crostini, the all-purpose Tuscan antipasto made of thin slices of pane raffermo dressed, like open-faced sandwiches, with whatever the cook has on hand—leftover greens or beans or, for more special occasions, a mash of chicken livers and spleen *(milza),* or simply a few anchovies rubbed to a paste and mixed with butter.

If you don't make Tuscan-style bread for the crostini and bread-based soups that follow, do seek out a baker who produces a similar dense crusty loaf that retains its shape and texture for a good many days after the initial baking.

Sweet Bread from Lucca
buccellato

12 TO 14 SERVINGS

An ancient bread from the region around Lucca, buccellato is first mentioned in a will or testament dated 1485. But the tradition is much older, possibly going back to Roman times, although whether the bread the Lucchesi called buccellato in antiquity is the same as the fifteenth-century bread or as the sweet bread of today is anyone's guess. In any case, buccellato has become the very symbol of this handsome town so cozily enclosed within its rosy brick walls, atop which the good burghers of Lucca make their passeggiata each day, often munching buccellato as they stroll. If you go to Lucca, stop at Taddeucci, a bakery in Piazza San Michele in Foro just behind the glorious Pisan Romanesque church of the same name, for a taste of the real thing.

Buccellato makes a great tea bread, and leftovers are wonderful toasted for breakfast the next morning.

1 teaspoon active dry yeast

1 cup warm water

3 1/2 to 4 cups unbleached all-purpose flour

5 tablespoons unsalted butter

2/3 cup whole milk

1/2 cup golden sultana raisins, soaked in warm water to plump

1 egg, lightly beaten

1 tablespoon rum

1 1/2 cups pastry flour

1/2 cup plus 1 tablespoon sugar

1 tablespoon fennel or aniseed, freshly crushed in a mortar or spice grinder

Grated zest of 2 oranges

Make a sponge by mixing the yeast with the warm water until it has dissolved, then stirring in 1 cup of the all-purpose flour. Stir with a wooden spoon to mix thoroughly, then set aside, covered, in a warm place to rise for about 1 hour.

When ready to continue with the recipe, combine 4 tablespoons (1/2 stick) of the butter and the milk in a small pan and set over low heat to warm the milk and melt the butter. (Do not let the milk come to a boil.) Drain the raisins and pat dry with paper towels. Mix the beaten egg with the rum.

Set aside 1 cup of the remaining all-purpose flour and put the rest in a large bowl with the pastry flour, $1/2$ cup of the sugar, the fennel or aniseed, raisins, and orange zest. Toss with a fork to mix well. Turn the sponge into the bowl and mix, first with a spoon and then with your hands, kneading the mixture in the bowl. Add the warm milk and butter, a little at a time, and continue mixing and kneading. When the liquid has been incorporated, add approximately half the egg and rum mixture and mix thoroughly with your hands. Spread the reserved cup of flour on a board and knead the dough, incorporating additional flour as necessary to make a soft but not sticky dough. Knead for about 5 minutes to develop the gluten.

Place the ball of dough in the clean bowl, sprinkled very lightly with flour, and set aside to rise, covered, for $1^1/2$ hours, or until doubled.

Use the remaining 1 tablespoon of butter to coat a baking sheet liberally, then sprinkle with about 1 tablespoon of flour. Punch down the risen dough and pull and stretch it into a snake about 20 inches long. Bring the ends together to make a fat ring and set it on the baking sheet. Cover lightly and let rise for about 30 minutes in a warm place.

Preheat the oven to 350°F. Paint the risen ring with the remaining egg and rum wash and sprinkle the surface with the remaining tablespoon of sugar. Slash the ring in a regular pattern and bake for 45 minutes to 1 hour, or until the top is golden and the buccellato is cooked through.

Remove and let cool to room temperature before slicing and serving.

Appetizers and Snacks
antipasti e merende

The antipasto course in Tuscany is a thing of great simplicity. Often, in fact, there's no antipasto at all and meals begin directly with the primo, or first course, a lightly sauced pasta or a small plate of hearty bean or vegetable soup. Only in restaurants, or at home when the family is entertaining, do antipasti come into their own. Not in variety, mind you—compared with other parts of Italy, the antipasto course in Tuscany tends to be restrained, like Tuscans themselves, and made up of simple things that every kitchen should have on hand, either in the larder or outside in the garden. When it exists, the antipasto is often little more than a platter with a few slices of salty home-cured ham or dry finocchiona sausage, perhaps along with crostini, slices of stale country bread piled like an open-faced sandwich with any number of combinations from leftover vegetables to a sort of coarse pâté made from the livers of a roasted chicken or rabbit.

A merenda, on the other hand, a snack lunch served outside regular mealtimes, is more substantial, especially in summer when country people rise early and work late and there may be a good many hours between meals. During the crucial periods of planting and harvest, a hearty merenda may be carried out to workers in the fields. Hearty, indeed, but usually also quite simple, sometimes just a sandwich made on the spot from good, rough bread, slabs of sheep's milk Pecorino, and sliced prosciutto; but sometimes, when days are longest, the merenda becomes more elaborate, a vegetable-and-bread combination like panzanella, ribollita, or acquacotta, something that's filling but needn't be served hot from the stove.

Years ago, when we first went to live in our little mountain village behind Cortona, our neighbors still raised their own wheat to grind into flour for bread and pasta, and the trebbiatura, when the grain was threshed, was an annual summer event of great excitement, a social occasion when families gathered together to help with the hot, dusty labor that went on from early morning until well into the afternoon.

Feeding the workers was as important as the threshing itself, each farmwife vying to serve the tastiest merenda for a late-morning snack, along with big straw-wrapped jugs of homemade red and white wine. Late in the day, when the rickety

A Tuscan Appetizer
UN ANTIPASTO TOSCANO

Assembling a Tuscan antipasto in this country takes some patience and considerable planning to seek out the very best products. Imported prosciutto di Parma, the only Italian cured ham available here, is a good deal sweeter than most Tuscan country hams, which are often quite salty. Nonetheless, prosciutto di Parma is a delicious, if expensive, contribution to the antipasto platter. Just make sure you are buying the genuine article, a finer and tastier product than most similar hams cured in this country or in Canada. (You can buy Italian prosciutto in this country but you cannot buy prosciutto in Italy to bring home with you. It is illegal to import any meat products, fresh or cured.)

A good prosciutto should have firm, compact flesh of a deep rose color surrounded by a fragrant layer of ivory-colored fat. (Don't cut the fat away—it's an important part of the flavor and in the quantity that it's consumed it does no harm at all to anyone who's not following a rigorous fat-free diet.) The best prosciutto is cured on the bone, but this is hard to find in America, and increasingly difficult in Tuscany as well. If you should be so lucky, and you have a cool, dry pantry or cellar rattle of the noisy old threshing machine had ground to a halt, the end of the task was celebrated with a copious feast created from the farm's own bounty—roasted chickens and rabbits, bread baked that morning in the wood-fired oven built into the outside wall of the farmhouse, vegetables and salads straight from the garden, and, as an introduction to the table, an abundant but simple antipasto.

This kind of country feasting is very close to Tuscan hearts, even the hearts of deeply urbanized Tuscans in the suburbs of Florence or farther afield in Milan or Turin or Rome. Restaurants throughout the region serve exactly the same kind of food, sometimes elaborated and made fancy by well-meaning chefs, but often with the same generous simplicity of my neighbors in Teverina. Ask in the fanciest restaurant for an antipasto and you will most likely be presented with a similar array of crostini in all their variety, along with thin slices of cured ham and sausages. But whatever the selection, it will be made up of appealingly simple and fresh ingredients, things that are close to hand and easy to assemble, that can be eaten with the fingers or piled on a crust of rustic, unsalted Tuscan bread. Companatico, these things are often called, meaning that which goes with the bread, especially the unsalted bread that is the very foundation of Tuscan cuisine.

to keep it in, you might want to invest in a whole prosciutto on the bone and slice it as needed. When all the meat is gone, the bone makes a wonderful base for soup.

Prosciutto should be thinly sliced but not so thin and papery that it shreds when you try to work with it. Overlap the slices—there should be at least two per person—on a big oval platter, perhaps with an equal number of thin slices of salami, or any other dry-cured sausage that is rich and slightly pungent with flavor. Then, if figs are in season, select fruits that are literally bursting with ripeness, along with sun-ripened melons or peaches full of sweet summer flavor. Split the figs or peaches in half, slice the melons thinly, and distribute the fruits over the cured meats. Count on at least half a fig, half a peach, and a thin slice of melon per person.

Serve this platter with nothing but a peppermill and some thinly sliced Tuscan country-style bread to accompany it.

For an even more authentic presentation, serve another platter with two or three among the following versions of crostini along with the prosciutto and sausage.

Crostini with Chicken Livers
crostini neri

Crostini neri, or black crostini, always used to be spread with a rich dark mixture of mashed chicken livers and milza, or spleen. Today spleen is hard to find in Tuscany, and most cooks use all chicken livers. Crostini neri are an invariable part of the restaurant antipasto platter, but they are also served frequently at home as appetite whetters before a celebration meal or Sunday lunch. Since chicken is almost always a part of that meal, chicken livers are a natural, but thrifty housewives will add rabbit or duck livers, too, when they have them.

3/4 pound livers, either all chicken or mixed chicken, duck, and rabbit

1/4 cup finely chopped flat-leaf parsley

1/4 cup finely chopped onion

1 clove garlic, finely chopped

2 tablespoons extra virgin olive oil

2 salted anchovy fillets, rinsed and chopped

1/4 cup dry vin santo, dry Amontillado sherry

Salt and freshly ground black pepper to taste

1 tablespoon finely grated lemon zest or conserva di pomodoro

1/4 cup dry white wine

2 tablespoons salted capers, rinsed and chopped

6 to 8 slices country-style bread

A little broth or lightly salted water for dipping, if desired

Pick over the chicken livers, cutting away any greenish bits. Rinse under running water, pat dry with paper towels, and set aside.

In a pan over medium-low heat, gently sauté the parsley, onion, and garlic in the oil until the vegetables are soft but not brown. Add the anchovies and cook, mashing them into the contents of the pan. When the anchovies are fully dissolved, add the livers and raise the heat to medium. Brown the livers, turning them frequently until they're thoroughly brown on all sides but still rosy in the middle.

Add the vin santo or sherry to the pan, raise the heat again, and cook until the liquid is reduced to a syrupy consistency and the livers are cooked through. Taste and add salt and pepper, along with the grated lemon zest or conserva.

Add the wine or stock and continue cooking, mashing the livers with a fork as they cook, until the liquid has been absorbed. You should have a thick but rather liquid paste, which will get thicker as it cools. If the livers are not thoroughly mashed, put them through the coarse disk of a food mill or process very briefly in a food processor. They should have considerable texture, however, and not be reduced to a purée. Stir the capers into the chicken livers. Taste again and adjust the seasoning.

Serve the chicken liver paste at room temperature. If you wish, briefly dip thin slices of country-style bread in broth or lightly salted water, then spread with the liver paste. Or toast the bread before spreading with liver paste.

Note: Salted anchovies, if available, are preferable to canned ones. To prepare, rinse thoroughly under running water to rid the anchovies of salt. The fillets strip away easily from the interior bones. Use the equivalent of 2 canned anchovy fillets, but do not salt the chicken liver paste until after the anchovy has been added, as it can add considerable salt to the recipe.

Crostini

You can make crostini with almost any topping, as long as you have the right dense, country-style loaf, like Tuscan Pane Sciocco (page 21). The bread, which should be raffermo, that is, firmed up rather than fresh, is thinly sliced. In the classic Tuscan tradition, the slices are then dipped briefly in a little broth, vin santo, or salted water to soften them before they're spread with the topping. Modern Tuscan cooks, however, often toast their bread instead of softening it, and I have even been served crostini featuring bread slices that have been quickly fried in olive oil.

Red Crostini with Tomatoes
crostini rossi

Red crostini are made at the summer's height, when fresh, garden-ripened tomatoes are available. Be careful of the red pepper—Tuscan food should be gently suffused with the heat of chiles, but not so hot you run for the water pitcher.

1 clove garlic, finely chopped
$1/4$ cup extra virgin olive oil
$1^1/2$ pounds tomatoes, peeled, seeded, juiced, and chopped
$1/2$ small dried hot red chile pepper, finely chopped,
    or $1/4$ teaspoon crushed red chile peppers
Salt and freshly ground black pepper to taste
6 to 8 (1-inch-thick) slices country-style bread
Basil leaves, for garnish

In a medium frying pan, gently sweat the garlic in 1 tablespoon of the olive oil until soft but not brown. Add the tomatoes and hot red chile pepper, stir, and simmer gently 10 to 15 minutes, then taste and add salt and pepper. Continue simmering for 45 minutes, or until the tomatoes are thoroughly dissolved and make a chunky sauce. Stir occasionally and add a little boiling water if the sauce gets too dry.

If you have a food mill, put the sauce through the disk with the largest holes. Or, process briefly in a food processor to make a sauce with a good texture, thick but not too smooth. If the sauce is too liquid, return to the pan and simmer again until most of the liquid has boiled away and the sauce is a dense paste.

Slice the bread about the thickness of a finger and cut each slice in two. Toast the bread on both sides and drizzle with the remaining olive oil; or, if you wish, sauté the bread in the olive oil. Garnish with leaves of fresh basil if you wish.

Crostini with Black Cabbage or Broccoli di Rape
crostini con cavolo nero o con broccoletti

6 TO 8 SERVINGS

A wintertime version of crostini is made with cavolo nero. This translates as black cabbage but the vegetable, which is a cold-weather staple throughout Tuscany, is really a form of kale. You can find cavolo nero in some markets, or I substitute either kale or broccoli di rape.

This extremely humble dish is actually a fine way to show off your best Tuscan estate-bottled extra virgin olive oil.

> 6 to 8 (1-inch-thick) slices country-style bread
> 1 bunch broccoli di rape
> 1 clove garlic, finely chopped
> $1/2$ dried hot red chile pepper
> 3 tablespoons extra virgin olive oil, plus more for garnish
> Salt and freshly ground black pepper to taste
> A little broth or lightly salted water for dipping, if desired

Lightly toast the bread slices and cut them in half. Arrange on a platter and set the platter in a warm oven while you prepare the broccoli di rape.

Pick over the greens, discarding any yellowing or wilted parts and cutting away tough stems. Rinse thoroughly and place in a large saucepan over medium heat. The water clinging to its leaves should be sufficient to cook it, but if not add a few tablespoons of water to the pan. Cover and steam for about 15 minutes or until the vegetable is thoroughly wilted.

Meanwhile, in a sauté pan large enough to hold the broccoli di rape, gently sweat the garlic and chile pepper in the oil over medium-low heat until the garlic is soft but not brown. Using tongs, remove the broccoli di rape from its cooking liquid and add to the garlic in the pan, stirring to coat the greens well with oil. Add about $1/4$ cup of cooking liquid to the pan, raise the heat to medium, and cook for an additional 5 to 7 minutes, or just long enough to meld the flavors. Season to taste.

If you wish, dip thin slices of country-style bread in broth or lightly salted water, then pile the vegetable, with its juices, on top. Or toast the bread before mounding the broccoli di rape over it. Serve immediately, garnished with a little more olive oil. (This is a little messier than most crostini and should be eaten with knife and fork.)

An Etruscan Banquet

Modern Tuscans are inordinately proud of their Etruscan origins. It's no coincidence, they say, that the Renaissance had its beginnings precisely in that part of Italy where Ancient Etruria flourished. (So much for Renaissance popes, many of whom were Tuscans anyway!) Romantic though the theory may be—and profoundly irritating to other Italians—there's more than a germ of truth to the claim, even though Tuscans today are descendants of many tribes, including the British and German hordes who, seduced by the sun, the wine, the country estates that once could be bought for a song, have become a permanent presence throughout this century. So it's not surprising if the people of Murlo choose to celebrate their Etruscan heritage with an open-air banquet in the cobbled square of their little hilltop village each year when the full moon of September rides high in the night sky over the hills where Etruscans once trod.

Murlo *is* an Etruscan village—the present tense is deliberate. A few years ago, a scientist of some renown identified what was said to be an Etruscan genetic marker and found more of the historic DNA in the blood cells of the Murlani than in any other part of Tuscany. No one in town found that the least remarkable because, after all, you had only to clothe the mayor in a toga and pose him in banquet-style semi-recline, as a French photojournalist immediately did, to see how close *his* Etruscan origins are—the mayor could top a funerary urn in Murlo's fine little Museo Etrusco any day of the week and not look out of place. (When he's not actually mayoring, he also runs a first-rate pizzeria and restaurant, the only place to eat in town. The pizza is cooked in a wood-fired oven and, if it's not Etruscan—but who knows for sure?—it's still awfully good.)

The September moon bathes the walled town in its tranquil radiance, moon-glow competing with torches that flare from walls surrounding the village square while terra-cotta oil lamps flicker gently down the long banquet tables. In the center of the square, smoke rises from haunches of meat set to roast over the embers on massive iron grills like so many ritual burnt offerings. But the moonlight seems most appropriate: Surely the ancient Etruscans banqueted by moonlight on warm summer nights, and why should their modern descendants, gathered in the square to celebrate their Etruscan heritage, not do the same?

Surrounded by fields of corn and tobacco, neither of which were known for at least another two millennia after the Etruscan heyday, Murlo, with its imposing walls and towers, looks more medieval than Etruscan. Nearby, on a neighboring hilltop, is the ancient site of Poggio Civitate, where the American Etruscologist Kyle Phillips excavated a remarkable Etruscan settlement that some think was a fortified agricultural village, possibly inhabited by a single extended clan, and that others claim was a ritual gathering place where the chiefs of many clans came together annually to plan campaigns, resolve disputes, salute the gods, and generally chew the fat.

Just like their ancestors, the people of Murlo gather each year on a balmy summer night to rediscover their Etruscan origins and, not incidentally, to garner support for their delightful museum, housed in a sixteenth-century bishop's palace that crowns the village. Here the domestic remains of Poggio Civitate are displayed including enigmatic, larger-than-life size terra-cotta figures that once adorned the gables of Poggio Civitate's buildings as well as bowls, spoons, cups, jugs and pitchers, small clay ovens and baking dishes, votive figurines, and impressed terra-cotta tiles, one of which shows an Etruscan banqueting scene not too different from the scene set in the moonlit piazza this very night.

But what did the Etruscans really eat? Not corn, potatoes, tomatoes, beans, or peppers, all staples of the modern Tuscan table, for sure, but the banquet laid is not all that strange to a contemporary Tuscan palate. The menu, based on local ingredients, local flavors, is decidedly in the Tuscan/Etruscan manner, beginning with an antipasto of fresh figs with cured wild-boar prosciutto, aromatic olives, boiled eggs, their yolks crushed and mixed with wild herbs like mint, rosemary, and thyme, and a wilted salad of wild greens.

Did the Etruscans know farro, the ancient strain of wheat that is newly popular with Tuscan cooks? Some say not, but farro was one of the earliest domesticated grains and a zuppa di farro seems appropriate, especially with an *intingolo,* a sauce of minced wild mint, celery, citronella, sorrel, and capers, heated in olive oil and drizzled over the thick and fragrant soup. Pasta may have been more of a stretch for the ancients—the origins of pasta are a subject of constant dispute— but, made with farro flour and smothered in a fragrant sauce of wild rabbit, pasta too is not out of place.

Not unexpectedly, it's in the meat course that modern and ancient Tuscan tastes come most closely together. Knowing as little as we do of Etruscan diets, we can still be pretty certain they loved meat as much as did their near contemporaries, the heroes of Homeric Greece, who needed only the slightest excuse to drop what they were doing, slaughter a calf, and throw it on the fire, offering the fat and thigh meat as a sacrifice to the gods and gleefully consuming everything else. On the tables of the Etruscan poor, perhaps, meat was not much in evidence, but for a high-class banquet like the one at Murlo, nothing else would do. Modern meat may pale in flavor compared to the gamy flesh consumed in days of old, but tonight we feast on grilled steak and haunches of fire-roasted lamb impregnated with the intense aroma of crushed wild juniper berries harvested from the site of Poggio Civitate itself, and feel ourselves a little closer thereby to the culinary hearths of our ancestors in Ancient Etruria.

"Etruscan" Egg Crostini
crostini all'etrusca

6 TO 8 SERVINGS

Did the Etruscans really eat crostini? Did they make this version of what we might call Etruscan egg salad? No one really knows for sure, but it's a nice conceit. At Murlo, a hilltop village south of Siena with an unassailable Etruscan pedigree, crostini like these are often served at the annual "Etruscan" banquet in the village's main square. Etruscans, of course, would have used wild green herbs, but modern Tuscans use culinary herbs growing outside their kitchen doors.

> 4 extra-large eggs
> 2 tablespoons freshly chopped green herbs, including flat-leaf parsley, sage, basil, and, if available, a little mint
> 3 teaspoons extra virgin olive oil
> 1/4 teaspoon aged red wine vinegar
> Salt and freshly ground black pepper to taste
> 6 to 8 (1-inch-thick) slices country-style bread, crusts removed

Simmer the eggs in water to cover for at least 10 minutes, or until they are hard-boiled. Rinse in cold water and as soon as the eggs can be handled, peel the shells away. Separate the whites from the yolks and mash the yolks in a small bowl, adding the chopped green herbs, the oil, and the vinegar. Taste and adjust the seasoning, adding salt and pepper as desired. Finely chop the egg whites.

Cut each slice of bread in half and toast the slices very lightly on both sides, using a grill or broiler. Spread with the paste of the herby yolks, top with the chopped whites, and serve.

Fresh Sage Omelet
torta di salvia o salviata

2 TO 4 SERVINGS

This recipe comes from a magnificent two-volume compilation on Tuscan food, Giovanni Righi Parenti's *La Cucina Toscana*. Salviata is made in late springtime when the young sage leaves sprout. You could also use other fresh early herbs, such as thyme, basil, or young nettle tops. Serve it as a first course or for a light lunch or supper.

> 6 extra-large eggs
> 2 tablespoons freshly grated Parmigiano-Reggiano
> 1/2 cup whole milk
> 2 tablespoons unbleached all-purpose flour
> 1 bunch fresh sage, leaves only, finely chopped to make 1/4 cup
> Salt and freshly ground black pepper to taste
> 1 tablespoon unsalted butter

Beat the eggs with a fork and mix in the grated cheese and milk. Sprinkle the flour over the eggs and fold in. Then stir in the chopped sage. Add salt and pepper to taste.

If you wish to bake this in the oven, preheat to 325°F. Use the butter to grease generously an earthenware pie dish about 9 inches in diameter. Pour in the egg mixture and bake 15 to 20 minutes, or until the eggs are set but the top is still a little loose and creamy.

Or cook like a conventional Italian frittata, on top of the stove. Melt the butter in a frying pan over medium heat and when the foam subsides, pour in the egg batter. Cook by constantly shaking the pan over medium heat, lifting the cooked egg from the bottom to let the uncooked portion run underneath, and running a narrow palette knife around the edge of the pan to keep it loose. When the egg is mostly set except for the top, invert the pan onto a dish and slide the omelet back into the pan to cook the other side. Or simply run the pan briefly under a broiler to set the upper surface of the frittata lightly. Don't overcook. The top should remain slightly creamy.

Leek Pie
la porrata

Tuscan porrata (from *porri,* leeks) will remind you of a French quiche, but it is much simpler and lacks the butter and cream that give so much heft to the French version. Be attentive to the leeks—browned leeks develop an unattractive bitter flavor.

For the dough:
1/4 teaspoon active dry yeast
2 cups plus 2 tablespoons all-purpose flour
1 egg, lightly beaten
3 to 4 tablespoons extra virgin olive oil
Salt to taste
For the pie filling:
1 1/2 pounds (untrimmed weight) leeks
1/4 cup extra virgin olive oil
Salt and freshly ground black pepper to taste
2 eggs, lightly beaten
3 tablespoons freshly grated Parmigiano-Reggiano
Butter to grease the pan
1 to 2 ounces imported prosciutto or baked ham, cut in lardons

Place the yeast in a cup with 6 tablespoons of warm water and set aside to dissolve.

Place the flour in a bowl, make a well in the center, and mix in the dissolved yeast, egg, 3 tablespoons of the olive oil, and salt. Knead all the ingredients together until the dough is soft and a little spongy, using a little more olive oil if necessary. Form the dough into a ball and set aside in a warm place, covered with a dampened cloth, for at least an hour or until ready to use.

Clean the leeks very well, getting rid of any internal sand. Slice them fine, discarding the dark green tops. You should have about 1 pound (4 cups) sliced leeks.

Warm the olive oil in a frying pan over low heat. Add the leeks, a pinch of salt, and pepper to taste. Cook very gently, covered, until the leeks are thoroughly softened, 30 to 40 minutes. Stir frequently and do not let the leeks brown. Once the leeks are done, set the pan aside to cool, then stir in the eggs and grated cheese.

Preheat the oven to 375°F.

Lightly butter a 9- to 10-inch straight-sided pie or quiche pan not more than about 1½ inches high. Roll out the dough in a circle large enough to cover the bottom and sides of the pan and fit the dough into the pan, crimping the edges around the top. Distribute the ham over the bottom of the pan and pour the egg-leek mixture over it. Bake in the preheated oven for about 30 minutes, or until the filling is firm but not hard. Remove from the oven and let sit for about 15 minutes before cutting into pie-shaped wedges for serving.

Pinzimonio
RAW VEGETABLES DIPPED IN EXTRA VIRGIN OLIVE OIL

Tuscan cooks have developed a number of fine ways to appreciate the splendid extra virgin olive oil that is the pride of this region. This is an early summer dish, when the vegetables are crisp and new from local gardens and the oil harvested the previous winter has lost its bitter edge and grown sweet and fragrant with fruit. No ordinary olive oil will do for this dish; use only the very finest estate-bottled oil, something like Castello di Ama, Capezzana, or Badia a Coltibuono's Albereto oil.

You will also need garden-fresh vegetables from your own or a nearby farmer's fields. The variety, of course, depends on what is available, and should include, but not be limited to, young spring onions, baby carrots, crisp white celery, and fragrant ripe red and yellow peppers. With a little imagination you can extend the selection to include baby beets and little purple-topped turnips, peeled and quartered; young artichokes in which the choke has not yet formed; small cucumbers, peeled or not depending on the bitterness of the skins; firm, crunchy radishes; sugar snap peas; raw green beans when they're slender and crisp; slim spears of asparagus; or any other vegetable that is sweet with youth and dewy with freshness.

Prepare the vegetables and arrange them on a handsome platter or tray moments before serving. Nothing else is required but a jug or cruet of fine olive oil, some crunchy sea salt, and a peppermill filled with fragrant black peppercorns. Each guest mixes his or her own oil, salt, and pepper on a plate, then selects vegetables to dip in the oil and eat out of hand. A plate of fine prosciutto and thin slices of bread are a nice accompaniment, but anything else is gilding the lily.

Crisp-fried Sage Leaves
stuzzichini di salvia

6 SERVINGS (2 STUZZICHINI EACH)

A neighbor of mine makes these when the furry-textured sage leaves on the bush out-side his kitchen window are about three inches long, and puts them out for nibbling before dinner. Little morsels of crisply fried sage leaves sandwiched around a bit of anchovy, they are astonishingly good with a glass of chilled white wine. My neighbor counts on two to a person, but you may want to increase the proportions to three or four per person—they're that good.

> 24 large fresh sage leaves
> 3 whole salted anchovies, or 6 oil-packed anchovy fillets
> 1/2 cup flour
> Oil for deep-fat frying
> 1 egg

Rinse the sage leaves under running water and set them aside on a kitchen towel to dry thoroughly.

If using whole salted anchovies, rinse them under running water to rid them of excess salt, and strip away the central bones. (You needn't be too fussy about this as anchovy bones are softened by the salting process.) If using oil-packed anchovies, drain them well.

Make a pastella, or flour and water batter: Place 1 cup water in a medium bowl and sift the flour over it, beating with a fork. Use just enough flour to make a thick cream.

In a heavy frying pan over medium-high heat, bring about an inch of oil to frying temperature, about 360°F. (Test it with a cube of bread—when the bread sizzles and quickly turns golden, the temperature is right.)

While the oil is heating, beat the egg with a fork in a small bowl. Dip a sage leaf in the beaten egg. Place a piece of anchovy on the leaf and cover it with a second leaf dipped in the beaten egg. Fasten the two leaves together with a toothpick. Dip the sage sandwich in the pastella and drop in the hot oil. Fry quickly on both sides and when the sandwich is golden, remove to a piece of absorbent paper to drain.

Serve immediately, removing the toothpicks beforehand if you wish—otherwise, warn guests of what to expect.

Variation: If you don't care for the flavor of anchovies, use small slices of mozzarella instead.

Rice-stuffed Tomatoes
pomodori ripieni

6 SERVINGS

Toward the end of August when the tomatoes in their gardens are ripe and succulent, my neighbors in Teverina make these stuffed tomatoes first thing in the morning before the day heats up. As frequently as they serve pomodori ripieni for an antipasto, they also offer them as a light lunch or supper dish requiring no further cooking.

6 round naturally ripened red tomatoes, weighing about $1/2$ pound each
$1/2$ cup raw medium- or long-grain rice such as Carolina rice
2 tablespoons finely chopped fresh basil
2 tablespoons finely chopped flat-leaf parsley
1 small onion, finely minced
1 small clove garlic, finely minced
$1/4$ cup freshly grated Parmigiano-Reggiano or aged Pecorino Toscano
Salt and freshly ground black pepper to taste
Extra virgin olive oil
1 cup water or light chicken stock

Preheat the oven to 350°F.

Cut a cap off the top of each tomato and set it aside. Place a sieve over a bowl and gently squeeze the tomatoes to release the juice and seeds. Discard the seeds. Add to the juice in the bowl all the other ingredients except the oil and water or stock, and mix well.

Use about a tablespoon of olive oil to grease lightly a baking dish large enough to hold all the tomatoes close together but not touching. Arrange the tomatoes in the dish.

Bring the water or stock to a boil. Meanwhile, spoon the rice mixture into each tomato, filling the tomatoes only about two-thirds full to leave room for the rice to expand. Add about $1/2$ teaspoon oil to each tomato, cover with the caps, and pour the boiling liquid into the baking dish. Bake for about 40 minutes, or until the tomatoes are tender but still firm and the rice is thoroughly cooked. Raise the heat to 450°F., remove the little caps, and continue baking the tomatoes until the tops are crisp and brown.

Remove from the oven and set aside to cool to room temperature, or a little warmer, before serving.

Roasted Sweet Peppers
peperoni arrostiti

MAKES 2 PINTS

This is a favorite summertime antipasto at Grattamacco, a wine and olive oil estate sited high on a breezy hill overlooking the enchanting town of Castagneto Carducci and the bright blue, sail-speckled Tyrhennian off in the distance. Paola Meletti Cavallari, who owns the estate with her husband Piermario, naturally uses Grattamacco olive oil, a light, flowery oil characteristic of this region with its seaside exposure, and serves the peppers with a fresh, lightly chilled Grattamacco bianco produced from vermentino and trebbiano grapes.

9 firm sweet bell peppers, preferably red and yellow
4 cloves garlic, peeled and very thinly sliced
1 tablespoon coarsely chopped fresh oregano, leaves only, or 1 teaspoon crumbled
   dried oregano
1 teaspoon salt, more or less, or to taste
1 cup extra virgin olive oil

Prepare the peppers by roasting them over charcoal or wood coals or a gas flame; set the peppers on a grill about 4 inches above the hot, glowing coals. Turn them frequently until their skins are thoroughly blackened and blistered. Use a long-handled fork if roasting over a gas flame.

Once the peppers are black, put them in a paper bag or cover them with a kitchen towel and set them aside to rest until they're cool enough to handle.

Peel the peppers by pulling and rubbing away the blackened skin, using your fingers or a sharp knife if necessary to get rid of stubborn bits. Do not do this under running water as it washes away much of the flavor. Cut the peppers in half, discarding seeds and white membranes, and slice the pepper halves into long strips about the thickness of your index finger.

Have ready 2 pint jars (or 4 half-pint jars), scrupulously rinsed with boiling water and wiped dry. Layer the pepper strips in the jars, sprinkling each layer with garlic, oregano, and a little salt. When the jar is full, pour over enough olive oil to cover. Set aside in a cool place for at least two days to develop the flavors before using.

Since the peppers are not processed, they are best kept in the refrigerator, but they should be brought to room temperature before serving. They may be served as they are, with thin slices of bread to cushion them, or they may be layered in a glass bowl with strips of anchovy fillet and a few capers scattered among them.

Tuscan Bread-and-Tomato Salad
panzanella

6 TO 8 SERVINGS

Another of the many delicious uses for leftover pane raffermo, this will please anyone who's ever taken a bit of bread to sop up the juices in the bottom of the salad bowl. Use your finest oil for this.

> 1 pound stale (firm but not dried-out) country-style bread, about
>   four 1-inch-thick slices
> 4 large very ripe and flavorful tomatoes
> 1 large red onion, finely sliced
> 1 or 2 cucumbers, peeled, quartered lengthwise, and chunked
> 1 cup firmly packed fresh basil, very coarsely chopped or torn
> $\frac{1}{2}$ cup extra virgin olive oil
> 3 tablespoons aged red wine vinegar
> Salt and freshly ground black pepper to taste

Soften the bread slices in a bowl of cool water, then squeeze each slice gently to rid it of excess liquid. Tear the bread into chunks, discarding the thick crusts, and drop the chunks into a salad bowl. Slice the tomatoes thickly or cut in chunks and add to the bowl. Add the onion, cucumber, and torn or chopped basil.

In a separate small bowl, beat the oil and vinegar with a fork to emulsify, adding salt and pepper to taste as you beat. Pour the dressing over the salad and mix well, using your hands. Set aside in a cool spot to let the flavors develop (but do not refrigerate) for at least 30 minutes before serving.

Fresh Bean and Tuna Salad
fagioli con tonno

4 TO 6 SERVINGS

Borlotti beans are sometimes called cranberry beans in America. In Tuscany, as in America, they're favorite beans for drying, but they're also wonderful shelled and eaten fresh at the height of summer when their pods have turned a creamy ivory color streaked with dark pink. The beans are dried on the plant in late summer, then threshed and stored for winter, but in August they're cooked up quickly to make a hearty salad that can be part of an antipasto or a first course for an important meal, or, accompanied by a fresh green salad perhaps, served as a light main course for lunch or supper.

Although tuna is the traditional garnish for this salad, salted anchovies or canned sardines are sometimes used instead, and Florentines, in an extravagant gesture that recalls their Medicean past, sometimes serve this humble country salad with a healthy dollop of caviar.

Beans for this purpose should be cooked very plainly, with little more than salt, pepper, and olive oil, though some cooks insist that a branch of fresh sage must be added to the bean pot. And you don't need to wait for fresh shell beans, either—dried winter beans will do just as well so long as they're thoroughly soaked and cooked at a very slow temperature so they don't burst in cooking.

You will need 2 to 3 pounds of beans in the pod, depending on the size of the beans, to get 2 cups shucked.

2 cups shelled fresh beans
2 bay leaves or 1 sprig fresh sage
3 tablespoons extra virgin olive oil
1 tablespoon red wine vinegar
Salt and freshly ground black pepper to taste
1 (6-ounce) can best quality oil-packed tuna
1 tablespoon capers, if desired
1 tablespoon finely minced flat-leaf parsley
1 medium red onion, very finely sliced

Bring a pot of lightly salted water to a rolling boil, add the beans to the pot with the bay leaves or sage, and cook until the beans are tender but still firm and not falling apart—about 15 minutes, depending on the size and age of the beans. Drain thoroughly, discarding the aromatics, and transfer to a bowl.

Dress the warm beans immediately with the oil and vinegar. Add about 1 teaspoon salt, or to taste, and plenty of black pepper. Mix well and taste, adjusting seasoning.

Now flake in the tuna and add the capers and parsley to the beans. Toss to mix well and strew the red onion slices over the top. Arrange on a platter and serve immediately while the beans are still warm, or let cool to room temperature.

Variation: There's no reason to wait for summer to make this salad, but if you use dried beans, be careful not to overcook them. Once dried beans have soaked in water overnight, 1 cup will expand to 2. Drain the beans and put them in a pot with fresh cool unsalted water to cover to a depth of 1 inch. Bring to a boil over medium heat, then lower the heat so the beans just barely simmer until done—about 45 minutes to 1 hour, but it all depends on the size and age of the beans. When the beans are tender but not falling apart, drain thoroughly and transfer to a bowl. Dress and season as above while still warm.

Oven-braised or Grilled Skewered Liver
fegatelli

6 TO 8 SERVINGS

A winter dish, fegatelli are one of the immediate delights of the annual slaughter of the family pig, which usually takes place between mid-November and Christmas. The pork liver we get here in this country is quite gamy in flavor, unlike the sweet livers of Tuscan pigs that have grazed in the forest on acorns and beech mast. When I make fegatelli here, I usually substitute calf's or lamb's liver, which is easier to find and sweeter in taste.

Caul fat, which you can order from a good butcher, is the lacy membrane of fat that lines the abdominal cavities of sheep and swine. It's widely used in Europe to bard very lean meats (like liver, small birds, or very lean fresh sausages) and to keep them from drying out while cooking. By the time the meat is cooked, the caul fat should be almost completely melted. Don't worry if you can only buy caul fat in large quantities; it keeps well in the freezer.

Tuscan cooks favor the use of fennel pollen, or the crushed flowers of wild fennel, to flavor all sorts of pork dishes. If you're traveling in Tuscany, look for little plastic bags of the stuff in country markets. It doesn't seem to exist in this country (although wild fennel grows by the roadside in California) but ground fennel seeds may be substituted. They'll be best if freshly ground in a mortar just before adding them to the dish.

½ pound caul fat
1½ pounds calf's or lamb's liver
Salt and freshly ground black pepper to taste
1 teaspoon powdered fennel, preferably fennel pollen
6 or 8 bay leaves, preferably fresh

Put the caul fat to soak in a bowl of tepid water while you prepare the liver.

Cut the liver in large bite-size chunks, discarding any membranes or filaments. Sprinkle the chunks liberally with salt, pepper, and fennel, rolling the liver chunks in the aromatics to coat them well.

Cut fresh bay leaves in half. On a board or work counter, carefully spread out a piece of lacy caul fat large enough to wrap around a liver chunk. Place a piece of liver in the center of the caul fat, top it with half a fresh bay leaf, wrap the caul fat around the meat, tucking the ends in as if you were wrapping a package, and secure it with a toothpick. The little packages may also be skewered, three or four pieces to a skewer, each piece separated from the others by a bay leaf.

If you have a charcoal grill or wood fire, build up a thick bed of hot coals or glowing embers. Set the livers on a grill 4 to 5 inches from the heat source and grill them, turning frequently, until they are done to taste (some people like their liver well done while others prefer it pink in the middle) and most of the caul fat has melted away.

The fegatelli may also be roasted in the oven. To do this, preheat the oven to 450°F. Set the skewers or separate chunks in an oven dish and place in the oven for 15 to 20 minutes, turning at least once, until the livers are done to taste and most of the caul fat has melted away.

Serve immediately, with plenty of thinly sliced bread for sopping up juices.

First Courses: Soups

i primi: zuppe

Tuscan soups are robust affairs from the country wife's kitchen, where they often form the *piatto unico,* the sole dish on the table, especially at the evening meal. Combinations of vegetables thickened with beans, pasta, or potatoes, they are most often served over a slice of crusty bread, usually stale, sometimes toasted, rubbed with a cut clove of garlic, then laved with olive oil (extra virgin, naturally, the dense green unguent of local production), a bruschetta in the bottom of the bowl to add further substance to an already substantial dish.

Hearty soups like these formed the backbone of the country-man's diet, served almost every day of the year and made each day in much the same way, starting with a soffritto or battuto of aromatics (onion, garlic, celery, parsley, and/or carrot), finely minced and browned in the bottom of the pot with a little olive oil and some chopped rigatino, the leanest part of the pancetta or pork belly, salted, peppered, and hung to dry-cure just like a prosciutto. When the odors of the soffritto begin to rise from the pot, vegetables are added, in summer straight from the garden, in winter from the pantry and the cantina, the cellar where the housewife stores her pride, rows and rows and rows of pomarola, the fragrant tomato sauce put up in bottles and jars late in the summer.

Stocks and broths made from meat or chicken are not usually added to the family minestra, partly for reasons of economy but also because a meat or chicken stock would overpower the good flavors of the vegetables. Bean broth or bean purée is, however, another matter entirely. Next to the soup kettle on the hearth in the country kitchen a pot of beans was always simmering, especially in wintertime. Beans are an essential and all-purpose protein on the Tuscan table, and just about every minestra has a *mestolo di fagioli,* a ladleful of beans or bean broth, added to it.

It is often an all-day affair, this soup. Preparation begins right after breakfast, and ingredients are added throughout the day until suppertime. But it doesn't require a great deal of attention, so the cook can accomplish a dozen other tasks while the elements of the soup come together. The last ingredient, the bread, toasted or not, goes in when the soup is served.

Of course, not all Tuscan soups are of this nature, but enough to give a sense of similarity to the soup course wherever you go in the region. Some might call it monotonous, but on the contrary, as you'll see immediately, even as all-encompassing a soup as acquacotta changes ingredients from one valley to the next. In one Tuscan recipe book I counted twenty-six different versions of acquacotta alone. And that's only the beginning.

Bread Soup with Ricotta from Monte Amiata
acquacotta di santa fiora

6 TO 8 SERVINGS

Here's a simple, homey version of acquacotta like that made in Santa Fiora, a sweet little medieval town on the slopes of Monte Amiata. Potatoes give body to the soup, which is enriched with a dollop of fresh sheep's milk ricotta. Goat's milk ricotta is a little easier to find in this country, and just as tasty. (See the Source Guide, page 276.) Wild bitter greens such as dandelion greens will give an authentic touch, but if you're not up to harvesting wild greens, use cultivated dandelion or other bitter greens instead. In a pinch, green chard may be substituted for the bitter greens, but of course the soup will not have the same bite.

2 medium yellow onions, thinly sliced

1 stalk celery, including green top, thinly sliced

2 cloves garlic, peeled and coarsely chopped

2 ounces pancetta, diced, or use blanched slab bacon

2 tablespoons extra virgin olive oil

1½ pounds potatoes, peeled and sliced or cut in small chunks

3 or 4 plum tomatoes, skinned, seeded, and chopped, or 1 cup canned tomatoes, chopped, with their juice

1 cup cooked beans (see page 67)

1 dried hot red chile pepper

Salt and freshly ground black pepper to taste

1 bunch bitter greens, rinsed and slivered, to make 3 to 4 cups

1 cup fresh ricotta

6 to 8 (1-inch-thick) slices country-style bread, very lightly toasted

⅓ cup freshly grated aged Pecorino or Parmigiano-Reggiano

A little olive oil, for garnish

In a heavy soup kettle, gently sauté the onion, celery, garlic, and pancetta in the olive oil over medium heat until the vegetables are soft but not brown. Add the potatoes, tomatoes, cooked beans (with any cooking liquid), and dried red chile pepper. Add 3 cups of boiling water to cover the vegetables to a depth of 1 inch, and salt and pepper. As soon as the liquid comes to a simmer, lower the heat, cover the pan, and cook at a slow simmer for about 40 minutes. Now stir in the greens with the water clinging to their leaves and simmer, stirring occasionally, until the greens are thoroughly wilted, about 15 minutes longer. Taste and adjust the seasoning.

Just before serving, mix in the ricotta, breaking it into lumps. Place a slice of toasted bread in the bottom of each bowl and pour the soup over it. Serve immediately, with grated cheese and olive oil to add at the table.

Variation: Restaurants in Santa Fiora sometimes offer a choice of acquacotta with ricotta or with an egg (never both). To make the soup with eggs, drop an egg per serving into the simmering broth just before dishing up. As soon as the whites are set, remove the eggs, place one in each bowl on the slice of bread, and pour the steaming soup over. (This is actually easier if you poach the eggs separately in simmering water and put one in each serving bowl.)

Acquacotta
TUSCAN BREAD SOUP

The name means, simply, cooked water. It's the humblest of soups, as the name reflects, originally perhaps nothing but stale bread cooked in water with a few sliced onions and some wild greens or mushrooms, sustenance for woodsmen cutting trees and making charcoal in the chill damp of the winter forest, or for shepherds passing the night in a hut at the edge of fallow fields. It has many versions, each one of which claims to be uniquely authentic. "Delicious," my visitors from Arezzo proclaimed of the acquacotta with wild porcini served in a Cortona osteria, "but of course it's not really acquacotta. It's mushroom soup."

The Maremma, the broad coastal plain around Grosseto, only in the last century drained of its invidious malarial marshes, claims to be the motherland of acquacotta. But so does the Casentino, the rocky highland above Arezzo. And so does the region around Monte Amiata, Tuscany's highest mountain, a spent volcano that soars above the Maremma in southern Tuscany. About all that can be said with certainty is that it may have originated in all three—or perhaps somewhere on the crisscrossing routes that connect them, routes that have been traveled regularly, quite possibly since Etruscan times, by shepherds, woodsmen, and charcoal-burners. Nowadays the shepherds and charcoal-burners are mostly relics of the past and even woodcutters are more celebrated in fiction than in real life. But acquacotta lives on, a cold-weather dish whose robust flavors fill hungry stomachs when wind-driven rain and sleet slash against the windows of stone cottages.

above: **Tomato-Bread Soup** PAGE 62

opposite: **Prosciutto with Melon and Peaches**

overleaf: **Bread with Olive Oil and Coarse Salt**

above: **Tuscan Bread** PAGE 21

above: **Polenta with a Wild Mushroom Sauce** PAGE 104

above: **Oven-roasted Guinea Fowl with Pancetta and Herbs** PAGE 150

opposite: **Ingredients for Salt Cod with a Tomato Sauce** PAGE 140

overleaf: **Cantucci Biscotti di Prato with Vin Santo** PAGE 246

Bread Soup with Wild Mushrooms
acquacotta della montagna cortonese

MAKES 6 SERVINGS

Aquicker version of acquacotta from the mountains behind Cortona in eastern Tuscany, almost in Umbria. These steep wooded hills once supplied a living for dozens of charcoal-burners, whose lives were full of long intervals when there was precious little to do except watch the earth-covered mound in which green wood was slowly turning to charcoal. Thus, there was plenty of time to scavenge for the mushrooms, wild greens, and other forest treasures in which this region is still so rich.

1¼ pounds fresh wild mushrooms, cut in large chunks or ½ pound fresh shiitake
    mushrooms with one ½-ounce package dried wild porcini
¼ cup plus 3 tablespoons extra virgin olive oil
3 cloves garlic
3 sprigs wild mint (nepitella, similar to pennyroyal), or 5 fresh sage leaves
Salt and freshly ground black pepper to taste
½ pound drained canned plum tomatoes, coarsely chopped (about 1 cup)
6 (1-inch-thick) slices firm country-style bread, toasted on each side
6 eggs
½ cup grated aged Pecorino or Parmigiano-Reggiano, plus additional for serving

Place the fresh mushroom chunks in the bottom of a soup kettle with ¼ cup of the oil and sauté gently over medium heat until the mushrooms have absorbed the oil and released it again. Add 2 cloves of the garlic, the wild mint (nepitella) or sage, salt, and lots of pepper, and cook, stirring, until all the ingredients are well blended, about 10 minutes. Add the tomatoes, then stir in 4 cups hot water. (If using refreshed dried mushrooms, add them at this point along with ¼ cup of their soaking liquid.) Cover the pan and cook for about 15 minutes. Taste and adjust seasoning, adding more of the mushroom soaking liquid, as well as additional salt and pepper, if necessary.

Have the toasted bread slices ready. Cut the remaining clove of garlic and rub each slice with the cut garlic; then drizzle a little of the remaining oil over each slice. Place one slice in the bottom of each soup bowl.

Beat the eggs with the cheese in the bottom of a heated soup tureen or similar serving dish. Beat a ladleful of hot soup into the egg-cheese mixture and keep adding ladlefuls until the mixture is very hot. (This is called tempering the eggs, to make sure they don't scramble on contact with the boiling soup.) When the egg mixture is well heated, pour the remaining boiling soup over it, stir well to thicken the soup, and serve immediately, ladling the thickened soup over the toasted bread. Pass more grated cheese to garnish.

Bread Soup from the Casentino
acquacotta casentinese

4 TO 6 SERVINGS

This is the simplest acquacotta of all, probably close to the woodsman's or shepherd's original, as made in the Casentino, the high mountain valley that embraces the Arno north of Arezzo. Or so I thought. But after I'd eaten acquacotta at I Quattro Cantoni, a splendidly funky truck stop restaurant in Pratovecchio, and praised the soup's magnificent flavor, Marta Goretti told me that she puts her acquacotta in the oven to develop the flavors and pull it together, which of course shepherds and woodsmen could never do. It's more like a savory bread pudding than a soup, so thick you could eat it with a fork.

To finish this, you'll need a deep, heavy dish that can go in the oven—a soufflé dish will do as well as anything.

    1 thick slice pancetta or blanched bacon
    1 clove garlic
    1 small stalk celery
    1 medium carrot, peeled
    1 bunch flat-leaf parsley, leaves only
    1 tablespoon plus 1 teaspoon extra virgin olive oil
    4 or 5 medium red onions, very thinly sliced (about 1½ pounds)
    2 tablespoons tomato paste
    Salt to taste
    1 small dried hot red chile pepper
    4 to 5 cups light chicken broth or water
    1 cup grated aged Pecorino or Parmigiano-Reggiano
    1 pound stale country-style bread, very thinly sliced

Chop together the pancetta, garlic, celery, carrot, and parsley until very fine. Add with the tablespoon of oil to a heavy kettle and gently sauté over medium-low heat until the vegetables are very soft. Stir in the sliced onions and continue to cook, stirring frequently, until they are very soft and translucent, about 30 minutes. Do not let the onions brown.

When the onions are thoroughly softened and wilted, stir in the tomato paste—there should be just enough to give the onions a rosy color and no more. Add a pinch of salt and the chile pepper, broken in two, then pour in the chicken broth or water—just enough to cover the onions to a depth of about $1/2$ inch. (You may not need all of the stock to start with.) When the liquid has come to a simmer, cover the pan and continue to cook.

Let the soup simmer gently for about 30 minutes while you grate the cheese and slice the bread, crusts and all, as thinly as possible. (All of this may be done ahead of time but the onions should be simmering when you are ready to continue.)

Preheat the oven to 375°F. Spoon a little of the hot onion broth into an oven dish and fit as many slices of bread as you can across the bottom in one layer. Spoon about $1/3$ of the onion broth over the bread and sprinkle about $1/3$ of the grated cheese over the broth. Add more bread slices, again in one layer, then add another third of the onion broth and another layer of cheese. Make a final layer of bread, add the remaining onion broth, and sprinkle on the rest of the cheese. Fill the casserole with the remaining broth—it should come just to the top of the bread slices. Drizzle the teaspoon of oil over the top layer and place in the oven for 30 minutes to meld the flavors and lightly brown the top.

Serve immediately, passing more grated cheese if you wish.

Variation: When the stock or water is added to the onions, add 1 bunch of green chard, trimmed and very thinly sliced, to cook with the onions.

Tomato-Bread Soup
pappa al pomodoro

6 TO 8 SERVINGS

As with so many Tuscan recipes, the trick to making a fantastic pappa al pomodoro is in selecting the raw material, in this case tomatoes. This is one of those dishes that should really be made only when fresh, red, utterly ripe tomatoes are available from local farms or, better yet, your own garden. The Tuscan tomato season lasts a good deal longer than it does in most parts of the United States; still, the minute the tomatoes are ripe, good cooks drop everything and turn to pappa. This is a very dense soup, more like an old-fashioned porridge than a liquid broth.

2 pounds fresh red ripe tomatoes, cut in chunks

1 medium yellow onion, peeled and coarsely chopped

1 medium carrot, coarsely chopped

1 stalk celery, coarsely chopped

4 or 5 sprigs flat-leaf parsley

Salt and freshly ground black pepper to taste

$1/4$ cup extra virgin olive oil

2 cloves garlic, peeled, crushed with the flat blade of a knife, and chopped

$1/2$ pound country-style bread, crusts removed

1 stalk basil

Pinch of sugar

Extra virgin olive oil and basil leaves, for garnish

Place the tomatoes, onion, carrot, celery, and parsley in a soup kettle with about $1/4$ cup water. Bring to a boil and cook, uncovered, for about 20 minutes, or until the vegetables are all very soft. Midway through the cooking, taste and add salt and pepper. Add a little boiling water to the pan from time to time if necessary to keep the vegetables from sticking. When the vegetables are tender, remove the kettle from the heat and allow to cool a little. Then put the sauce through the fine disk of a food mill. Strain the resulting purée, if desired, and set aside. You should have about 3 cups.

Heat the olive oil in a soup pot over medium-low heat. Add the garlic and cook, stirring, until it softens. (Do not let it color.) While the garlic is cooking, tear the bread into big pieces and add to the pan, together with the basil and 2 cups boiling water. Cook the bread and basil in the water, stirring with a wooden spoon to break up the bread and adding more boiling water from time to time, up to 1 cup more. When the bread has thoroughly broken down and absorbed the water, add 2½ cups of the tomato purée and stir it in. Taste again and adjust the seasoning if necessary, adding a little sugar if desired. Cook over very low heat, stirring frequently, for 1 hour longer, adding a little more boiling water or hot tomato sauce to keep the soup from sticking. It should be very dense but still possible to eat with a spoon.

When the soup is done, set it aside to cool to room temperature (do not refrigerate). Remove and discard the basil. Taste the soup and adjust the seasoning if necessary. Serve each portion with a bit of extra virgin olive oil, garnished with a few basil leaves.

In Search of Ribollita

Ribollita simply means something that's reboiled—leftovers, in other words, and most often in Tuscany, leftover cabbage and beans. Hardly the stuff of gourmandise, yet there's not a restaurant worth its salt anywhere in the region that doesn't vaunt its own particular version. Ribollita can be first course, main course, or anything in between—a *piccolo assagio,* a little taste sent out by an acclaimed restaurant chef just so you can see how well he does it, or a mid-morning merenda for hard-working farmers engaged in field tasks. Far more than bistecca alla fiorentina or crostini or even the deliciously simple bruschetta rubbed with the first of the new season's olive oil, ribollita is what makes Tuscans Tuscan, and in its engaging use of leftovers, including leftover stale bread, it sums up all there is to say about the economy and frugality of the Tuscan table. Yet there are many ways to make a ribollita.

Carlo Cioni, chef and owner of Ristorante da Delfina, is a self-proclaimed authority on the subject of ribollita. Da Delfina nestles against the flank of Artimino, a diminutive hilltop village that overlooks the fresh green valley of the Arno west of Florence and the cream-colored walls of a Medici villa known as *cento camini* for its hundred chimneys. The restaurant has been in this spot for a good sixty years, since it was established by Cioni's grandmother, the original Delfina, who had been a cook at the villa, so Carlo has the weight of tradition very much on his side.

And he is unmistakable in his conviction: *"La ribollita è fatta in padella!"* Index finger raised like a Renaissance pope, he announces this in a thundering voice that immediately draws the attention of everyone seated around us on the sunny restaurant terrace. "Ribollita is made in the frying pan!" This goes counter to everything I've ever heard about ribollita. But here we have another authority, ninety-two-year-old Delfina herself, sitting quietly in the vestibule of the restaurant shelling fresh cannellini beans. If anyone knows ribollita, surely it is Delfina. And, she nods modestly, she has taught her grandson all her considerable secrets.

Here's how Carlo explains the process:

First, you make a minestrone or zuppa di verdura, an ordinary vegetable soup in which at least 60 percent of the ingredients consists of cabbage, mostly cavolo nero, the Tuscan black cabbage, which is not really cabbage at all but a pungent and savory kale, a wintertime staple on the tables of rich and poor alike. Other cabbages play a role too, but the place of honor goes to cavolo nero. The rest of the vegetables includes any or all of the following: zucchini, chard, garlic, nettles, borage, fennel, bitter greens, carrots, even a healthy spoonful of tomato conserve, and beans, of course, because without beans it would not be a true Tuscan zuppa di verdure. That's for the first day, and you eat what is necessary and put the rest aside.

The second day, you set the leftover soup on the stove to warm up. Then you slice as thinly as possible some good country-style bread that is slightly stale but not hard and crusty. (You can toast the slices if you want, but it's not vital.) Spread a layer of bread in the bottom of a soup tureen (better yet a terra-cotta baking dish) and spoon some of the hot leftover soup on top. Another layer of bread slices and another layer of hot soup. Cover the tureen and set aside for 20 minutes or so for the bread to absorb all the flavors of the soup. Eat what is necessary and put the rest aside.

The third day, warm up the bread soup while you slice very thinly some crisp white onions. Spread the onions over the top of the soup, drizzle with a very little olive oil, and place in a hot oven until the onions turn golden. Eat what is necessary and put the rest aside.

On the fourth day, just skim the surface of a frying pan with a little olive oil—*a punta di cucchiaio,* just the edge of a spoonful, of oil. That's the way the frugal old farmwives did it, says Carlo. Now take what's left of the soup, add it to the frying pan, place over low heat, and cook until it forms a little crust, then turn it and cook it some more until it forms another little crust, and keep turning it and cooking it to form crusts until you have a nice mixture of soft vegetables with bits of brown crust distributed throughout. (At this point I am remembering the way my mother made corned beef hash, which, in its origins, is not too far from ribollita.) Serve it in its glory with just a few drops of oil on top and eat it all.

"And that," says Carlo, "is a genuine ribollita."

In many Tuscan restaurants, ribollita is served with lashings of olive oil; indeed, it often seems like nothing but an excuse to consume alarming quantities of delicious green Tuscan oil. But Carlo Cioni's point is well taken. This is a farmhouse dish, and Tuscan farmers, until well into this century, were cash-poor even when their tables were laden with the products of fields, gardens, and forest. Olive oil was a precious commodity, to be sold for the coins that would be stashed in the farmer's mattress. Such frugality (some might say stinginess) demanded imagination and skill from cooks like Delfina, who evolved an inventive cuisine from humble ingredients, even from leftovers.

Ribollita

THE FOLLOWING is my own version of ribollita. It begins with beans, and here I must confess that I learned this method of cooking beans from Mario Batali, chef-owner of the tiny Ristorante Po on Cornelia Street in Greenwich Village. The technique seems to me so superior to others that I recommend it, even though it's not particularly Tuscan. Mario covers the dried beans with water, refrigerates them to keep them from sprouting, and soaks them for two days, then brings them to a simmer and just barely simmers them for an hour or until they're tender. (For a more traditional Tuscan method see Paola's Tuscan Pasta and Bean Soup [page 70].)

As for the beans themselves, Tuscans use a variety of different beans depending primarily on what they happen to grow in their own particular regions—white cannellini are the best known to us here, but there are also borlotti, the particolored beans that are favorites both freshly shucked and dried, and zolfi or zolfini, a pale creamy yellow bean from the upper Valdarno around Montevarchi that is considered absolutely essential to a successful Montevarchi ribollita. (These may be the same as the beans we call sulfur beans in Maine, but you probably can't get those in your local market either.) In general, almost any dried beans will do as long as they're not too old and hard. For this reason I generally buy dried beans at a health-food store with a fairly brisk turnover. Maine yellow-eyes or soldier beans are just about perfect. For authenticity's sake, the beans should not be deeply colored; hence, no black beans, no red kidney beans—but this is purely an aesthetic consideration.

I should also note that when I prepare beans in the United States, whether Tuscan fagioli or Maine baked beans, I use Poland Spring water for both soaking and cooking. Not that my local water isn't safe to drink, but I do believe the softer unchlorinated spring water yields better beans, just as it's better for bread. Use whatever locally bottled spring water is available in your area.

Tuscan Beans for Soup or on Their Own
fagioli alla toscana

4 TO 5 CUPS BEANS; 3 TO 4 CUPS LIQUID

2 cups dried beans

2 cloves garlic, peeled and crushed with a flat knife blade

3 sprigs fresh sage

2 tablespoons extra virgin olive oil

Freshly ground black pepper to taste

Salt to taste

Rinse the beans under running water if they look a little dusty. Place in a large bowl and add 2 cups of water (preferably spring water), or enough to cover the beans to a depth of about 1½ inches. Cover with plastic wrap and set in the refrigerator for 6 to 8 hours or overnight. Next day, check the beans and add more water if necessary—this time just top them up to a depth of ½ inch. Put back in the refrigerator and leave overnight again. They should soak for two days, more or less, and should be checked from time to time to see that they haven't absorbed all the water during this period. (Refrigeration is necessary to keep the beans from either fermenting or sprouting.)

When ready to cook, transfer the beans, *with their soaking liquid,* to a large, heavy pot—enameled cast-iron is perfect. Add more water if necessary, to a depth of about ½ inch, and the garlic, sage, oil, and pepper. Cover the pot with a tight-fitting lid and set over medium-high heat. Bring to a boil, let boil for 60 seconds, then lower the heat and cook *without removing the lid* very, very gently, just barely simmering, for 1 hour. At the end of the hour, stir in salt to taste. Test the beans and if they are not sufficiently tender, continue to simmer gently until done. (It is hard to predict what beans will do, since so much depends on the age of the beans, a factor that, unless you've grown them yourself, is often hard to determine.)

The beans may be served as is, with a drizzle of fresh green olive oil and, if you wish, chopped raw garlic, chopped anchovies, flaked canned tuna, thinly sliced red onion, and plenty of black pepper, along with slices of grilled bread. Beans like this are often served as a side dish to accompany roast pork, game, or grilled sausages. Or they may become the basis of other dishes.

Vegetable Soup
zuppa di verdura

12 TO 14 CUPS, TO SERVE 8 TO 10

3 cups cooked beans plus 1½ to 2 cups cooking liquid

2 tablespoons extra virgin olive oil plus more to garnish

1 medium onion, peeled and finely chopped

2 cloves garlic, peeled and finely chopped

2 stalks celery, finely sliced

2 medium carrots, scraped and finely sliced

1 leek, cleaned and finely sliced

4 fresh ripe flavorful tomatoes, peeled (or 1 cup canned tomatoes with juice)

3 medium potatoes, peeled and cut in small chunks

Salt and freshly ground black pepper to taste

1 bunch green chard, finely sliced

1 bunch kale or cavolo nero, finely sliced

½ small green cabbage, quartered and finely sliced

1 teaspoon fresh thyme or ¼ teaspoon dried thyme

8 slices stale country-style bread, if desired

Drain the cooked beans, reserving the liquid in which they cooked. Set aside about 1 cup of the beans and purée the remainder along with the bean liquid. Reserve.

In a heavy soup kettle, heat the oil. Add the onion, chopped garlic, celery, carrots, and leek and cook, stirring occasionally, until the vegetables are soft but not brown. Chop the tomatoes coarsely and add them and their juice to the vegetables. Stir in the potatoes and add 1½ cups boiling water. Taste and add salt and pepper as desired. Cook, covered, for 5 to 10 minutes, or until the potatoes just start to soften.

If you are using large leaves of chard, kale, or cavolo nero, remove the thick stalks and discard them, then sliver the greens. Together with the slivered cabbage, you should have 4 to 5 cups of greens. After the potatoes have started to soften, add the greens, the bean purée, and the reserved cup of whole beans, along with the fresh or dried thyme, stirring to incorporate everything well.

Lower the heat to low, cover the kettle, and cook at a bare simmer for 30 minutes to 1 hour, or until the vegetables are very soft. Add *boiling* water from time to time as necessary to prevent the bean purée from sticking to the kettle.

Serve as is or over toasted slices of garlic-rubbed bread. Drizzle each serving with a little extra virgin olive oil.

Twice-boiled Vegetable and Bread Soup
ribollita

6 SERVINGS

8 cups leftover Vegetable Soup (previous page)
8 thin slices country-style bread
1 clove garlic, unpeeled, cut in half
2 to 3 tablespoons extra virgin olive oil, plus more to pass

Heat the leftover zuppa di verdura to simmering. Grill the bread slices until they are toasted brown, and rub each slice on one side with the cut clove of garlic. Place 4 of the slices in the bottom of a soup tureen and drizzle on about 1 tablespoon of oil. Ladle half the soup over them. Top with the remaining bread slices and remaining oil, and cover with the rest of the soup. Let rest for a few minutes in a warm place (a turned-off oven is fine) so that the bread can absorb the soup, then serve immediately, passing more oil so that each person can add as much or as little as desired.

Or set the soup aside in a cool pantry to serve at room temperature, a nice thing to do in summertime.

Paola's Tuscan Pasta and Bean Soup
pasta e fagioli di grattamacco

8 SERVINGS

Paola Meletti Cavallari, who with her husband Piermario makes wine and olive oil at Grattamacco in the rolling hills of the Maremma, is a home cook of rare distinction. Although originally from Bergamo in the north, Paola has mastered the classics of Tuscan cuisine. And nothing could be more classically Tuscan than this bean soup. Beans—cannellini, borlotti, toscanelli, piattelli, zolfini, and a dozen other varieties—are the great staples of the Tuscan table. Paola uses borlotti beans (sometimes called cranberry beans in America) from her own garden, dried and put by for the winter, but any light-colored dried beans, such as white cannellini or Maine soldier beans, will do for the dish; for aesthetic reasons, dark-colored kidney beans or black beans are not so good.

If you don't want to make your own pasta, small shapes of dried pasta such as ditalini cook best in this thick soup.

1½ cups dried beans, soaked overnight
3 tablespoons extra virgin olive oil, plus a little more for garnish
1 branch fresh sage, leaves only
1 branch fresh rosemary
For the pasta:
2 cups unbleached all-purpose flour
1 large egg
Water
Pinch of salt
Olive oil
Or: 1 cup dried commercial pasta such as ditalini
2 small onions, minced
2 stalks celery, minced
1 medium carrot, minced
¼ cup tomato sauce, or 2 tablespoons tomato concentrate diluted with
　　2 tablespoons water
Salt and freshly ground black pepper to taste
1 clove garlic and 1 tablespoon chopped flat-leaf parsley, minced together

Put the beans in a saucepan with water to cover to a depth of 1 inch—about 4 cups should do it. Add 1 tablespoon of the oil, the sage, and the rosemary, bring to a simmer over low heat, and cook, covered, until the beans are tender. Time varies depending on the age of the beans, but count on at least 45 minutes and as much as 1 hour and 15 minutes. This will make about 5½ cups beans.

While the beans are cooking, make the pasta if you wish. Mound the flour on a board, make a well, crack the egg into it, and add some water and a pinch of salt. Pull the flour into the well and mix gently with your hands. Knead briefly on the board, then rub all over with olive oil, cover with plastic wrap, and set aside to rest.

In a saucepan large enough to hold the beans, gently sweat the onions, celery, and carrot in 2 tablespoons of the oil until the onions have turned golden but not brown.

Set a vegetable mill over the saucepan and, using the fine disk, pass the cooked beans, with their cooking liquid, into the vegetables in the pan. Mix well and add the tomato sauce, salt, and pepper. Add 2 cups boiling water, bring the soup to a simmer, and cook 15 minutes, stirring frequently.

While the soup is cooking, roll out the pasta about ⅛ inch thick and cut it with a knife into the irregular (anyhow) shapes that are called *maltagliati,* "badly cut." Add the fresh pasta to the soup and cook briefly, about 5 minutes, until the pasta is done. (If using dried pasta, add it to the simmering soup and cook according to package directions.)

When the pasta is done, serve the soup, garnishing each bowl with a sprinkling of minced garlic and parsley and a thread of extra virgin olive oil.

Variation: You can make Chickpea Soup (Zuppa di Ceci) by following this recipe but using 1½ cups dried chickpeas soaked overnight, then drained and cooked as above, with a bunch of rosemary but no sage. When the chickpeas are tender (they will take up to 1½ hours to cook), remove the rosemary and purée the soup.

In a sauté pan sweat 3 finely chopped cloves of garlic in 3 tablespoons extra virgin olive oil. When the garlic is soft but not brown, add 5 drained canned tomatoes, breaking them up with a fork or wooden spoon. Cook until the sauce is thick, then purée it through a vegetable mill directly into the chickpea purée, add about 1 cup small pasta shapes, and cook until the pasta is tender. Serve with a healthy drizzle of extra virgin olive oil.

Soup from the Olive Mill
zuppa frantoiana

6 TO 8 SERVINGS

Made in the early winter when the peppery olive oil, fresh from the press, is available, this soup, Tuscans say, is one of the best ways to taste the new oil. Use the finest oil you can find, preferably one of the current season's offerings, which usually arrive in U.S. markets in February or March. More and more, the best oil producers are dating their products so customers can select for freshness. (This by no means implies that an oil one or two years old is bad, but rather that the vivid flavors of the young oil will have softened and settled down.)

The beans used here are borlotti, also called *scritti* because the red markings look like scribbling on the pale ivory beans. If you can't find borlotti, use white cannellini beans or Maine yellow-eyes.

1½ cups dried beans, soaked overnight
1 medium carrot, cut in chunks
½ medium yellow onion
1 stalk celery, cut in chunks
Salt and freshly ground black pepper to taste
1 clove garlic, chopped
About ¾ cup extra virgin olive oil
3 or 4 leaves kale or cavolo nero
1 medium potato, peeled and cut in cubes
1 cup cubed pumpkin or dark yellow winter squash
1 medium carrot cut in large cubes
½ teaspoon crushed fennel seeds or fennel pollen
6 to 8 thin slices country-style bread
1 clove garlic, cut in half

Drain the beans and put them in a soup pot with about 3 cups of water and the chunks of carrot, onion half, and celery stalk. Bring to a gentle simmer and cook, covered, at a bare simmer until the beans are tender. Time will vary depending on the age and size of the beans; count on something between 45 and 75 minutes.

Once the beans are tender, remove and set aside about ¹/₂ cup whole beans. Put the remaining beans and vegetables, together with any cooking liquid, through the fine disk of a food mill and return to the rinsed-out soup pot. Taste and add salt and pepper as desired.

In a small saucepan, gently sauté the chopped garlic in 2 tablespoons of the olive oil; when the garlic is soft but not brown, add it to the puréed beans, along with the oil in the pan. Strip the tough center ribs from the kale or cavolo nero and chop the leaves coarsely. Add the chopped leaves, cubed potato, pumpkin, and cubed carrot to the soup pot. Bring to a simmer and cook gently, covered, until the vegetables are tender, then stir in the crushed fennel or pollen, the reserved beans, and add more pepper if you wish.

While the vegetables are cooking, toast the bread slices under a broiler (or over fireplace embers). Rub the slices with the garlic halves. When ready to serve, drizzle a liberal dose (at least 1 tablespoon) of olive oil over one side of each slice of toasted bread and set a slice in the bottom of each soup plate. Spoon the hot soup over the bread and add another dollop of oil (at least a teaspoon) to the center of each serving without stirring it in. Serve immediately.

Cornmeal, Kale, and Bean Soup
farinata di cavolo nero

8 SERVINGS

Tato, vammi a cercar du'funghi dietro casa che stasera ti faccio la farinatina." Eyes sparkling with enthusiasm, Fabrizia Fabbroni is imitating a Tuscan grandmother preparing farinata, an all-purpose soup made from cornmeal and any other grains available: "Grandpa," she translates, "go find me a couple of mushrooms behind the house so I can make a little farinata for your supper tonight." Grannies in the Casentino make their farinata, Fabrizia says, from whatever flour they have on hand—a little wheat flour, a little semolina, a handful of cornmeal, and maybe some wheat bran from the corner cupboard.

Like a soupy polenta, farinata is often not much more than meal and water. A little salt, a little oil, some mushrooms, tossed in an old black iron kettle over the wood fire and cooked long and slowly so the separate ingredients disintegrate into a soft and savory porridge. Granny, Fabrizia explains, never learned measurements—she talks of a handful of meal, a pinch of salt, a thread of oil, and that amusing, frustrating notation throughout Italy, "q.b.," *quanto basta,* meaning "as needed." Water as needed, salt as needed, flour as needed. If, like those grandmothers, you make these dishes day after day, you never need to measure. The eye, the hand, the nose will tell you quanto basta. Here, though, are more precise measurements for a farinata made with cornmeal and beans.

½ cup dried beans, soaked in water to cover overnight
1 (6-inch) strip fresh pork rind (cotiche) or 2 tablespoons extra virgin olive oil
1 small bunch kale or cavolo nero
2 ounces pancetta, chopped
½ medium onion, peeled and chopped
1 stalk celery, chopped
1 carrot, chopped
½ cup chopped flat-leaf parsley
1 clove garlic, peeled and flattened with a knife
2 tablespoons chopped rosemary
2 tablespoons extra virgin olive oil, plus more for garnish
2 medium potatoes, peeled and cut in cubes
½ teaspoon fennel seeds, crushed

Salt to taste

½ pound (1 cup) coarsely ground cornmeal

6 to 8 thin slices country-style bread, toasted or fried in extra virgin olive oil

Grated aged Pecorino or Parmigiano-Reggiano, for garnish

Drain the beans and place in a small saucepan with the pork rind or olive oil. Cover with water to a depth of 1 inch. Bring to a boil and simmer, covered, until the beans are tender but not falling apart, adding a little boiling water if necessary from time to time. When they are done, remove the pork rind and discard. Set the beans aside in their cooking liquid.

Remove and discard the tough central ribs from the kale or cavolo nero. Sliver the leaves—you should have about 4 cups, tightly packed. Rinse the leaves well but do not dry. Set aside.

Chop together the pancetta, onion, celery, carrot, parsley, garlic, and rosemary until the mixture is very fine. In a soup kettle, gently sauté the chopped mixture in 2 tablespoons of oil until the vegetables are soft but not brown. Add the boiled beans with all their liquid and stir to mix well. Now add the slivered kale, the potatoes, and fennel. Add salt to taste and 1½ to 2 cups boiling water and simmer the soup over gentle heat for about 20 minutes, or until the potatoes are cooked through and the other vegetables are very soft. The farinata may be prepared ahead of time up to this point.

When ready to continue, heat the vegetable mixture to simmering, adding a little more water if necessary.

Turn the cornmeal into a bowl and add 2 cups of cold water. Stir until the cornmeal has absorbed the water, then turn the cornmeal into the simmering soup, stirring all the while, until all the cornmeal has been blended in. Continue cooking, stirring frequently, for 40 minutes, to make a very thick, porridgy soup, but still a soup, that must be eaten with a spoon.

Serve the farinata immediately, over slices of toasted bread or bread that has been fried in olive oil. Garnish with a drizzle of olive oil and a little freshly grated Pecorino or Parmigiano-Reggiano.

Like polenta, this is sometimes spread on a board to firm up, then sliced when quite cold, and the slices fried in abundant olive oil.

Variation: The ingredients of a farinata vary with the seasons. Instead of wintertime kale or cavolo nero, in summer cooks will add 2 large, fresh, ripe tomatoes, peeled, seeded, and chopped, or in autumn (as grandmother does) 2 large, fresh, wild porcini mushrooms, cleaned and sliced. (Don't make the mistake of thinking that if one of these ingredients tastes good, all of them combined will taste better—they won't, and you'll only muddy the purity of the dish.)

Hearty Farro Soup
minestra di farro

6 TO 8 SERVINGS

The word *farro* comes from a generic Latin word for wheat, *farrum* or *far,* which itself is derived from the Indo-European root *bhares-* (from which in English we get barley and barn). Farro is sometimes (I believe wrongly) translated as spelt, a type of wheat once widely grown in colder regions of Europe. The farro that is today grown and used in Tuscany and Umbria is more properly identified as emmer wheat. Although spelt and emmer are related, and both are ancient grains, among the first ever cultivated, they are genetically distinct. Farro gives a soft, low-gluten flour, not particularly good for bread or pasta but excellent for porridge, which is, after all, a kind of protobread.

Elio Capecchi, a farmer in the Val di Chiana, the broad, fertile valley that runs south of Arezzo, has been experimenting with farro for years. Its use died out, he told me, because each individual grain has a tough, indigestible outer husk, called a glume, that was hard to remove before the advent of modern milling equipment. When buying farro, look for clean, whole grains with the glume removed. The best farro in Tuscany comes from the Garfagnana, the mountainous region that follows the valley of the Serchio River northeast of Lucca, where farro has been cultivated for millennia.

If you can't find farro, you could substitute kamut, another type of wheat, or wheatberries in this recipe. Properly cleaned Tuscan farro will not need to be soaked, but other wheat grains must be soaked several hours or overnight to soften them.

1 cup dried beans, such as borlotti or cannellini

Salt to taste

1 medium onion, coarsely chopped

1 medium carrot, coarsely chopped

1 stalk celery, coarsely chopped (including leafy top)

2 ounces pancetta or blanched slab bacon, diced

2 tablespoons extra virgin olive oil, plus more for garnish

3 tablespoons finely chopped canned plum tomatoes

4 fresh sage leaves

¾ cup farro (see headnote for substitutes)

3 large leaves kale or cavolo nero

Freshly ground black pepper to taste

¼ cup finely minced flat-leaf parsley, for garnish

¼ cup freshly grated Pecorino or Parmigiano-Reggiano, for garnish

The night before cooking, put the beans to soak in cool water to cover to a depth of 1 inch. (If you are using wheatberries instead of farro, set them to soak in a separate bowl.) Next morning, drain the beans and place in a saucepan with fresh water to cover to a depth of 1 inch. Bring to a simmer, cover, and simmer gently until the beans are tender. Timing will depend on the age of the beans, and can take from 45 to 75 minutes. Add boiling water as the beans absorb what is in the pot. When the beans are soft, stir in salt to taste.

Meanwhile, chop together the onion, carrot, and celery. In a soup kettle, gently sauté the pancetta in 2 tablespoons of the olive oil over medium heat. When the pancetta starts to release its fat, stir in the chopped vegetables and continue cooking gently until they start to soften. Add the tomatoes and sage and 2 cups of water, bring to a boil, cover, reduce the heat, and simmer very gently for 30 minutes, stirring occasionally.

Set aside about ½ cup beans to be added to the soup later. Purée the remaining beans and their liquid in a food processor or a vegetable mill and add to the vegetables in the soup kettle. Stir in the reserved beans. Place over low heat, and when the soup starts to simmer, add the farro or soaked and drained wheatberries and stir to mix well. The liquid should be fairly dense but not sticking to the bottom of the pan. Add a little boiling water if necessary to thin.

Cover the pan and cook the farro or wheat for about 45 minutes, or until the grains are swollen and soft. Check frequently and add a little boiling water if the purée starts to stick. After 30 minutes add the thinly slivered kale and black pepper to taste.

When done, serve immediately, garnishing the soup with a sprinkle of parsley and a drizzle of extra virgin olive oil. Pass the grated cheese at the table.

Variation: One year at the annual Banchetto Etrusco in the little hill town of Murlo, southeast of Siena (see page 40), the "Etruscan" zuppa di farro was served with an *intingolo,* a mixture of very finely chopped wild mint, celery, citronella (lemongrass), sorrel, and capers, heated in about ½ cup extra virgin olive oil. This was drizzled over the soup at the moment of serving.

Wild Mushroom Soup
zuppa di funghi porcini

6 TO 8 SERVINGS

In the long and balmy Tuscan autumn, when the hills are alive with the sound of funghi hunters in search of wild porcini mushrooms, cooks turn these prized and often elusive specimens into sauces, stews, and simple grills. Porcini, also known as cèpes (their French name) and boletes (from their botanical name, *Boletus*), are easy to find in this country, too, and because of their unmistakable characteristics, they are one of the least threatening, most user-friendly of all wild mushrooms. Consult any good mushroom guidebook for information, or seek out a local mycological society for help. Other kinds of wild mushrooms may also be used in this recipe, alone or in combination, but porcini are the real prize.

Wild mushrooms should be carefully cleaned by brushing away any earth with a soft brush. Don't wash them, however, as they will absorb the water and become spongy. Slice the mushrooms thickly before using and discard any that are riddled with wormholes.

> 3 tablespoons extra virgin olive oil
> 1 red or yellow onion, peeled and finely chopped
> 2 stalks celery, finely chopped
> 1 medium carrot, scraped and finely chopped
> 1 tablespoon unbleached all-purpose flour
> About 1 pound wild porcini or other mushrooms
> 6 cups light chicken broth, heated to a simmer
> Salt and freshly ground black pepper to taste
> 6 (1-inch-thick) slices country-style bread, lightly toasted and rubbed with a cut
>   clove of garlic
> 2 or 3 tablespoons finely minced flat-leaf parsley

In a soup kettle or heavy pot large enough to hold all the ingredients except the bread, gently sauté in the oil the chopped onion, celery, and carrot. When the vegetables are soft but not brown, sprinkle with flour, stirring to mix well. Add the mushrooms, cut in small pieces, and turn them in the savory fat. The mushrooms will absorb a good deal of the fat and then release it again, along with their juices.

When this happens, pour in the simmering broth and stir to mix well. Taste and add salt and pepper as desired. Cover the pan and cook at a slow simmer for about 20 to 30 minutes, or until the broth is impregnated with the flavor of the mushrooms.

Put the garlic-flavored bread slices in the bottom of a soup tureen, or put one slice in the bottom of each soup plate. Pour the simmering soup over the bread and serve immediately, garnished with sprinkles of parsley.

Note: If you can't find wild mushrooms, the soup may be made with a combination of fresh cultivated shiitakes and a small, $1/2$-ounce packet of dried wild funghi porcini, soaking the porcini as described on pages 104–105, and adding them, with their strained soaking liquid, when you add the broth.

Tuscan Onion Soup
carabaccia

6 TO 8 SERVINGS

One of the enduring myths of Tuscan gastronomy concerns the role of Caterina de' Medici (or Cathérine de Médicis), who taught the hitherto backward French everything they needed to know about fine cuisine when she married the future Henri II in 1533. Were it not for Caterina, they say, the French would remain to this day unenlightened about, among other things, forks, petit pois, parsley, artichokes, and soupe à l'oignon.

It's true that there are ancient Tuscan recipes for onion soup, one of which, from a fourteenth-century manuscript called *L'Anonimo Toscano,* sounds very much like the soup made in Tuscany today. Whether it's the ancestor of soupe à l'oignon or not, it's a first-rate example of how the simple good things of the countryside (the work of humble farmhouse cooks) have persisted over the centuries. This is the recipe from *L'Anonimo Toscano* in its entirety:

Togli cipolle tagliate e lavate bene con acqua calda, e metti a cocere con carne e cascio, pepe e zaffarano; e ppoi ponevi ova dibattuto, pepe e croco e, se vuoli, spezie in scudelle. ★

And this is the recipe for a modern Tuscan onion soup.

2 ounces pancetta, cut in small dice
2 carrots, scraped and coarsely chopped
2 stalks celery, coarsely chopped
1/4 cup minced flat-leaf parsley
2 tablespoons extra virgin olive oil
2 pounds red or yellow onions, peeled and very thinly sliced
Salt and freshly ground black pepper to taste
4 cups light chicken or meat broth, or broth and water mixed
1/2 cup dry white wine
1/3 cup freshly grated Pecorino or Parmigiano-Reggiano, plus additional for passing
Slices of toasted bread

Combine the pancetta, carrots, celery, parsley, and oil in a saucepan over medium-low heat and sauté very gently until the fat starts to run. Add the onions, with salt and pepper, and cook very gently, covered, for 1 hour, while the onions soften and give off considerable liquid. If the liquid is insufficient and the onions start to brown, add a little of the broth or plain water. The onions should not brown but rather reduce to a soft, golden mass.

At the end of the cooking time, add the wine, and when the alcohol has evaporated, add the remaining broth. Cook, uncovered, an additional 15 minutes. Stir in the cheese, taste, and adjust the seasoning. Serve immediately over toasted bread slices, passing more grated cheese at the table.

* Take onions that have been sliced and washed well with hot water, and place them to cook with meat and cheese, pepper and saffron, and then add beaten eggs, pepper and saffron crocus and, if you wish, spices.

Spring Vegetable Soup from the Lucchesia
garmugia

6 TO 8 SERVINGS

Abeautiful springtime soup that pulls together all the flavors of the season, garmugia is made only when cooks have access to fresh green peas, sweet fava beans, asparagus, and the smallest violet-colored artichokes. A specialty of the hills around Lucca, garmugia *could* be made with frozen peas and asparagus imported from Mexico, but take the trouble to seek out the freshest and most flavorful spring vegetables and you'll begin to understand what I mean when I say that Tuscan flavors begin not in the kitchen but in the marketplace, if not in the garden itself. Don't feel constrained by the list of ingredients: If you can't get fava beans, use diced young carrots or fresh string beans instead, or if you find some small new potatoes, add them to the whole. The point is to take advantage of the best of the new crop rather than to spend time chasing down elusive items.

Fava beans (sometimes called broad beans), if they are sufficiently young and tender, may be topped and tailed and cut into chunks like string beans, but unless you grow them yourself it's hard to find beans that young in American markets. If the pods are no longer tender, shell the beans and discard the pods. Some recipe books recommend removing the delicate peel around each individual bean as well, but to my mind that is overly solicitous, especially since the peel has a lot of earthy flavor.

3 tablespoons extra virgin olive oil

4 fresh white spring onions with green tops still attached, or 1 fat leek,
    trimmed and chopped

2 ounces prosciutto, including the fat, or 2 ounces pancetta,
    cut in thin lardons, or 1 small Italian pork sausage

½ pound very lean ground veal or beef

3 to 4 pounds fresh spring vegetables, such as:

1 pound young fava beans, cut in chunks or shelled

1 pound young green peas, shelled

4 small chokeless artichokes, trimmed and cut in half
    (or the hearts of 2 globe artichokes trimmed and diced)

½ pound fresh asparagus, trimmed and cut in small pieces

Or the equivalent in baby carrots, white turnips, green beans, new potatoes, and the
   like, peeled if necessary, and cut in small pieces
6 cups chicken stock
Salt and freshly ground black pepper to taste
6 slices country-style bread, toasted and cut in thick fingers
Freshly grated Parmigiano-Reggiano, for garnish

In a saucepan or soup kettle large enough to hold all the ingredients except the bread, heat the oil over medium-low heat. Add the chopped onions and prosciutto and sauté gently 5 to 10 minutes until the onions are soft and the fat starts to melt. Add the ground meat, raise the heat slightly, and cook, stirring, until the meat is browned, about 5 minutes.

Add all the vegetables and cook for about 5 minutes, stirring constantly, until the vegetables are well coated with fat and starting to soften. Pour in the stock and bring to a very slow simmer. Cover the pan and cook gently until the vegetables are soft, 10 to 15 minutes depending on the size of the vegetable pieces. Taste, adding salt and pepper as desired.

The soup may be prepared several hours ahead of time up to this point. When ready to serve, bring it back to a slow simmer, but do not overcook. The fresh flavors of the vegetables will be most apparent if they are just barely done. Distribute the toasted bread fingers among 6 or 8 soup plates. Pour the soup over the bread in each plate and serve immediately, passing freshly grated Parmigiano-Reggiano if desired.

Note: A more delicate but savory vegetarian version of this soup can be made simply by omitting the meats and using vegetable broth instead of chicken broth.

Chickpea Stew
cacciucco di ceci

6 SERVINGS

Cacciucco most often refers to a fish stew (see page 125), but in the mountains of the Maremma, where the blue green expanse of the Tyrrhenian Sea is far away on the distant horizon, fish is at a premium, and cacciucco is made instead with chickpeas.

1 cup chickpeas

1/2 pound green or red chard

1/3 cup extra virgin olive oil

4 salted anchovies, split and rinsed in running water, or 8 oil-packed anchovy fillets

1 large onion, peeled, halved, and thinly sliced

2 cloves garlic, peeled and coarsely chopped

1/2 dried hot red chile pepper, crumbled, or 1/4 teaspoon crushed red pepper flakes

Freshly ground black pepper to taste

1 tablespoon canned tomato paste

6 (1-inch-thick) slices crusty country-style bread

1 clove garlic, cut in half

1/4 cup freshly grated Pecorino Toscano or Parmigiano-Reggiano or more to taste

Put the chickpeas to soak for at least 6 hours or overnight in abundant cool water.

When ready to cook, slice the chard in ribbons and rinse well in running water. Place in a saucepan and cook in the water clinging to its leaves, adding a little more if necessary, until it is tender, about 20 minutes. Drain if necessary and set aside.

In a soup kettle, heat 3 tablespoons oil. Chop the anchovy fillets and add to the oil, stirring and pressing with the back of a spoon until they have melted into the oil. Add the onion and chopped garlic and cook gently, stirring occasionally, until the vegetables are soft but not brown.

Drain the chickpeas and add them to the oil, stirring to coat them well with the mixture. Add the chard and chile pepper and cover to a depth of about 1/2 inch with boiling water. Stir in lots of ground black pepper and the tomato paste, cover, and cook over gentle heat, so that the soup is just barely simmering, for about 2 hours or until the chickpeas are very soft and the flavors are thoroughly blended.

Lightly toast the bread slices on a grill or under a broiler. Rub one side of each slice with the cut clove of garlic. Place a slice of garlic toast in the bottom of each soup plate and drizzle over it some of the remaining olive oil. Pour the hot soup over the bread and sprinkle with a little grated cheese. Serve immediately.

Butter and Egg Soup for Newlyweds
ginestrata

4 SERVINGS

Tuscan cuisine is so rigorously based on olive oil and pork fat that it may come as a surprise to find lots of butter in this beautiful yellow soup from the Chiantigiana. Butter, says Dario Cecchini, the Panzano butcher (see pages 172–173), was a feature of early summer dishes because the Chianina calves, born in spring, were taken off their mothers' milk in June and the excess milk, rich with cream, was used to make butter.

Traditionally this soup, with its odd mix of medieval spices, was an ancient restorative, intended to pick up the flagging spirits of bride and groom the morning after their wedding. Thus, you'll often find recipes written in quantities for two, with the stipulation that it be served in the household's most beautiful pair of soup bowls. It's called ginestrata because it's the same clear brilliant yellow as the fragrant blossoms of Scotch broom, the shrub that carpets Tuscan hillsides in June (genus *Genista*) and fills the air with a haunting, delicate perfume.

The spices in this soup will be more fragrant if they are freshly ground just before you add them.

6 cups chicken stock
½ cup dry vin santo or dry Amontillado sherry
1 tablespoon sugar or honey
4 egg yolks
Pinch of ground cinnamon
Pinch of grated nutmeg
4 tablespoons (½ stick) unsalted butter

Beat together the chicken stock, vin santo, sugar or honey, and egg yolks, then strain through a fine sieve into a soup kettle. Add the cinnamon and nutmeg and set the kettle over very low heat. Stirring constantly with a wooden spoon, add the butter, a little at a time. Keep stirring as the butter melts and dissolves into the soup, just as it would with a hollandaise sauce. Continue stirring until the soup thickens. Do not let it come to a boil as it will curdle. When the soup is thick, pour into soup bowls and serve immediately, sprinkling the surface, if you wish, with a scrape of nutmeg and a few grains of sugar.

First Courses: Pasta, Polenta, Farro, and Rice Dishes

i primi: pasta, polenta, farro, e riso

An old lady I once knew in Teverina told me of a woman from our village, or perhaps she came from the neighboring town, who made pasta for Sunday lunch—or who had an aunt who made it, or could it have been her grandmother?—in any case, this quasi-mythical figure made her pasta using thirty eggs to every kilo (2.2 pounds) of flour. This was told with an air of wonder as an astonishing feat but, the teller of the tale assured me, a feat that was not without the possibility of achievement by women who were truly blessed with a gifted hand for making pasta. That it would be a woman who would achieve it, and that the achievement would be divinely conferred and not something learned and practiced over time, went without saying, for the ability to make a light, savory, egg-rich pasta, one that dances with the sauce, is truly considered a gift from the gods.

With such an attitude, it almost goes without saying that pasta is not an every-day meal in the Tuscan countryside, but almost always a Sunday or holiday tradition—and not a very old tradition at that. Eggs, after all, were a source of income for farm families and it must often have seemed more sensible to sell the eggs and *magari,* buy a piece of meat or a new pair of shoes rather than waste the precious things on pasta. Not pasta but bread, as we have seen, was always the starchy base of the country diet, bread and bread's near cousin, polenta.

Centuries ago, polenta meant a dull but fundamental porridge, not unlike the cornmeal mush we know today but made mostly from barley or chestnut flour, rarely from wheat, and sometimes, in periods of famine, from a flour ground from dried acorns or even tree bark. It was the universal dish of poor people, not just in Tuscany but all over the Italian peninsula, especially in mountainous regions where wheat, the noble grain, failed to thrive. The arrival in Europe of American maize corn, mistakenly called *granturco,* Turkish grain, in Italian, created new possibilities for the humble dish, but polenta was still disparaged, nonetheless, as the food of the rustic poor. My neighbor Bruno Antolini won't eat polenta because it reminds him of a time when that was all there was to eat—and that time for him is still uncomfortably close. When his daughter Anna makes a family favorite, Polenta with a Wild Mushroom Sauce (page 104), Bruno eats the sauce and pushes the polenta to one side.

Elsewhere, however, cornmeal polenta has regained favor, and you'll often find it on Tuscan restaurant menus, as you will another old grain, much older than granturco—farro (see page 76).

Rice, on the other hand, is not found much in Tuscan country kitchens. I don't recall ever being served a dish that included rice in any home I've ever visited, although risotto is a restaurant favorite and there are risotti that are considered, with some justification, to be Tuscan. I've included one of these, the charmingly titled High-Summer Risotto (page 114), simply because it's an interesting technique. Only in the Lunigiana, the mountainous finger of Tuscany that hovers over eastern Liguria, does rice play a more important role, especially in the Rice Bombe (page 110), an elaborate rice timbale that belies the humble peasant traditions of this region.

One pasta preparation has been left out of this section, with my apologies. *Pici* (sometimes called *pinci*) are handrolled pasta made in the region between Siena and Arezzo and down the Val di Chiana to Chiusi, and if you travel in that part of southern Tuscany you should seek them out. They're not easy to find, although at La Chiusa in Montefollonico, between Chiusi and Pienza, they're regularly on the menu of this internationally famous restaurant, and the pici maker often comes out to the dining room to demonstrate her skill. Skill it is, too, for the pasta dough should be made of just flour and water, no eggs at all, and rolled, quickly and delicately, with the palms of the hands over a lightly floured board. In some towns, pici are rolled as fat as angleworms, while in others the makers vie with each other to roll them as thin as possible. I don't give a recipe because it is almost impossible to describe the making of these things in any way that makes sense.

Ribbon Pasta with Duck Sauce
pappardelle all'anatra

6 TO 8 FIRST-COURSE SERVINGS

Pappardelle sulla lepre is the original, an old-fashioned dish of homemade ribbon pasta with a rich sauce of stewed hare. It is definitive of Tuscan country cuisine—that is, when you ask other Italians about Tuscan food, pappardelle sulla lepre is the second dish that comes to mind (the first is always beans). "The most famous Tuscan *pasta asciutta*," says an old gastronomic guide in my library, "and possibly the only autocthonous one." Since most recipes are of the "first catch your hare" genre and include specific quantities of blood, heart, lungs, and liver of the beast, and since not many people, in Italy or elsewhere, have access to a freshly killed young hare these days, our recipe instead is made with duck.

Pappardelle al'anatra is associated with Arezzo, capital of the easternmost province of Tuscany. An ancient Etruscan town dominating the high mountain valleys that surround it, Arezzo represents the sober side of the Tuscan character, old-fashioned, conservative, practical, close-mouthed, but with a rich culinary tradition. The sauce, which actually benefits from being prepared a day ahead and refrigerated until you are ready to use it, is rich and gamy, even when made with duck instead of hare. Traditional cooks add an even boskier flavor with about $1/2$ ounce dried porcini mushrooms soaked in warm water until they soften. The water is strained through a sieve directly into the sauce, while the softened mushrooms are rinsed to rid them of any grit or sand, then coarsely chopped and added to the sauce with the tomatoes.

In the recipe, I've described a process used by restaurant chefs, who cook the pasta until about two-thirds done, then stir it into the sauce, adding a little of the pasta water, to finish cooking, so that the pasta itself absorbs flavors from the sauce. If you prefer a more traditional, less complicated cooking method, simply cook the pasta fully, drain it, and toss with half the sauce, then serve with the remaining sauce piled on top. Pappardelle are rather wide strips of pasta with ruffled edges (sometimes with a ruffled edge on one side only). If you can't find them, use any wide ribbon pasta.

As with other recipes, if pancetta is not available, substitute blanched slab bacon, and if the duck you buy comes without liver, use a couple of chicken livers in its place.

1 duck, weighing about 2 ½ pounds, with its liver

1 stalk celery, chopped

2 small carrots, scraped and chopped

1 medium onion, chopped

4 large fresh sage leaves , coarsely chopped

2 ounces diced pancetta (about ¼ cup)

1 tablespoon extra virgin olive oil

1 ½ cups dry white wine

1 (28-ounce) can tomatoes, or 2 cups peeled, seeded, and diced sweet, ripe, fresh
   tomatoes

⅓ cup finely chopped flat-leaf parsley

½ cup or more chicken or duck stock, if desired, or water

Salt and freshly ground black pepper to taste

1 tablespoon finely chopped wild mint (nepitella) or pennyroyal

1 pound pasta, preferably pappardelle or wide ribbon noodles

About ½ cup freshly grated Parmigiano-Reggiano

If possible, have the butcher chop the duck into 4 to 6 pieces (two wings, two legs, and the body halved). Remove any clumps of fat from the duck cavity. Discard the fat or render it and refrigerate for cooking fat. (Duck fat is great for sautéing potatoes.) Coarsely chop the duck liver. Set the duck and its liver aside.

Chop the celery, carrots, onion, sage, and pancetta together to make a coarse paste. Over medium-low heat, gently sauté this mixture in the oil until the vegetables are thoroughly softened, about 15 minutes. Push the vegetables out to the edge of the pan, add the duck pieces (but not the liver), raise the heat to medium-high, and brown the duck pieces on all sides, turning frequently.

Add the wine, a little at a time, and cook rapidly, stirring occasionally, until it has thrown off its alcohol and is reduced to a few tablespoons in the bottom of the pan.

Drain the tomatoes, reserving the liquid in the can, and chop the tomatoes coarsely. Add them to the pan with the liver and parsley, lower the heat till the sauce is just simmering, and cook, covered, for 1 hour. Check the sauce from time to time to see if there is sufficient liquid, adding a little of the reserved tomato juice if necessary. (If you're using raw tomatoes, add either a little chicken or duck stock or plain water.) After 1 hour, taste the sauce, adding salt and pepper as desired, and the mint. Raise the heat slightly and cook the sauce, uncovered, an additional 30 minutes to thicken it, again adding tomato juice, stock, or water if the sauce becomes too thick. When the sauce is ready, remove the duck pieces and set aside. Set the sauce aside or refrigerate to cool.

While the sauce is cooling, remove the duck meat from the bones and discard the bones and the duck skin. Chop the duck meat coarsely. Remove and discard any visible fat on the surface of the cooled sauce and put the sauce through a food mill, using the coarsest disk. Return the sauce to the pan, add the duck meat, and set the pan over medium heat to warm for serving. Taste again and adjust the seasoning.

When ready to serve, bring 4 quarts lightly salted water to a rolling boil. Add the pappardelle and cook until it is just al dente, tender but with a little bite. Drain and immediately turn the pasta into the simmering sauce, stirring to coat the pasta. Cook another 2 to 3 minutes until the pasta is tender and impregnated with the sauce. Turn into a warm serving bowl and serve immediately. Pass the Parmigiano separately to be sprinkled in small quantities over the pasta.

Oven-baked Pasta
pasta al forno

8 TO 10 SERVINGS

Because it can be made in great quantities to serve lots of hungry workers after their labors are done, this dish reminiscent of lasagne is a big favorite at the trebbiatura, when the harvest of summer wheat is threshed, or indeed at any other time of the year, harvest or not, when there are lots of mouths to feed. At times like these, my neighbor Mita Antolini always wears a little smile of special pride as she accepts her neighbors' compliments. Her layers of pasta are as thin and fine and elegant as a silk handkerchief, a far cry from the stodgy lasagne most Americans are used to.

This may look like a long, complicated recipe, but much of it can be done in advance. You could, for instance, make the ragù several days before you need it, and mix the pasta dough the morning of the day you plan to serve it. Then it's just a question of making the *besciamella* (a well-seasoned white sauce) and assembling the dish, which can also be done several hours before baking. Mita's daughter-in-law Maura, who has a full-time job running a clothing stall in the traveling local street markets, often puts her time and the family freezer to good use by making two of these at once and freezing one (unbaked) to be brought out and cooked whenever the occasion demands.

A word of advice if you're going to make this all at once: It's easiest if you first make the ragù, then put the milk to steep with its flavorings, and make the pasta while the milk steeps. Then continue with the besciamella while the pasta rests. If you must make the besciamella in advance, press a piece of plastic wrap directly on the surface of the sauce to keep a skin from forming.

This pasta is best of all when it's baked, literally, al forno, in the outside oven after the bread has come out, when a slight smokiness from the wood-fired oven impregnates the dish. But it's darned good baked in a conventional kitchen oven too.

For the ragù:
2 tablespoons extra virgin olive oil
1 medium carrot, scraped and finely chopped
1 medium onion, finely chopped
1 stalk celery, finely chopped
1 sweet Italian sausage

1 pound lean ground beef or veal

1 $\frac{1}{2}$ cups tomato purée

2 cups whole canned tomatoes, with their liquid

Salt and freshly ground black pepper to taste

For the pasta:

1 pound (3 $\frac{1}{2}$ to 4 cups) unbleached all-purpose flour

3 or 4 large eggs

1 tablespoon extra virgin olive oil

For the white sauce:

4 cups whole milk

2 bay leaves

1 small onion, peeled but left whole

1 small carrot, peeled but left whole

$\frac{1}{2}$ medium stalk celery

$\frac{1}{4}$ pound (1 stick) unsalted butter

1 cup unbleached all-purpose flour

Salt to taste

Freshly grated nutmeg to taste

For the final assembly:

1 tablespoon extra virgin olive oil

2 cups freshly grated Parmigiano-Reggiano

Salt and freshly ground black pepper to taste

First, make the ragù: Heat the olive oil over medium-high in a saucepan and while it's heating, chop together the carrot, onion, and celery. Add the vegetables to the oil in the pan and sauté gently, turning the heat down if necessary, until the vegetables are soft but not beginning to brown. Meanwhile, open up the sausage, discarding the sausage skin, and when the vegetables are soft, add the sausage meat to the pan, breaking it up with a fork. Cook, tossing and stirring the sausage meat with the vegetables. When the sausage has lost its pink color, add the ground meat and continue in the same manner, tossing and stirring the meat to mix with the vegetables until it is thoroughly browned.

Stir in the tomato purée. Coarsely chop the whole tomatoes and add them with their juices to the pan. Add a pinch of sea salt and several grinds of black pepper, or to taste. Bring to a simmer, lower the heat to medium-low, and cook at a steady, even, but not vigorous bubble for about 20 minutes, or until the tomatoes have cooked down to a thick sauce. If the sauce gets too thick, stir in a few tablespoons of boiling water. If the sauce doesn't thicken sufficiently, raise the heat to medium-high and continue cooking, uncovered, an additional 10 minutes.

When the sauce is done, taste and adjust the seasoning. Set aside until ready to proceed with the recipe. (You can make the sauce well in advance and refrigerate it, but heat it very hot before assembling the recipe.)

Make the pasta: Mound about ¾ of the flour on a board or wooden work counter and make a well in the center. Break the eggs into the well and slowly mix the flour into the eggs, adding 1 tablespoon of water from time to time as the dough comes together. Once the eggs and about ¼ cup of water are incorporated, knead the dough on the board for at most 5 minutes. (Too much kneading will develop the gluten and make the pasta very stiff.) You're aiming for a soft but not sticky mix, but don't worry if the dough is stiff, as it will relax while it rests. Form the dough into a ball, rub the olive oil in the palms of your hands, and rub it all over the outside of the ball. Cover loosely with plastic wrap and set aside to rest at least 15 minutes. (In warm weather, refrigerate the dough to keep it from getting too soft if you need to keep it more than 15 minutes or so, but bring it back to room temperature before rolling it out.)

Finally, make the besciamella, the white sauce that binds together all the elements of the dish: In a medium saucepan, combine the milk, bay leaves, onion, carrot, and celery. Place over medium heat and bring just to the boiling point, but do not let boil. Set aside, covered, to steep for at least 30 minutes. When ready to continue, the flavored milk should be very hot. If necessary, return to the heat before continuing with the recipe, but do not let the milk boil.

In a saucepan large enough to hold the milk, butter, and flour, melt the butter over medium-low heat. When it is completely melted and just beginning to foam, add all the flour at once, stirring vigorously with a wooden spoon to get a thick paste. Continue stirring for 5 minutes or so to cook off the raw taste of the flour, but if the flour starts to turn color, remove from the heat.

Skim out and discard the solids from the very hot milk and begin adding the milk, in ladlefuls, to the flour-butter paste, whisking constantly, with the pan set over medium-low heat. As soon as one ladleful of milk has been smoothly incorporated into the sauce, add another. Continue until all the milk has been combined, then add a pinch of salt and a very little freshly grated nutmeg, and continue cooking over very low heat and stirring constantly until you have a thick sauce, in consistency somewhere between heavy cream and sour cream.

When ready to assemble the dish, use the olive oil to grease a 9- × 13-inch Pyrex or enamel oven dish, like a lasagna dish. Preheat the oven to 350°F.

Use any remaining flour to dust the work surface lightly. Unwrap the pasta dough and cut out a piece about ¼ to ½ cup in size. (Those who are new to pasta-making will find it easier to work in smaller batches.) Pat the pasta dough into an oblong and pat it lightly in the flour on the board. Now, either roll the pasta out in a long oblong sheet, as thin as you can make it without letting it fall apart, or put it through a pasta machine, starting with the widest opening and gradually decreasing until you get to the smallest and finest sheet. Ideally, two sheets of pasta, slightly overlapped, will be just a little larger than the pan in which it will bake. Have ready a kitchen towel spread out on a tabletop and lightly dusted with flour. Lay the sheet of pasta on the towel to dry and continue with the rest of the pasta. Leave the pasta sheets to dry for about 15 minutes, or just long enough to tighten them up a little and lose their softness but not to become dry and brittle.

Bring a large pan of water to a rolling boil, and have ready a bowl of cold water next to the stove. Drop two of the pasta sheets into the boiling water for a few seconds, removing them with a slotted spoon or scoop just as soon as they float to the top, then transferring them to the bowl of cold water to stop the cooking instantly. Lay the sheets in the bottom of the prepared baking dish. Spread about $^1/_2$ cup white sauce over the layer—you don't have to cover it completely. Sprinkle a scant $^1/_4$ cup grated Parmigiano-Reggiano over the sauce and add a little salt and pepper. Repeat with another two sheets of pasta, spreading on some of the ragù instead of the besciamella. Continue in this fashion, alternating thin layers of ragù with the besciamella and cheese until you have at least ten layers. The topmost layer should be white sauce and cheese.

Bake in the preheated oven for 30 to 45 minutes, or until the top is golden and the sauce is very bubbly. Remove from the oven and let rest for 5 minutes or so, then serve.

Potato-stuffed Pasta with Ragù
tortelli di patate al mugello

10 TO 12 SERVINGS

High in the Appenines north of Florence, the Mugello is a wide grassy valley through which the Sieve River wends its way down to join the Arno at Pontassieve, east of the Tuscan capital. This is part of the *contado fiorentino,* the Florentine countryside, since the fourteenth century a favored playground for moneyed Florentine merchants and aristocrats. The Medici traced their origins to the Mugello; Villa Cafaggiolo at San Piero a Sieve was a favorite retreat of both Cosimo Il Vecchio and Lorenzo Il Magnifico. Giotto was born in the village of Vespignano in 1267, and Fra Angelico came from nearby Vicchio more than a century later.

Beyond the last layer of hills to the north lies Emilia Romagna and the wide, flat valley of the Po, so it's understandable that many of the food traditions of the Mugello are shared with the richer region to the north. Whether it's the proximity of Emilia Romagna or influence from an aristocratic urban kitchen, dishes here tend to be less austere than in other parts of Tuscany. There's no better example of this than tortelli di patate, in origin a dish of poor country folk (the very idea of stuffing pasta with potatoes seems to come directly from la cucina povera) that is enriched with a flavorful sauce and further garnished with an opulent ragù.

Mirella Settori, whose recipe this is, runs the kitchen at La Casa di Caccia, a hunting reserve that sits on a steep forested spur looking over the Mugello at Vicchio. Her menu, naturally enough, features game, often birds, wild hare, even boar shot on the reserve and brought to Mirella's kitchen for her expert attention. Sundays throughout the long Tuscan hunting season you're apt to see groups of camouflage-clad hunters relaxing by the fire while they wait for their catch to come out of the kitchen.

I've never been a big fan of game, which, even in Mirella's skilled hands, seems to me tough and rank. For my taste, the glory of her kitchen are these much more civilized tortelli di patate; the rich ragù was her mother's specialty and, unlike the usual Tuscan quick-cooked sauce, it's the result of long hours of slow braising to develop the dense flavors that marry so well with the tortelli. This is a lengthy but not a particularly difficult procedure. Take heart, though—it's worth every bit of time and effort you can put into it.

For the ragù:

3 medium red onions, chopped

2 stalks celery, finely chopped

2 medium carrots, scraped and chopped

1/2 cup extra virgin olive oil

1 pound very lean beef, twice ground

1 cup red wine

3 cups canned whole tomatoes, chopped, with their liquid

Salt and freshly ground black pepper to taste

For the pasta stuffing:

3 pounds potatoes, preferably yellow-fleshed varieties

1/2 head of garlic, peeled and chopped

1/2 cup chopped flat-leaf parsley

2 tablespoons extra virgin olive oil

3 tablespoons dry white wine

1 tablespoon tomato paste

Salt and freshly ground black pepper to taste

Freshly grated nutmeg to taste

1/2 cup freshly grated Parmigiano-Reggiano

For the pasta dough:

2 pounds (7 to 8 cups) unbleached all-purpose flour

6 to 8 large eggs

Salt to taste

1 tablespoon extra virgin olive oil

To prepare the ragù, mix together the onions, celery, and carrots and chop very fine. Turn the chopped vegetables into a colander and set aside to drain for at least 1 hour.

In a large, heavy-duty cooking pot, mix the drained vegetables with 1/4 cup oil and set over low heat. Cook very slowly for at least 3 hours, adding a little water from time to time if necessary to keep the vegetables from sticking. At the end of this time, add the remaining 1/4 cup oil and the ground beef, stir together, and return to low heat to continue cooking very slowly. After 40 minutes, add the red wine and cook, stirring, while the alcohol evaporates, about 10 to 15 minutes. Now stir in the chopped tomatoes with their liquid. Add salt and pepper to taste, bring to a boil, and leave to cook slowly, uncovered, for 6 hours. Add more water as the liquid in the pan evaporates. At the end of the cooking time you will have a dense and aromatic sauce.

(Note that if it's more convenient, you may prepare this sauce in stages, starting with the battuto, which could be done two days ahead, then the meat added a day ahead, so that the ragù is entirely made ahead before you start the pasta.)

To make the stuffing for the pasta, scrub the potatoes and place in a pot. Cover with boiling water and cook, uncovered, over medium-high heat until they are tender. Drain, and just as soon as they can be handled but while they are still hot, peel them and put them through a ricer or mash with a potato masher.

While the potatoes are cooking, make another battuto by further chopping the garlic and parsley, then cooking the mixture very slowly in the olive oil over medium-low heat until the vegetables are tender; do not let them burn. Once the garlic is soft, add the wine and tomato paste, along with salt, pepper, and 3 tablespoons of water. Bring to a simmer and let cook very slowly until the potatoes in the other pot are done—about 10 minutes.

As soon as the potatoes are riced, mix in the battuto, taste, and adjust the seasoning, adding a few scrapes of grated nutmeg and the grated cheese. Mix together with your hands or a wooden spoon, trying to keep the mixture light. Set aside, covered, but do not refrigerate.

Make the pasta: In a large bowl mix together about ¾ of the flour (reserving the remaining flour for dusting the board) and the eggs, using a wire whisk at first and then, when the dough gets stiff, your hands. Add a healthy pinch of salt and the olive oil and turn the dough out on a lightly floured board or work counter. Knead for 10 to 15 minutes until the mixture becomes soft and elastic, then cover with plastic wrap and set aside to rest for at least 15 minutes.

When ready to proceed, roll out the pasta on a lightly floured board ("as thick as a scudo," says Mirella, referring to an old-fashioned thin coin), or put the pasta through a pasta machine, gradually decreasing the setting until you reach the thinnest. Spread a sheet of pasta on the lightly floured board and dot half the sheet at regularly spaced intervals with little blobs (about 2 tablespoons each) of the potato mixture. Fold the other half of the pasta over the potato stuffing. Use the side of your hand to mold and press around each of the tortelli to eliminate air pockets. Then cut in squares with a pizza roller or use a large, circular ravioli cutter to cut out rounds. Set the tortelli on a cake rack or on a board dusted with cornmeal or semolina to keep them from sticking.

Bring a large pot of lightly salted water to a rolling boil. If necessary, reheat the ragù until it is simmering. Drop the tortelli into the boiling water and cook until the pasta is done, about 7 to 10 minutes. Turn the pasta into a colander to drain, then serve on a preheated platter with the ragù on top and, if you wish, a handful of grated Parmigiano-Reggiano. Serve immediately.

Pasta with a Seaside Sauce
pasta allo scoglio

6 SERVINGS

With some exceptions, like the renowned fish stew called cacciucco (see page 125), Tuscany is not noted for fish and seafood dishes, but in the beachfront restaurants along the sea at Viareggio, and all down that remarkable coastline that curves southward into the Maremma, this tasty seafood sauce is served, usually over spaghetti. When I make it at home, however, I use penne or another type of short pasta, simply because the task of winding spaghetti strands around pieces of shrimp, clams, and mussels is daunting for many diners.

20 small manila clams

24 mussels

$1/2$ cup extra virgin olive oil

$1/4$ cup coarsely chopped garlic, plus 2 cloves garlic, minced

1 dried red hot chile pepper

$1 1/2$ cups finely chopped flat-leaf parsley, plus some for garnish

3 cups peeled chopped ripe red tomatoes, or well-drained canned tomatoes

$1/2$ pound small squid, cleaned

$1/2$ pound peeled medium-count shrimp

Salt and freshly ground black pepper to taste

$1 1/2$ pounds penne or other short dried pasta

Prepare the clams and mussels by rinsing and scrubbing them, debearding the mussels, and discarding any broken clams or mussels with gaping shells.

In $1/4$ cup of the olive oil in a large pan, sauté the quarter-cup of garlic with the chile pepper and 1 cup of the chopped parsley. When the vegetables are soft but not brown, add the tomatoes and cook, stirring frequently, until you have a dense but still liquid sauce. Remove from the heat and set aside.

In another deep sauté pan, sauté the remaining garlic and parsley in the remaining quarter-cup oil until the garlic is soft but not brown. Add the mussels and cook, stirring frequently, until they open. Remove each mussel as it opens and set aside in a bowl.

When all the mussels are done, add the clams to the pan and cook in the same way, stirring, until all the clams are done. (Discard any clams or mussels that fail to open.) Add the clams to the bowl holding the mussels.

Add the squid and shrimp to the pan and cook, stirring and turning frequently, until they are thoroughly cooked, 4 to 5 minutes. Do not overcook. Add the shrimp, squid, and all the cooking juices to the bowl with the clams and mussels. (The recipe may be prepared a few hours ahead of time up to this point.)

When ready to serve, bring a large kettle of water to a rolling boil; at the same time, reheat the tomato sauce to a gentle simmer. Place the seafood and its cooking liquid in another pan and warm over very gentle heat. Add 1 tablespoon of sea salt to the boiling water and drop in about 1½ pounds dried pasta. Cook until just al dente. Drain and immediately turn the pasta into the tomato sauce, tossing gently to mix well. Turn the pasta into a heated bowl and pour the seafood with its cooking juices over the top. Season with pepper. Garnish with a little more chopped parsley and garlic and serve immediately.

Potato Gnocchi
gnocchi di patate

6 TO 8 SERVINGS

Egg pastas are summertime dishes, made when the hens are laying and there's an abundance of eggs. But when there's less light in the atmosphere, the barnyard fowl stop producing, so in the dark days of winter eggs are in short supply. Then it's time for other types of first courses, like these potato gnocchi, which are simplicity itself and delicious when made with a flavorful potato variety like Yukon Gold or Yellow Finn.

Some cooks like to roll the gnocchi over the large holes of a cheese grater or the tines of a fork to give them a pattern, one of those niceties that's fun to do if you have time, but not really necessary.

> 2 pounds yellow-fleshed potatoes, such as Yukon Gold
> Salt to taste
> 1 ¾ cups unbleached all-purpose flour
> Tomato sauce or ragù and grated cheese to dress the gnocchi

Scrub the potatoes and place them, unpeeled, on a vegetable rack set over but not in a large pot of boiling water. Steam until tender all the way through but not falling apart. It's important that the potatoes not be overcooked. (Overdone, they will absorb too much water and take up so much flour that the gnocchi will sink like heavy little stones to the bottom of the stomach.)

As soon as the potatoes are tender enough to push through a vegetable mill, remove them from the rack and when they can be handled, but while they're still hot, peel them and pass them through the vegetable mill into a large bowl. (Don't be tempted to try a food processor for this—it will turn them to glue.)

Add a healthy pinch of salt and all the flour to the potatoes, working in the flour with a wooden spoon; then knead the dough gently for about 5 minutes on a lightly floured board or wooden work surface. Taste and knead in more salt if you wish, but be careful not to overwork the dough—it should be soft and supple.

Divide the dough into 6 or 8 equal pieces. Roll each piece into a snake about ³/₄ inch in diameter and 8 to 10 inches long. Cut each snake into regular pieces about ³/₄ inch long. Continue until all the dough has been rolled and cut. If you wish, roll each gnocco (yes, that's the singular of gnocchi) over the large holes of a cheese grater or along the tines of a fork to impress the soft dough with a pattern.

Bring a large pot of lightly salted water to a rolling boil and drop in the gnocchi. (Do this in two batches if it's easier.) Boil the gnocchi until they rise to the top, then remove them with a slotted skimmer and transfer them to a heated platter or bowl. Serve immediately, with a meat and tomato ragù such as the ones listed on page 117, or with a plain tomato sauce. Spoon half the ragù or sauce over the gnocchi and mix gently, then garnish with the remaining sauce or ragù and a little grated cheese, if desired.

Spinach and Ricotta Gnocchi
ravioli 'gnudi o strozzapreti

6 TO 8 SERVINGS

Elsewhere in Italy, these are known as *gnocchi di spinaci e ricotta*. In Florence, however, they're called *strozzapreti,* priest-stranglers, presumably because the priest ate so many of the delicious morsels that he strangled himself. In the rest of Tuscany, they are *ignudi,* or *'gnudi,* nude ravioli, simply because they have no pasta "clothing" wrapped around the filling. They are usually dressed simply with melted butter and grated cheese, though sometimes a light tomato sauce is used instead. If you can't get a good, flavorful goat's or ewe's milk ricotta, boost the flavor with additional grated Parmigiano-Reggiano (about ½ cup more should do it).

The trick with 'gnudi is to drain the spinach very, very well, squeezing out the liquid, then to chop it very fine by hand and drain again; otherwise the mixture may be too liquid to handle easily.

> 2 pounds fresh spinach
> 1 pound fresh ricotta, drained overnight
> 1 cup freshly grated Parmigiano-Reggiano
> 2 eggs, lightly beaten
> Salt, freshly ground black pepper, and freshly grated nutmeg to taste
> ¼ pound (1 stick) unsalted butter
> Flour for the board

Carefully stem and clean the spinach, washing it in several changes of water until not a trace of sand is left. Cook the spinach in the water clinging to its leaves in a large covered pot over medium heat until it is very tender. Drain it very well in a colander and chop it in the colander (if it's tender enough, you can chop it with the edge of a plate) to get rid of excess liquid. Press it in your hands to release even more of the liquid.

Transfer the drained spinach to a cutting board and chop fine. (The spinach must be chopped by hand, not in a food processor, in order to rid it of as much liquid as possible.) Once it is chopped, squeeze it again between your palms to eliminate any remaining liquid. You should have about 2¼ cups finely chopped spinach.

In a mixing bowl, gradually combine the spinach with the ricotta, ³/₄ of the grated cheese, the eggs, and the seasonings, beating the mixture well with a wooden spoon after each addition.

Bring a large pot of lightly salted water to a rolling boil. While the water is heating, melt the butter gently in a small saucepan; do not let it sizzle and fry. When the water is ready, form the 'gnudi. Shake a liberal quantity of flour over a bread board. Using two tablespoons, form a dollop of the ricotta-spinach mixture into an egg shape and roll it in the flour to coat it lightly. Toss each one between your lightly floured hands to shake off any excess flour and set aside on a lightly floured plate. (Don't make these ahead of time, as the damp dumplings will absorb the flour coating and you'll have to start all over again.)

Drop the 'gnudi, a few at a time, in the pan of rapidly boiling water and cook briefly after the water returns to a boil. They will rise to the surface when they are done; let cook another 30 seconds or so on the surface and then remove with a slotted skimmer and set in a heated serving platter or oven dish. When all the dumplings have been cooked, pour the melted butter over them and sprinkle with the remaining cheese. They may be served as is, or you can run the oven dish under a preheated broiler just to glaze the surface and melt the cheese.

Serve immediately.

Note: If you wish, you may clothe the naked gnocchi by making a sfoglia, a sheet of pasta, mixing together well 1 pound (3 to 4 cups) of unbleached all-purpose flour, 3 to 4 large eggs, about ¹/₃ cup of water, and 1 tablespoon of extra virgin olive oil, as described in the recipe for Oven-baked Pasta (page 92). Roll the pasta dough out on a very lightly floured board, or put through a pasta machine, and cut into 3- to 4-inch disks with a glass. Place a dollop of the spinach-ricotta mixture in the center of each disk, fold over, and seal the edges with a fork. Cook in rapidly boiling, lightly salted water for about 6 or 7 minutes, drain, and serve with a sauce of melted butter in which a few sage leaves have been steeped.

Polenta with a Wild Mushroom Sauce
polenta con ragù di funghi porcini

6 TO 8 SERVINGS

Nowadays, you'll find cornmeal polenta in some of Tuscany's most chic restaurants, but you'll still find it in farmhouses, too. Anna Antolini makes this version with what I call Teverina wild mushroom sauce.

The second part of the recipe describes a basic technique for cooking a smooth polenta, which is by no means as difficult as it's often made out to be. Older cookbooks sometimes suggest cooking polenta for a very long time, but with freshly ground meal, 30 minutes should be plenty. The mushroom sauce can be made ahead of time and, in fact, is as good with a plain pasta like taglierini or fettuccine as it is with polenta. And the polenta, of course, can be served with any of the ragù or tomato sauces in this book, as well as with a plain garnish of freshly grated Parmigiano-Reggiano and, for a change, a dollop of fine unsalted butter, softened to room temperature. It's also delicious with a spoonful of what's sometimes called *burro toscano,* Tuscan butter: soft lard beaten to a cloud with salt and chopped fresh herbs like rosemary and thyme.

1 1/2 ounces dried porcini mushrooms

1 pound sweet Italian sausages, preferably fennel-flavored

2 tablespoons extra virgin olive oil

1 medium onion, minced

1 medium carrot, peeled and minced

1 stalk celery, minced

1/4 cup minced flat-leaf parsley

1 (28-ounce) can plum tomatoes with their liquid, coarsely chopped

1 teaspoon finely minced fresh rosemary

2 sage leaves, finely minced

Salt and freshly ground black pepper to taste

1 1/2 cups coarsely ground cornmeal

Cover the dried porcini with very warm water in a bowl and set aside to soak for 30 minutes.

While the mushrooms are soaking, slice the sausages no more than $1/2$ inch thick. In a heavy skillet over medium-high heat, sauté the slices in the oil, stirring and turning frequently, until they lose their pink color. Remove the sausage slices with a slotted spoon and set aside to drain on paper towels.

Drain the mushrooms in a sieve lined with cheesecloth placed over a bowl to catch the liquid. Rinse the drained mushrooms under running water to rid them of any residual sand or grit, then chop them coarsely. Reserve the chopped mushrooms and the strained soaking liquid.

Add the onion, carrot, celery, and parsley to the oil in the skillet and sauté gently until the vegetables are soft but not brown. Stir in the tomatoes, rosemary, and sage. Simmer gently, uncovered, until the sauce is thick, about 20 to 25 minutes, then add the mushroom liquid, the mushrooms, and the sausage slices. Continue cooking, uncovered, for another 15 to 20 minutes. The sauce should be very thick. Taste and add salt and pepper if necessary.

Bring 6 cups of water to a rolling boil, stir in 1 tablespoon of salt, and lower the heat to just simmering. Stirring with a wooden spoon, slowly pour in the cornmeal, stirring continuously while you pour, and continuing to stir for an additional 20 minutes while the cornmeal cooks, reaching with the spoon all over the bottom of the pan—this is tedious but necessary to prevent lumps from forming in what is essentially a cornmeal porridge. (Protect your stirring arm with an oven mitt: The boiling polenta sometimes sends up volcanic spatters of burning hot polenta.)

After 20 minutes, the polenta should be a thick, puddinglike mass, but if it is still too liquid, continue cooking for up to 10 minutes longer, remembering that polenta firms up considerably once it's removed from the heat. When it has reached the right consistency, stop stirring but leave the pan sitting on very low heat (warm setting, if using electric heat) for $1/2$ to 2 minutes, just to tighten it. Then turn it out on a heated platter or, for a more traditional presentation, onto a wooden board, and serve with the mushroom ragù.

Polenta with Fried Croutons of Bread
polenta con ciccioli di pane

6 TO 8 SERVINGS

Montisi is a delightful village set amid the bare, lion-colored dunes of the Crete Senese, the hills southeast of Siena. Despite the number of English-speaking foreigners who have bought property around the town in recent years, Montisi retains its Tuscan character, most of all in local dishes and traditions of which this polenta, garnished with crisply fried cubes of bread and served with a chicken liver ragù, is one.

1 pound stale bread

$1/4$ cup extra virgin olive oil

1 medium onion, chopped

1 clove garlic, thinly sliced

1 small carrot, scraped and chopped

2 tablespoons coarsely chopped flat-leaf parsley

$1/4$ pound chicken livers, cleaned and coarsely chopped

$1/4$ pound very lean ground beef

$1/2$ cup dry white wine

2 sage leaves, coarsely chopped

$1/4$ teaspoon powdered fennel

2 cups tomato purée

Salt and freshly ground black pepper to taste

$1 1/2$ cups coarsely ground cornmeal

Grated Parmigiano-Reggiano or Pecorino Toscano

Slice the crusts from the bread and discard them. Cut the bread into approximately $1/2$-inch cubes. Heat the oil in a frying pan over medium-high heat. When the oil starts to shimmer on the surface, add the bread cubes, in two or more batches if it's easier. Fry until golden brown on all sides. Remove from the oil with a slotted spoon and set aside on paper towels to drain.

Make the ragù: Add the onion, garlic, carrot, and parsley to the oil remaining in the frying pan and cook gently over medium-low heat until the vegetables are soft. Raise the heat to medium and add the chicken livers and ground beef. Stir the meats with the vegetables and continue cooking until the meats are brown, then add the wine and $^1/_2$ to $^3/_4$ cup water. Raise the heat to high and cook rapidly, stirring, until the liquid has reduced to a few tablespoons. Stir in the sage, fennel, and tomato purée. Mix well, taste, and add salt and pepper if necessary. Lower the heat to simmer, cover the pan, and continue cooking until the sauce is thick, about 20 minutes. (The sauce may be made ahead and reheated when ready to serve.)

When ready to make the polenta, bring 6 cups of water to a rolling boil, stir in 1 tablespoon salt, and lower the heat to just simmering. Stirring with a wooden spoon, slowly pour in the cornmeal, stirring continuously while you pour and continuing to stir an additional 20 minutes while the meal cooks, reaching with the spoon all over the bottom of the pan—this is tedious, but necessary to prevent lumps from forming. (Protect your stirring arm with an oven mitt: The boiling polenta sometimes sends up volcanic spatters of burning hot polenta.)

At the end of 20 minutes, the polenta should be a thick, puddinglike mass, but if it is still too liquid, continue cooking for up to 10 minutes longer, remembering that the polenta firms up considerably once it's removed from the heat. When it has reached the right consistency, remove from the heat and stir in the fried bread cubes, folding to distribute them thoroughly.

The polenta may be served immediately, turned onto a serving platter with some of the ragù poured over and the rest in a bowl on the side. Or pour the polenta into a loaf pan and set aside to firm up and cool thoroughly. Once the polenta is cool, invert it onto a cutting board and slice it into approximately $^3/_4$-inch-thick slices. Sliced polenta may be warmed up in the oven with the ragù or the slices can be painted lightly with olive oil and grilled or broiled for about 5 minutes to a side until they are toasty brown. Serve grilled polenta slices with the ragù as an accompaniment, along with freshly grated Parmigiano-Reggiano or aged Pecorino Toscano.

Polenta or Cornmeal

Don't bother with industrially processed cornmeal or with the stuff that's imported from Italy; most of it is too old and stale to make a tasty polenta. You'll be better off buying freshly stone-ground meal from a mill you can trust, like Gray's Grist Mill in Adamsville, Rhode Island, or Morgan's Mills in East Union, Maine (see the Source Guide, page 276). A coarse grind, called in Italian *bramata,* makes a more authentic Tuscan polenta.

Lunigiana Pancakes with Pesto
testaroli e panigacci al pesto

12 PANCAKES, SERVING 6

S o," said Faith as we tucked into a plate of *testaroli* in the rain-soaked medieval borghetto of Bagnone, "I guess this is a first, huh? Boiled pancakes?"

Faith married an Etruscan and went to live in Florence many years ago, but not long enough to tarnish her highly polished American brass. We were on the road together, heading north toward Pontremoli, a major town in the steep valley of the Magra River that drops down to the ruins of ancient Luni on the coast, when heavy rains and impending darkness drove us to take shelter at a restaurant called simply da Lina that, the guidebook promised, also offered rooms. Indeed it did, and charming ones with views over the rushing Magra and the fairy-tale castle that soars over the river and Bagnone's Roman bridge. More to the point, it had Lina Ricci in the kitchen, and it was her testaroli we were sampling for the first time.

And, yes, they are a little like boiled pancakes, but a rare treat nonetheless. The name *testaroli* comes from the *testi* on which they are baked, low earthenware griddles that look a little like saucers to put beneath plant pots. Once upon a time, the testi were placed in the embers of the fire to heat, then the batter was dropped on, a lid was clapped on top, and the cakes baked on the hot clay surface. I have read of batters made with eggs or with an admixture of other flours, like fine cornmeal or ground farro, but what you're most likely to find (and you won't find them easily) are testaroli, or their smaller sisters called *panigacci,* made like Lina Ricci's from nothing but flour, water, a little salt, and a drop or two of oil.

And the griddle part is only the beginning, for once the crêpelike things are baked, they are cut, in strips or quarters depending on their size, left to dry slightly, then dropped briefly in boiling water to soften and reheat them before being served with a rich, old-fashioned pesto made properly in a mortar. Thus they combine two distinctive traditions, flour-and-water griddle cakes that are made throughout the Appenines, and fragrant basil pesto from neighboring Liguria. But the combination is strictly from the Lunigiana, an enchanting part of Tuscany that's unknown even to most Tuscans.

Panigacci, because they're smaller and don't need to be covered, are easier to produce in kitchens outside the Lunigiana. You'll need an 8-inch crêpe pan or a similar flat, well-seasoned iron skillet.

For the pancakes:

1 teaspoon salt

2 cups unbleached all-purpose flour

2 cups water

For the pesto:

1 cup fresh basil

2 cloves garlic

Salt, if desired

$\frac{1}{2}$ cup roughly chopped walnuts or pine nuts, or the two mixed

$\frac{1}{2}$ cup extra virgin olive oil, or more to taste

2 tablespoons freshly grated Pecorino Toscano or Parmigiano-Reggiano,
   plus more for serving

1 teaspoon extra virgin olive oil

Toss the salt with the flour to mix well. Slowly add the water, a little at a time, stirring it in gradually with a wooden spoon to prevent lumps from forming. Once all the water has been added, stir the batter 100 times (a ritual number) to develop the gluten. Cover the bowl and set the batter aside to rest 1 hour.

While the batter is resting, make the pesto: Coarsely chop the basil leaves and garlic and place in a mortar with a pinch of salt. Pound the basil, garlic, and salt together to a smooth, homogeneous paste. As you work, gradually add nuts and pound them in with the other ingredients. Once the nuts have been thoroughly crushed, start to add the olive oil, a few drops at first, then a steady, thin thread, exactly as you would for a mayonnaise. When all the olive oil has been incorporated, stir in the cheese. Taste and add more salt if necessary. (Yes, of course you can make this in a food processor, though I guarantee that the flavor is better the old-fashioned way.)

When the batter is ready, set a crêpe pan or similar flat iron skillet over medium heat. When it's very hot, grease the pan lightly with a little olive oil. (In the Lunigiana, home cooks dip a cut potato in olive oil and rub it over the surface of the pan.) Make the panigacci just as you would crêpes, dropping a few tablespoons of batter in the center of the hot pan and quickly tilting the pan to cover the surface with batter. As soon as the top starts to skim over, turn the crêpe, using a long, narrow spatula, and cook the other side very briefly. Remove from the pan and set aside.

When all the panigacci have been cooked, cut them in quarters (or in strips if you prefer, but Lina Ricci cuts hers in quarters). Bring a large pot of lightly salted water to a boil and drop in the panigacci for just 2 minutes. Drain and serve immediately with the pesto sauce and a little more grated cheese to sprinkle on top.

Rice Bombe or Timbale from the Lunigiana
bùmba d'rîs

SERVES 6 TO 8

Those who are familiar with the elaborate rice timbales of Naples and the south will immediately recognize their cousin in this bomba di riso. It seems oddly extravagant for a poor mountain district like the Lunigiana, but I suspect it traveled from farther away, perhaps from some port city on the coast, where it's since been forgotten.

$^3/_4$ pound sweetbreads (one pair)

$^1/_4$ cup extra virgin olive oil

$^1/_2$ pound sweet Italian sausages

1 pound lean veal, finely ground

1 medium onion, finely chopped

1 medium carrot, scraped and finely chopped

1 stalk celery, including green top, finely chopped

Salt and freshly ground black pepper to taste

$^1/_2$ teaspoon freshly ground cinnamon

2 cups whole canned tomatoes, coarsely chopped, with their canning liquid,
   or 2 cups fresh ripe tomatoes, peeled and coarsely chopped

2 cups raw rice

Juice of $^1/_2$ lemon

2 tablespoons capers, rinsed and coarsely chopped

$^1/_2$ cup freshly grated Parmigiano-Reggiano

3 extra-large eggs

2 tablespoons unsalted butter

$^1/_4$ cup plus 2 tablespoons toasted bread crumbs

Prepare the sweetbreads: Bring a pan of lightly salted water to a boil and drop the sweetbreads in. Let boil 5 minutes, then "shock" the sweetbreads by draining and immediately plunging into a bowl of very cold water. Peel off and discard the outer membrane and dice the sweetbreads in $^1/_4$-inch dice.

Add the oil to a heavy saucepan or skillet and place over medium-high heat. Remove the sausages from their skins and crumble into the oil. Stir the sausage meat and brown it, then add the ground veal and mix with the sausage meat. When the veal pieces are nicely brown, stir in the diced sweetbreads. Mix all together and cook for about 5 minutes, then remove the meats with a slotted spoon and set aside.

Lower the heat to medium-low. To the oil remaining in the pan, add the onion, carrot, and celery and cook gently until the vegetables are soft but not brown. Return the meats to the pan and mix with the vegetables, sprinkling with salt, pepper, and cinnamon. Add the tomatoes and their liquid to the pan. Reduce the heat to low and simmer the sauce for 1 hour, uncovered, adding up to 1½ cups water as the sauce cooks down. It should be very thick when done, but you will need about ¾ cup liquid to add to the rice (see below). (The sauce may be prepared ahead of time but should be reheated before continuing with the recipe.)

Bring a large saucepan of lightly salted water to a boil. Add the rice and boil 10 minutes, then drain immediately in a colander, tossing the rice to rid it of as much heat as possible. Set it aside to cool, but don't refrigerate—the rice should be slightly warmer than room temperature. Mix the rice in a bowl with the lemon juice, capers, cheese, and eggs.

When the sauce is almost cooked, remove about ¾ cup of the cooking liquid and mix with the rice.

Preheat the oven to 350°F.

Butter the bottom and sides of a 3-quart mold (a soufflé dish is fine for this) and dust with ¼ cup of the bread crumbs. Pack the flavored rice around the bottom and sides of the dish, using about ¾ of the rice. Add the meat sauce to the middle and cover with the remaining rice. Sprinkle the remaining 2 tablespoons of bread crumbs over the top and dot with about 1 tablespoon of butter. Bake in the preheated oven for 45 minutes.

You may serve this immediately or let it cool to slightly warmer than room temperature before serving.

Rice and Onion Tart
turta d'ris e sîgul

8 SERVINGS

Savory tarts like this are typical of the Lunigiana, the steep hill country that climbs up to a watershed between the broad valley of the Po River and the Ligurian coast. Though this miniregion is little known today, centuries ago the Lunigiana was an essential link in the route that led pilgrims and tradesmen from northern Europe down to Rome and beyond to the riches of the Eastern Mediterranean. The cuisine of the Lunigiana reflects a dual heritage, based on Tuscan rustic traditions like chestnuts, polenta, cabbages, wild game, and foraged mushrooms, but with a distinctive overlay of more sophisticated ingredients—rice, lemons, cinnamon—that reflects the region's links with more cosmopolitan parts of the Mediterranean.

For the pastry:
7 1/2 tablespoons unsalted butter
1 1/4 cups unbleached all-purpose flour
2 egg yolks
3 to 4 tablespoons cold water
Extra virgin olive oil

For the filling:
3 pounds white onions, thinly sliced
2 tablespoons extra virgin olive oil
1 1/2 cups rice, preferably medium-grain (not risotto rice)
Salt and freshly ground white or black pepper to taste
1 pound ricotta (preferably made from goat's or ewe's milk, drained if necessary)
3 eggs, beaten together
1/2 cup freshly grated Parmigiano-Reggiano

1 egg yolk

Mix the pastry: Cut the butter into the flour and mix together quickly, being careful not to overwork. Stir in the egg yolks and the water. Put the dough on a lightly floured board and knead very briefly, no more than 10 strokes, until the ingredients come together. Rub a few drops of the olive oil in the palms of your hands and shape the dough into a ball. Cover with plastic wrap and refrigerate for at least 1 hour.

In a sauté pan over low heat, sweat the onions gently in the oil. As soon as they start to soften, cover the pan and leave the onions to cook, very gently, for about 30 minutes, adding a very little water if they start to stick. In the end you should have a very soft, melting mass of onions. Remove from the heat and let cool slightly.

While the onions are cooking, parboil the rice. Bring 5 or 6 cups of lightly salted water to a rolling boil and add the rice. Cook just 5 minutes, then drain, tossing lightly in a colander.

Season the onions with salt and pepper to taste, then stir in the parboiled rice. Let the mixture cool at least 30 minutes before ricing the ricotta (pushing it through the large disk of a food mill) and adding it to the onion–rice mixture along with the eggs and grated cheese. Mix well.

Preheat the oven to 375°F.

Divide the pastry in two unequal portions. From the larger portion, roll out a bottom crust and use it to line the bottom and sides of a 9- or 10-inch pie plate. Fill with the onion–rice mixture and top with a lattice made from the remaining crust. Beat the egg yolk with $1/2$ teaspoon water and use it to paint the lattice. Bake for 1 hour, or until the top is golden brown. (If necessary, turn the heat down to 325°F. after the first 20 to 25 minutes.)

Serve immediately or let cool to room temperature before serving.

High-Summer Risotto
risotto al sol d'agosto

8 SERVINGS

This is based on a recipe in Giovanni Righi Parenti's great book *La Cucina Toscana,* which should be in the library of anyone who loves Tuscany and Tuscan food. "Sol d'agosto" refers to the leonine sun of August, when tomatoes are at their peak of perfection. I have changed the recipe a little in order to use the aromatics available in American markets and gardens, but that brilliant touch at the end, the addition of raw tomatoes and aromatics to finish the dish, is straight from Righi Parenti's description.

1 medium white onion, finely chopped
1/4 cup finely chopped basil, plus 2 tablespoons slivered basil leaves
1/4 cup finely chopped flat-leaf parsley
2 tablespoons finely chopped sage
2 tablespoons extra virgin olive oil
2 cups arborio, carnaroli, or vialone nano rice
Salt and freshly ground white pepper to taste
1/2 cup dry white wine
2 1/2 cups peeled, seeded, and chopped perfectly ripe, sweet, fresh tomatoes
1 cup hot chicken stock, or more if necessary
1/2 cup freshly grated Pecorino Toscano or Parmigiano-Reggiano
2 cloves garlic, finely minced

In a large heavy saucepan over medium-low heat, sweat the onion with the finely chopped basil (the slivered basil will be added later), parsley, and sage in the oil until the vegetables are very soft. Do not let them brown. Mix the rice into the vegetables and add salt and pepper. Stir slowly and when the rice starts to turn opaque, pour in the wine.

As soon as most of the wine has been absorbed by the rice, add about half the tomatoes to the dish, stirring to mix well. Continue to cook the rice, stirring frequently; as the liquid in the tomatoes is absorbed, add hot chicken stock, 1/4 cup at a time. (You may not need all the chicken stock to finish the risotto.)

The risotto is cooked when the grains of rice are still separate and slightly resistant to the bite but bathed in a thick sauce. At this point remove the pan from the heat and quickly stir in the cheese, the remaining tomatoes, the slivered basil, and minced garlic. Cover and let rest for 10 minutes, then serve immediately.

Farro Tart
torta di farro

4 TO 6 SERVINGS

If you can't find farro, this simple tart can be made with wheatberries or with kamut, a type of wheat that is often available in health-food stores.

To toast a small amount of bread crumbs, remove the crusts from a slice of slightly stale country-style bread. Toast the bread in the oven until it is brown on both sides, then process to crumbs in a food processor; or put the toasted slice in a paper bag and pound to crumbs with a rolling pin.

> $^1/_2$ cup farro
> $^1/_2$ pound ricotta (preferably made from goat's or sheep's milk, drained if necessary)
> $^1/_2$ cup freshly grated Parmigiano-Reggiano
> 1 tablespoon finely chopped fresh marjoram
> 6 large basil leaves, coarsely chopped
> 2 tablespoons finely chopped flat-leaf parsley
> $^1/_4$ teaspoon freshly grated nutmeg, or to taste
> Salt and freshly ground black pepper to taste
> 2 extra-large eggs
> 2 tablespoons unsalted butter
> $^1/_4$ cup bread crumbs, toasted

Put the farro in a small saucepan and cover with boiling water to a depth of 1 inch. Boil for 10 minutes, then drain immediately and set aside to cool.

Put the ricotta through the large disk of a food mill to rice it. Stir the cooled farro into the ricotta and add the cheese, marjoram, basil, parsley, nutmeg, salt, pepper, and eggs, mixing well to make a light but homogeneous mixture.

Preheat the oven to 300°F.

Melt the butter and use it to coat an 8-inch quiche pan or straight-sided pie tin about $1^1/_2$ inches deep. Add the bread crumbs to the pan and shake to coat the bottom and sides with crumbs and melted butter. Turn the farro mixture into the pan and smooth the top gently. Bake 40 minutes in the preheated oven, or until the mixture is firm. Remove from the oven and cool to slightly warmer than room temperature before serving. This may be served with a little plain tomato sauce or pomarola on the side.

Potato and Leek Tart
turta d'patàc e pòri

8 SERVINGS

For the pastry:

7 ½ tablespoons unsalted butter

1 ¼ cups unbleached all-purpose flour

2 egg yolks

3 to 4 tablespoons cold water

Extra virgin olive oil

For the filling:

1 pound leeks, white and pale green only

1 tablespoon salt

2 pounds potatoes, peeled and cut in chunks

½ cup freshly grated Parmigiano-Reggiano

½ cup milk

1 large egg

Freshly ground black pepper to taste

Extra virgin olive oil to paint the pastry

Make the pastry: Cut the butter into the flour and mix together quickly, being careful not to overwork. Stir in the egg yolks and the water. Put the dough on a lightly floured board and knead very briefly, no more than 10 strokes, until the ingredients come together. Rub a few drops of olive oil in the palms of your hands and shape the dough into a ball. Cover with plastic wrap and refrigerate for at least 1 hour.

Trim the leeks and rinse out any sand. Coarsely chop the leeks, then toss with the salt and set aside for 30 minutes to soften.

Bring a saucepan of lightly salted water to a rolling boil and drop in the potatoes. Let boil for 10 minutes, or just long enough to soften them but not cook them through. Drain immediately and chop coarsely.

In a large bowl, mix the salted leeks and chopped potatoes together, then add the cheese and toss to combine. With a fork beat the milk and egg together, then stir into the mixed vegetables. Taste and add salt, if necessary, and freshly ground black pepper.

Preheat the oven to 400°F.

Remove the pastry dough from the refrigerator and roll out on a lightly floured board in a circle large enough to cover the bottom and sides of a 9- to 10-inch quiche pan or straight-sided pie tin, leaving about 1½ inches of pastry hanging over the edge of the pan. Turn the vegetable mixture into the pan and smooth the top. Now fold the edges of the pastry over the edge of the filling so that it is partially covered. Paint the exposed pastry with a very little olive oil.

Bake 45 minutes in the preheated oven. Remove and let cool slightly, to somewhat warmer than room temperature, before serving.

Sauces for Pasta

ALTHOUGH HANDMADE egg pasta is the pride of Tuscan cooks, many nowadays use commercially produced pasta instead. There are a number of good imported pastas to be found in this country, among them widely available brands like Barrilla (Italy's best-selling commercial pasta) and De Cecco, both of which are on the shelves of well-stocked supermarkets. More artisanally made pastas, like Martelli (made in Tuscany), Benedetto Cavalieri, Rustichella d'Abruzzo, and Latini, can be found in many specialty food stores and through mail-order outlets. Commercially made pastas, whether industrial or artisanal, are definitely not to be scorned. Since they are, by law, made from hard durum wheat, they are far superior to most of the freshly made pasta that's available in this country, all too often an extruded, soft-wheat pasta that doesn't hold up well to cooking. The following pasta sauces may be used with these commercial pastas, or if you want to make pasta yourself at home (and it's not all that difficult with a little practice), these sauces marry well with handmade egg pasta.

To make pasta at home, follow the directions in either the recipe for Oven-baked Pasta (page 92) or Potato-stuffed Pasta with Ragù (page 96). Once the basic dough has been mixed, it can be rolled out by hand and cut in whatever shape pleases you, or put through the pasta machine to produce tagliatelle or linguine or anything in between.

The fundamental Tuscan sauces for pasta, hearty and tasty, are made from plain ground beef or veal, or from ground meat with chicken livers (fegatini) or from ground meat and sausage, almost always with tomato in some form (whole, puréed, or in concentrate) added, and flavored with Tuscan seasonings like rosemary and sage.

You'll find a number of ragù sauces in recipes throughout the book (see especially Oven-baked Pasta [page 92], Potato-stuffed Pasta with Ragù [page 96], Polenta with a Wild Mushroom Sauce [page 104], and Polenta with Fried Croutons of Bread [page 106]), any of which will go well with other kinds of pasta. Other sauces follow.

White Sauce
sugo bianco

2 TO 3 CUPS

This is called White Sauce simply because it has no tomatoes. It's made with shreds of wild boar, if available, or sausage or plain pork. I've had sugo bianco, sometimes called ragù bianco, with pici and gnocchi, as well as with more conventional pasta.

1 medium yellow onion, finely chopped

2 tablespoons extra virgin olive oil

2 sweet Italian sausages

2 large fresh porcini mushrooms, or use one 1/2-ounce package dried mushrooms and
   1/4 pound fresh shiitake mushrooms

1 medium zucchini

3 or 4 fresh sage leaves, coarsely chopped

3 to 4 tablespoons fresh cream

Salt and freshly ground black pepper to taste

In a saucepan over medium-low heat, gently sweat the onion in the olive oil until it is meltingly soft. While the onion is cooking, strip the skins away from the sausages and crumble the sausage meat with a fork or your fingers.

Add the sausage meat to the onions and continue cooking very gently, stirring occasionally, until the meat is thoroughly brown.

Meanwhile, clean the fresh mushrooms with a mushroom brush, cutting away any discolored parts, and chop coarsely; if using dried mushrooms, soak for at least 15 minutes in 1 1/2 cups very warm water. When they are soft, rinse under running water, and chop coarsely. Reserve the soaking liquid to be strained into the sauce.

Grate the zucchini, skin and all, on the large holes of a cheese grater to make about 1 1/4 cups. Add to the onion-meat mixture together with the chopped sage and stir to incorporate well. Continue cooking on medium-low heat until the zucchini bits are thoroughly softened, then stir in the chopped mushrooms. Strain the mushroom soaking liquid through a fine-mesh sieve directly into the pan. (If you are using only fresh mushrooms, add a few tablespoons of hot water at this point.) Raise the heat to medium and cook rapidly until most of the liquid has evaporated or been absorbed.

Away from the heat, stir the cream rapidly into the sauce, then return to the heat briefly, just to bring the cream to a simmering point. (If the sauce is too liquid, it may be boiled to thicken; if it is too thick, stir in a little more cream to thin it out.) Season to taste. Serve immediately over gnocchi, fusilli, or other short, curly pasta.

Fake Sugo or Meatless Ragù
sugo finto

2 TO 3 CUPS SAUCE

This is said to be "fake" sugo because it has no meat in it, but in fact I've never heard of a recipe that doesn't call for just a bit of carne secca, dried meat, in the form of prosciutto or pancetta, thus proving that Tuscans are such confirmed meat-eaters that even their vegetarian preparations are unthinkable without a *little* meat. You could leave the meat out and increase the amount of olive oil, but then you wouldn't have a sugo finto so much as a sugo vegetariano.

1 medium onion, finely chopped
1 clove garlic, finely chopped
1 stalk celery, including leafy top, finely chopped
1/4 cup minced flat-leaf parsley
2 tablespoons extra virgin olive oil
2 ounces prosciutto or pancetta, finely diced, or another 2 tablespoons extra virgin olive oil
1/2 cup dry white wine
2 (1-pound) cans peeled tomatoes
Salt and freshly ground black pepper to taste
2 tablespoons slivered fresh basil

In a saucepan over medium-low heat, gently sauté the onion, garlic, celery, and parsley in the olive oil until the vegetables are soft but not brown. Stir in the prosciutto or pancetta, if using, turn the heat to medium-high, and continue cooking, stirring frequently, until the meat dice just begin to brown. Add the white wine and cook vigorously until the alcohol has evaporated and the wine has reduced to a couple of tablespoons.

Drain the tomatoes, reserving the juice, and add the tomatoes to the saucepan. Lower the heat to medium-low and cook for about 45 minutes, crushing the tomatoes with a spoon as they cook down and adding a little of the reserved liquid if the sauce gets too dry. At the end of the cooking time, you should have a thick and fragrant sauce. Taste and add salt and pepper as desired. Away from the heat, stir in the basil.

Serve immediately as a sauce for gnocchi, polenta, or any kind of pasta.

Note: This sauce freezes well; if you freeze it, omit the basil, adding it only when ready to serve.

Tomato Sauce for Preserving
pomarola

3 TO 4 PINTS

Late in August, when the tomatoes in her garden are as ripe and red as they can get, Mita Antolini, my neighbor, makes a couple hundred jars of pomarola, tomato sauce, to be stored for use throughout the cold months until fresh produce comes around again in spring. This is an all-purpose sauce that can be used as is on pasta or gnocchi or as the basis for soups and stews throughout the winter; often a few spoonfuls of the sauce are mixed with steamed or sautéed vegetables to give them a little extra oomph.

Tomatoes are among the easiest things imaginable to put up like this; even people with little experience preserving will have no difficulty with the task. Moreover, tomatoes are one of the few garden products that are almost as good preserved as they are fresh from the garden—almost, I note, though nothing quite compares with the flavor of a just-picked, perfectly ripe fruit. Still, this sauce is much to be preferred over the out-of-season tomatoes available in our markets.

If you want to preserve your own tomatoes (and even a few jars will give an inestimable sense of pleasure and well-being), there are a few preliminaries to be observed and prepared. First of all, you'll need canning jars; the best are glass Mason-type jars with screw-on caps. (Mita uses the equivalent of half-pint, pint, and quart jars, to have varying quantities of pomarola on hand for whatever the occasion warrants.) Then you'll need a canning kettle large enough to hold at least 8 or 10 such jars. And of course you'll need tomatoes, preferably ones you've raised yourself or bought in quantity from a farmer or farm-stand. It goes without saying that the best are naturally raised, without pesticides or chemical fertilizers, and picked at the peak of ripeness, not even several days beforehand.

But this is also a good sauce to make in smaller quantities for a quick and easy evening meal of pasta with a fresh tomato sauce. The quantities I've given below will make 3 or 4 pints of sauce, but once you've read the recipe through, I think you'll see that it's easy to expand (or contract, if necessary) for the quantity of tomatoes you have on hand.

The puréed sauce may also be frozen—1-cup containers are very handy—though nothing beats the satisfaction of looking at all those well-filled jars glowing ruby red on the pantry shelves.

5 pounds ripe, red tomatoes

2 cloves garlic

1 or 2 medium yellow onions

1 stalk celery

1 medium carrot

Salt and freshly ground black pepper to taste

$^{1}/_{3}$ cup extra virgin olive oil

Wash the tomatoes well, remove the stems, and cut away any soft spots or bruises. Slice the tomatoes in chunks right into a heavy saucepan large enough to hold all the ingredients. Coarsely chop the remaining vegetables and add to the pan with about 1 tablespoon of salt, if desired, and pepper to taste. Add the olive oil and stir the contents of the pan to mix everything together.

Set the pan over medium heat, and when the tomato juices start to boil, cover and cook for about 15 minutes, occasionally removing the lid to give the contents of the pan a good stir. Lower the heat to medium-low or low so that the liquid simmers rather than boiling rapidly. Let cook, covered, for another 15 to 20 minutes, stirring occasionally, until the tomatoes are thoroughly soft and have yielded up all their juices. Now raise the heat to medium-high and cook rapidly, uncovered, to evaporate the juices and reduce the contents to a thick paste. The total time will depend on the juiciness and meatiness of the tomatoes.

When the tomatoes are soft and thick, remove from the heat and set aside to cool a little, then put through the large disk of a food mill (a better choice than a processor or a blender because it holds back seeds and skins that give the sauce a bitter flavor). Taste the sauce and add more salt and pepper if desired, or a very little sugar, which will bring out the natural sweetness of the fruit.

To preserve the sauce the old-fashioned way, in glass jars, have ready 4 scrupulously clean 1-pint (or 8 $^{1}/_{2}$-pint) glass preserving jars and lids. Stand the jars on a wooden board or on layers of newspaper or kitchen towels on the counter. Fill each jar with *boiling* water. Heat the sauce up to simmering. When you're ready to fill a jar with sauce, tip the water out and immediately fill it with *hot* tomato sauce. When all the jars are filled, screw the lids on tightly and set them in a preserving kettle or a large stockpot. Fill the kettle with boiling water to come just to the tops of the jars, set the kettle over medium-high heat, bring to a boil, and boil for 10 to 15 minutes. (Some people put newspaper or towels in the bottom of the kettle to keep the jars from rattling.) Remove the kettle from the heat and let cool slightly. Using tongs, remove the jars and set them on a rack or on the layer of newspaper or kitchen towels. Pretty soon you'll hear them start to ping and snap as the lids seal. (Any jars that don't seal can be refrigerated and used within a week.)

Seafood
pesce e frutti di mare

Let it be said up front and straight out, Tuscans are not great lovers of seafood. Historically a people of the *entroterra*, or hinterland, they eat fish mostly when they have to and not because they want to. If I say to you, truthfully, that for most Tuscans great fish traditionally means great salt cod *(baccalà* or *stoccafisso)*, I will have said it all. Or almost. Guido Gianni, writing about Arezzo's traditional cuisine, confirms the importance of salt cod with a story from World War I of a commandant of a prison camp who, tired of the unvarying supplies of salt cod provided for his Austrian prisoners, proposed an exchange with local peasants. According to Gianni, the contadini, delirious at the thought of all that delicious baccalà, willingly swapped their fattest and most succulent sausages and prosciutti for the dried salt fish. "Today," Gianni notes with equivalent dryness, "things might go a little differently."

Salt cod is still a Tuscan favorite, however, often to be found on restaurant menus, especially on Friday, the traditional fish day, and the repertoire of dishes is considerable. Interestingly, more and more American restaurant chefs are also discovering the versatility of this once disdained product, which, when it's properly cured, properly desalted, and combined with other flavors in an enlightened manner, is utterly delicious.

Nonetheless, there are a few great fresh seafood dishes from this region. Most are from the coast, naturally enough, and especially from around Livorno (inexplicably called Leghorn in English), the port city established by the Medici in 1577 after the silting of the Arno destroyed Pisa's importance as a great maritime trading center. Livorno's cacciucco (next page) is arguably one of the greatest of Mediterranean fish stews, with a rich complexity of flavors that can dazzle the palate. But once past cacciucco, most of the fish cookery of the coast is simplicity itself—fish and shellfish are grilled, roasted, deep-fried, served with a sprinkle of crunchy sea salt, a drizzle of the fine, light oil that comes from this area, a squeeze of fresh lemon. The emphasis is on the flavor of the freshest fish, nothing more.

One other method for cooking seafood, little known outside Tuscany (and of equal complexity with cacciucco) is the preparation called Pesce in Zimino (or Inzimino di Pesce), the pesce usually being calamari or squid but often other fish or even, deliciously, chunks of salt cod. The process, which seems to be an old one and is often attributed, like most odd and unexpected combinations of flavors, to an Arab origin, involves cooking masses of greens, whether spinach or chard, flavored with ginger or, in modern kitchens, a little hot red chile pepper, and then stewing the seafood in this—or sautéing the seafood apart and combining it with the greens. As with most old preparations, there are many versions, all fiercely disputed; up in neighboring Liguria there's even a dish called ceci (chickpeas) in zimino, though the Ligurian dish has nothing to do with the Tuscan.

More than seafood per se, Tuscans historically have treasured freshwater fish from the streams and lakes of the region, like the southeastern lakes of Chiusi and Trasimeno (officially in Umbria but nonetheless claimed as at least Tuscan once upon a time), the Lago di Vagli up in the Apuan Alps north of Lucca, an artificial lake that is periodically drained to reveal the drowned village of Fabbrica, and on the seacoast the Lago di Massaciùccoli west of Lucca, where Puccini lived in a lakeside villa while composing some of his best-known operas and, whenever operatic inspiration failed him, indulging in his favorite sport, shooting waterfowl.

Down on the shores of Lake Trasimeno, where once fishermen made something of a living by harvesting the lake's products, I now see advertised sportsmen's paradises where the sports can pay to stand on the edge of a square excavated pond that's been stocked with trout and cast a line for their catch—and this no more than a hundred feet from the shores of the vast and magically mysterious lake itself. But they're assured of a quick catch.

Fish Stew from Livorno
cacciucco

8 SERVINGS

Cacciucco is undeniably Tuscany's greatest seafood dish, which, if you've read the introduction to this chapter, perhaps isn't saying much. Yet a well-made cacciucco, with at least five or six different varieties of seafood, is a fish stew of great and deliciously complex flavors, although relatively easy in the execution, that will hold its own in any crowd of ichthyophiles.

The best cacciucco that I've had was served at the Trattoria Senese, in the beachside town of Cecina south of Livorno. Piero Falorno, chef and owner of the restaurant, starts his cacciucco with a *fumetto di pesce,* a Livornese version of a *fumet de poisson,* a broth made of fish heads and bones steeped with aromatics and wine. In this deeply flavorful fumetto, Piero cooks separately each element of the cacciucco, then finishes it off with a tomato sauce sparked liberally with peperoncino, the little dried hot red chile pepper that is so subtly prevalent in the Tuscan kitchen. All these elements are combined at the last minute and served, as is customary, over crisp slices of grilled or toasted bread liberally rubbed with garlic and doused with extra virgin olive oil.

A more conventional way of making cacciucco, and one that's more adaptable to the home kitchen, is the one that follows: Make the fish broth using racks (bony frames) and heads scavenged from an obliging fishmonger, along with an array of cheap, bony, small fish, simmering this until you've extracted all the flavors. Then strain the broth directly into the thick and savory tomato sauce. The fish is cooked in the sauce and served with the aromatic sauce over and around it.

Piero, naturally, uses varieties of seafood that he finds fresh in his local market, among them *gamberoni* (big shrimps), mussels, squid, clams, and *palombo* (a type of dog shark); other fish he might have used, had they been available the day I visited, were *scorfano* (scorpion fish, the fish the French call *rascasse* and consider vital to a good bouillabaisse), *sanpietro* (St. Peter's fish, called in English John Dory, a flat fish), *galinella* (gurnard), and *gatuccio* (another type of shark or dogfish).

Most of these are simply not available in North American fish markets, but the operative words here are not varieties of fish so much as "fresh" and "local." I have made cacciucco with halibut, haddock, fresh Maine shrimps, scallops (none of these to be found in Tuscany), squid, and the tentacles of an octopus that I purchased fresh from an Italian-

American fishmonger named Salvatore Fantasia who believes as strongly as I do that the fresher the fish, the better the dish, unless of course you're speaking of salt cod.

The dish is a delicious variant of fish stew found all over the Mediterranean, once made from leftovers at the end of the fishmonger's or fisherman's day. Today, even along the Tuscan coast, it's more likely to be made with fish purchased specially for the occasion, and the more varieties, the better it will be—some say as many as twelve or thirteen different fish, but six should be sufficient. Both the quantities and varieties of fish given on pages 127–128 are approximate. I have suggested certain types of fish, but feel free to use whatever looks good and fresh in the market. Just be sure to use both shellfish (mussels, clams, shrimps) and finfish (haddock, halibut, snapper), as well as some form of cephalopods (squid, octopus, calamari). What Italians call *pesce azzurro* (meaning blue fish), such as mackerel, bluefish, tuna, and the like, are best omitted, as their strong flavors will dominate the dish.

Ask the fishmonger for heads and racks of already cleaned fresh fish to make the broth. Rinse the pieces under cool running water before using. If the fishmonger has available some small, bony fish (but not mackerel or other oily fish), add a pound or so of those to the mix.

Note that both the fish broth and the tomato sauce may be made ahead and combined when you're ready to cook the fish.

> For about 10 cups fish broth:
> 2 medium white onions, coarsely chopped
> 1 stalk celery, including green top, coarsely chopped
> 1 medium carrot, scraped and coarsely chopped
> 2 tablespoons extra virgin olive oil
> 1 cup dry white wine
> About 2 ½ pounds fish heads and bones; or mix 1 ½ pounds heads and
>   bones with 1 pound small, bony fish
> 2 bay leaves, preferably fresh
> 6 large sprigs flat-leaf parsley

In the bottom of a 3- or 4-quart stockpot, gently sauté the onions, celery, and carrot in the olive oil over medium heat until the vegetables are soft and just beginning to brown. Add the wine, raise the heat to medium-high, and cook the wine rapidly until it has thrown off its alcohol and is reduced by about one-third. Add the fish heads and bones and stir to mix well. Add 8 cups cold water, or enough to cover the fish parts, along with the bay leaves and parsley. Bring to a simmer and lower heat to medium-low or low. The broth should simmer rather than boil, uncovered, for 30 minutes. Skim off any foam that rises to the top.

When the broth is done, strain through a fine sieve or a colander lined with cheese-cloth, pressing on the fish to release all the juices. Discard all the solids. (Any broth not used in the stew may be refrigerated or frozen for future use.)

For the tomato sauce:

1 medium yellow onion, finely chopped

4 cloves garlic, finely chopped

1/2 medium fennel bulb, coarsely chopped

1 medium carrot, peeled and finely chopped

1/4 cup extra virgin olive oil

1/2 cup red wine

8 to 10 fresh, red, ripe tomatoes, peeled, seeded, and coarsely chopped,
    to make 5 cups, or use drained canned tomatoes, chopped

1/2 teaspoon crushed red pepper flakes

1 1/2 cups fish broth, or more if necessary

1/4 cup chopped flat-leaf parsley

Salt and freshly ground black pepper to taste

In the bottom of a heavy 2- or 3-quart saucepan, gently sauté the onion, garlic, fennel, and carrot in the oil over medium heat until the vegetables are soft and just beginning to brown. Add the red wine and stir to mix well. Let the wine cook until it has thrown off most of its alcohol, then stir in the tomatoes, red pepper flakes, and 1 cup of the prepared fish broth. Add the parsley and stir to mix well. Cook, uncovered, over medium-low heat, stirring occasionally, until the tomatoes have reduced to a very thick sauce, like a chunky purée. This will take about 30 minutes. If the sauce dries too much during the cooking process and the tomatoes look as if they're going to burn, add a little more of the broth. At the end of the cooking time, you should have about 4 cups of dense and aromatic tomato sauce. If it's still too liquid, cook a little while longer. Add salt and pepper to taste and set the sauce aside.

Assembling the cacciucco:

2 pounds small manila clams, or mussels if you prefer

3/4 pound squid or calamari, cleaned (see below)

1 1/2 pounds octopus tentacles, if available

3 cups prepared fish broth, or more if necessary

4 cups prepared tomato sauce

8 (1/2-inch-thick) slices country-style bread

1 or 2 cloves garlic, unpeeled, cut in half

1½ pounds firm white-fleshed fish, such as monkfish

1 pound white-fleshed fish, such as halibut, haddock, sea bass, or red snapper, cut in steaks or thick chunks

1 pound scallops

1 pound fresh (not frozen) shrimp (headless, with shells on)

1 or 2 tablespoons extra virgin olive oil

¼ cup finely minced flat-leaf parsley

Rinse all the different kinds of fish briefly in cool running water and pat dry with paper towels. Pick over the clams or mussels, discarding any that have cracked shells or are gaping. Pull the beards off the mussels.

Clean the squid, if necessary, by pulling the innards and tentacles gently away from the hood. Rinse the hood under running water and remove the bone that looks like a piece of transparent cellulose running up the inside of the hood—make sure you get all of it. Cut the hood in inch-thick slices. Cut the tentacles away from the innards just below the eyes and discard the innards. Rinse the tentacles and set aside.

In a medium saucepan over medium-low heat gently poach the octopus tentacles for 40 to 50 minutes in 3 cups of simmering fish broth, or until tender. Remove when tender, cut in inch-thick slices, and set aside.

Remove and set aside 2 cups of the broth used to cook the octopus. Add the clams (or mussels, if using) to the broth remaining in the pan and cook over high heat just until the shellfish open, removing them as they open and setting aside. Discard any that do not open after about 5 minutes. When all the shellfish have been removed, strain the remaining broth in the pan through a fine-mesh sieve or a colander lined with cheesecloth to get rid of any sand. Add the strained broth to the tomato sauce, along with 1 cup of the broth in which you poached the octopus.

Toast the bread slices on both sides on a grill or under the broiler. Rub on one side only with a cut clove of garlic. Arrange the bread slices in a single layer in the bottom of an attractive oven dish, a terra-cotta casserole, or a large gratin dish, and set aside in a very warm place—a 300°F oven will do just fine.

In a pan large enough to hold all the fish, bring the tomato sauce to a steady simmer over medium heat. Add the firm-textured fish to the tomato sauce and poach for about 3 minutes, then add the softer fish (haddock, halibut, or other) and continue to cook an additional 3 minutes. Gently stir in the squid and scallops and cook for 3 to 5 minutes longer. Finally stir in the shrimp and cook 2 minutes. Remove from the heat and immediately stir in the reserved octopus slices and the clams and/or mussels. Arrange the seafood on top of the toast slices in the hot casserole and spoon the tomato sauce over and around. Drizzle with olive oil, sprinkle liberally with minced parsley, and serve immediately, very hot.

Mixed Fish Fry
fritto misto di pesce

6 SERVINGS

You don't need a great variety of seafood to create a distinctive fritto misto; rather, what you need is seafood of the most impeccable quality. I use fresh (unfrozen) squid, the smallest I can find, and fresh Maine shrimp when they're in season, along with $1\frac{1}{2}$-inch chunks of fresh halibut or small (6-inch) smelts. In other parts of the country, you might find snapper of better quality than halibut, or oysters more in evidence than shrimp.

How do you know it's fresh? Your nose alone should tell you. Previously frozen fish often has no fragrance at all, and a spongy, disagreeable texture that's readily apparent, whereas fresh fish should smell pleasantly briny, with clean, firm flesh. Fish that's over the hill will have a distinctively unpleasant ammonia smell that's a dead giveaway—discard anything that has even a hint of this. Fresh seafood of any sort, finfish, shellfish, cephalopods, always looks appetizing—clean, translucent flesh, with no hint of gaping or yellowing. (Mussels, clams, and oysters, like lobsters, should only be purchased live.) This is the ideal, and it's not often met. Less than ideal fish can still be used, especially in dishes where other strong flavors come into play, but not for a fritto misto, where you come up against the flavor and texture of the fish very directly.

For deep-frying use a less expensive extra virgin olive oil; many supermarkets now have house brands that are excellent.

About 1 pound firm, white-fleshed fish fillets (halibut, haddock, snapper, sea bass, wolffish, drum are all good choices)
About 1 pound fresh small (35 count) shrimp in the shell
About 1 pound fresh calamari or squid, the smallest available
3 to 4 cups extra virgin olive oil
$\frac{3}{4}$ cup unbleached all-purpose flour
$\frac{1}{4}$ cup cornmeal
Salt and freshly ground black pepper to taste
$\frac{1}{4}$ teaspoon crushed red pepper flakes, if desired
Sprigs flat-leaf parsley and lemon wedges, for garnish

Rinse the fish fillets and pat dry. Cut into smaller pieces, about 1 to 2 inches on the side. Set aside.

Peel the shrimp, discarding the heads and shells. (In Tuscany, small shrimp like these are fried with their shells still on, to be eaten shell and all. Most Americans seem to find this distressing, but if you're serving Italians, by all means, leave the shells on.) Set aside.

Prepare the calamari as in the recipe for cacciucco (page 125). If the calamari are very small, they should be left whole after cleaning, rather than sliced.

Put the oil in a deep frying pan and set over medium-high heat. Have ready a rack spread with paper towels on which to drain the fried seafood.

Mix the flour with the cornmeal, adding salt and pepper to taste and a small amount of finely crushed red chile pepper if you wish. Either spread the seasoned flour out on a plate or, better yet, put it in a brown paper bag. Working in batches, as soon as the oil has reached frying temperature (350° to 365°F.), put a big handful of prepared seafood into the bag and shake to coat the pieces lightly. Then drop into the hot fat. The seafood is done when the pieces are pale golden—don't wait for them to become deep brown, as they'll be overcooked. Remove from the hot fat with a slotted spoon and transfer to the rack to drain. When all the seafood has been fried, add a dozen or so sprigs of parsley to the hot fat and fry until crisp. Use them to garnish the fritto misto, along with lemon wedges and a good sprinkling of crunchy, granular sea salt.

Red Mullet in Tomato Sauce from Livorno
triglie alla livornese

6 SERVINGS

Triglie, or red mullet, are the same small (no more than half a pound) pink- or red-skinned fish that the French call *rouget* and the Spanish *salmonetes.* All over the Mediterranean they are prized for their sweet, delicate flesh, and they are sometimes available in this country in fine fish shops, flown in from the Mediterranean or from the Atlantic coast of Morocco. In Tuscany, the best are called triglie di scoglio and are caught just off the coast. When buying red mullet, count on at least two to a portion.

This technique, which involves nothing more than making a savory tomato sauce, frying the fish, then finishing the fish in the sauce, is simplicity itself and can be applied to a variety of fish, whether small, whole fish, fish steaks, or fillets.

12 red mullet, each $1/2$ pound or less
$1/2$ medium fennel bulb, finely chopped
$1/2$ cup finely chopped flat-leaf parsley
1 clove garlic, finely chopped
1 stalk celery, white part only, finely chopped
2 tablespoons plus $1/2$ cup extra virgin olive oil
1 cup canned whole tomatoes, with their juice, chopped
$1/4$ cup tomato purée, if necessary
Salt and freshly ground black pepper to taste
Unbleached all-purpose flour for dredging the fish
Minced flat-leaf parsley and lemon wedges, for garnish

Rinse the fish under cool running water and pat dry with paper towels. Set aside.

In a saucepan or skillet large enough to hold all the fish, gently sauté the fennel, parsley, garlic, and celery in 2 tablespoons of the oil over medium-low heat until the vegetables are soft. Stir in the chopped tomatoes with their liquid and simmer for 15 or 20 minutes, until the tomatoes have condensed to a thick but still liquid sauce, adding a little tomato purée or plain water if necessary as the tomatoes cook to keep them from sticking to the pan. When the sauce is done, add salt and pepper to taste. Set aside but keep warm while you prepare the fish.

Spread the flour on a plate and roll each fish in the flour, dredging to coat lightly. In another skillet or saucepan heat the remaining $1/2$ cup oil to frying temperature—about 350°F. When the oil is hot, fry the fish until they are crisp and lightly golden on both sides, about 2 minutes to a side. Do this in batches if it's easier. As you remove the fish from the pan, set them on a rack to drain.

When all the fish are done, heat the tomato sauce to simmering and add all the fish to the sauce. Cook for no more than 5 minutes, then serve immediately, sprinkled with fresh parsley. Garnish the platter with lemon wedges.

Oven-roasted Tuna Steaks with a Sweet Red Pepper Sauce
tonno alla livornese

6 SERVINGS

The red peppers in this sauce recall similar preparations from Catalonia and the Balearic islands, a reminder that Livorno was, in its heyday, one of the most cosmopolitan of Mediterranean ports, with a population that included Christians, Jews, and Arabs, freemen and slaves, artists, musicians, gypsy lovers, and merchants and traders from all over the Inner Sea.

If fresh tuna is not available, the sauce is equally good with swordfish or, as in the preceding recipe, with other varieties, other shapes. Use your imagination, and your judgment about cooking times.

3 hefty red bell peppers
1/2 cup finely minced white or yellow onion
1 clove garlic, finely minced
1/4 cup extra virgin olive oil
4 tomatoes, peeled, seeded, and chopped (to make 1 cup chopped tomatoes)
1/4 cup light veal or chicken stock
2 tablespoons dry white wine
Salt and freshly ground black pepper to taste
1/4 cup unbleached all-purpose flour
1 1/2 pounds fresh 1-inch-thick tuna steaks (6 steaks)

Prepare the red peppers by charring them, preferably over a charcoal or gas grill. Or hold each one at the end of a long-handled fork over a gas flame, turning regularly until the skin is thoroughly blackened and blistered. When all the peppers are charred, peel and rub the skin away. Cut the peppers in half, discarding the seeds and white membranes, and chop very fine.

In a saucepan over medium-low heat, gently sauté the onion and garlic in 2 tablespoons of the olive oil until they are soft but not brown. Stir in the chopped peppers and continue cooking until the peppers are very soft. Now add the chopped tomatoes, together with the stock and wine, and cook for 20 minutes or more, or until the sauce has reduced to a thick but chunky purée. Taste and add salt and pepper. (This may be done ahead to this point, but the sauce should be reheated before proceeding.)

Preheat the oven to 400°F.

Spread the flour on a plate and lightly dredge the tuna steaks. Sear the tuna steaks in the remaining 2 tablespoons of olive oil over medium-high heat, just long enough to lightly brown them on each side. Transfer them to an oven dish or terracotta casserole that will hold the tuna in one layer. Spoon the pepper sauce over and around the steaks. Place in the preheated oven and cook for 10 to 15 minutes, or until the tuna is done and the sauce is bubbly.

Serve immediately.

Squid Braised with Spinach or Green Chard
totani in zimino

6 SERVINGS

Fish prepared *in zimino* is an antique Florentine dish that has spread out to other parts of Tuscany and taken on many variations. I've also been served *anguilla* (eels) in zimino and baccalà (salt cod) in zimino. But what does zimino really mean? Fish cooked with greens, say some experts, since spinach or chard, chopped and mixed with the pieces of fish, is an almost constant feature. But not quite, for anguilla in zimino hasn't a trace of green in it but is simply eels in a tomato sauce. Some cooks swear by tomatoes as a biblical part of any zimino, while others say no way, tomatoes are *never* in the real thing.

As for the word itself, like many culinary puzzles, this one is solved by resorting to a spurious Arabic origin: Zimino, it's said, refers to cumin, *cimino* being the original name of the dish (ignoring the fact that cumin, in Arabic, is *ka'amoun*). If this is so, it's one of the few dishes, if not the only one, in all the tradition of Tuscan cooking that calls for that spice. (It does seem likely that dried powdered ginger was used in the original, and replaced by dried red chile peppers [peperoncini] when they came into vogue.)

The smallest squid, called *totani* or *moscardini,* are what's called for, but if you can't find tiny squid, use regular sizes and cut them in inch-thick slices. Traditionally this is served over the usual Tuscan slices of stale bread, lightly toasted, but it's also excellent with polenta.

1 medium white or yellow onion, finely chopped

2 tablespoons chopped flat-leaf parsley

1 medium carrot, scraped and finely chopped

$1/4$ cup extra virgin olive oil

2 pounds squid, cleaned as described on page 128; left whole if small,
  otherwise cut in rings

2 cloves garlic, finely chopped

1 small dried hot red chile pepper, or $1/2$ teaspoon crushed red pepper flakes, or to taste

1 cup red wine

$1/2$ cup prepared tomato sauce (page 127)

2 pounds fresh spinach or green chard (or half of each), thoroughly
  cleaned and chopped

Salt and freshly ground black pepper to taste

In a saucepan or deep frying pan large enough to hold all the fish, gently sauté the onion, parsley, and carrot in the olive oil over medium-low heat until the vegetables are soft but not brown, about 10 minutes. When the vegetables are done, push them out to the edges of the pan and add the squid to the middle. Raise the heat to medium and quickly cook the squid, turning and stirring until they are cooked through and browning a little on the edges. Remove the squid and set aside in a warm place.

Add the garlic and red chile pepper or flakes to the oil and vegetables in the pan and stir to mix well. Add the wine and bring to a boil. Cook rapidly, raising the heat if necessary, until the wine has thrown off its alcohol and reduced by about one-third. Now stir in the tomato sauce and let come to a simmer. Cook for about 5 minutes and add the greens, turning them in the juices in the pan to mix everything together well. (The greens may seem like too much at first, but they'll cook down rapidly.) Lower the heat to medium-low or low and cook the greens, stirring occasionally, until they have wilted.

Return the squid to the pan and stir to mix well. Cook for about 30 minutes, stirring frequently and adding a little more red wine or water if the mixture becomes too dry. The greens should be dissolving into a sauce that caresses the pieces of fish.

After 30 minutes of cooking, the squid pieces should be very tender and the sauce should be thick and very flavorful. If the sauce is still too liquid, raise the heat and boil for no more than 3 or 4 minutes to reduce some of the juices. Season with salt and pepper.

Serve over slices of toasted bread rubbed with garlic if you wish, or with soft polenta or thick slices of polenta toasted on the grill till golden on both sides.

Variation: To make Baccalà in Zimino, soak out a 1½- to 1¾-pound side of salt cod, as described in the recipe on page 138. When the cod is ready, cut it in 2-inch chunks, and dredge the chunks lightly in flour before frying till golden, like the squid above.

Drowned Trout
trote affogate

The shores of Lake Trasimeno were Hannibal's victory ground, where he defeated the Roman armies of Scipio in 217 B.C., and nearly brought Rome herself to her knees. Nearby Tuscan villages like Ossaia and Sanguinaia ("bony" and "bloody") recall the dreadful events that took place here, so it's understandable if Trasimeno seems a haunted place, especially in winter when tourists and campers have departed and the broad shallow waters are left to the waterfowl and the reed meadows that border it.

On modern maps, the lake is shown in Umbria but it is still Etruscan-walled Cortona that dominates the western shore, and Cortonese cooks like Maria Luisa Valeri, who gave me the following recipe, consider the lake's products and ways of cooking them part of their Tuscan/Etruscan heritage. Freshly caught lake fish like *persico* (perch), *tinche* (tench), and *luccio* (pike) are quickly sautéed and served in ways that are reminiscent of coastal regions.

Except around the Great Lakes, it isn't easy to find good fresh lake fish in most of this country, but this recipe is fine with farmed trout or Arctic char, or even with saltwater fish like small snappers or bluefish, although of course they are stronger in flavor, so they will give an entirely different cast to the dish. The fish should be small enough so that one will do for each serving.

> 6 boned trout or Arctic char, $^1/_2$ pound each
> 3 slices imported prosciutto
> 1 medium onion
> 1 sprig fresh rosemary
> 1 (1-inch-thick) slice stale country-style bread, crusts removed
> $^1/_3$ cup dry white wine
> $^1/_4$ cup unbleached all-purpose flour
> $^1/_4$ cup plus 2 tablespoons extra virgin olive oil
> 1 clove garlic, flattened with the blade of a knife
> 2 tablespoons unsalted butter

Wash the fish inside and out and pat dry with paper towels.

Chop the prosciutto, onion, and rosemary leaves to make a fine mince. Tear the bread into pieces and place in a small bowl. Cover with 3 tablespoons of the wine. When the bread has absorbed all the wine, squeeze it out and mix it with the prosciutto mixture. Put a couple of tablespoons of this inside each fish, close the fish up, and tie, if necessary, with butcher's twine or clean white thread in two or three places.

Spread the flour on a plate and roll each fish in the flour to coat lightly.

Heat ¼ cup of the olive oil in a skillet over medium-high heat and add the garlic. When the garlic has browned thoroughly, remove it and discard. Add the trout to the pan, preferably in one layer—or do this in two or more batches, keeping the first batch warm in the oven while you finish the remainder. Brown the trout on both sides, then lower the heat to medium and continue cooking an additional 5 minutes to a side, or until the trout is thoroughly cooked.

Meanwhile, in a smaller pan, combine the remaining 2 tablespoons oil, the butter, and the remaining wine. Heat over medium-high until the wine has bubbled and given off all its alcohol.

Remove the trout to a serving platter and pour the oil-butter-wine mixture on top. Serve immediately.

Salt Cod with Leeks
baccalà con porri

6 TO 8 SERVINGS

Salt cod is one of those ingredients commonly used all over the Mediterranean from which American cooks seem to shudder in horror. Unreasonably, I say, because salt cod, properly soaked and cooked, is an utterly delicious food, as more and more younger and more adventurous American chefs are discovering.

Salt cod is often available in cute little wooden boxes from Nova Scotia, but tempting as these are, the contents, I find, are too often composed of small pieces of rather yellowing cod. When I buy salt cod I get whole sides of clear white and very salty fish. My fish expert, Salvatore Fantasia of Cambridge, Massachusetts, insists that the best has the bones left in, but I find boneless sides easier to handle. Two or three days before I'm ready to cook the fish, I start to soak it in water to plump and refresh the fish and remove much of the salt. I put the fish in a big plastic dishpan filled with cool water, then change the water in the pan every six hours or so for two or three days. Once the cod is refreshed, it can be refrigerated for another two or three days, if necessary, before using.

In Italy you will see references in markets and restaurants alike to both baccalà and stoccafisso. There is a difference, although it's not always observed. Baccalà is truly salt cod, fish that has been preserved by salting and drying. Stoccafisso (an Italianization of the German *stockfisch* or stick-fish, an apt description), on the other hand, is air-dried cod; Italian chefs say they prefer stoccafisso in any recipe, but to my taste (and nose) it has a peculiarly rank aroma that is difficult to love. If you want to try stoccafisso, you'll find it in food shops catering to West Africans and West Indians. Baccalà is more widely available in stores in Italian, Spanish, and Portuguese neighborhoods.

In Tuscany, both baccalà and stoccafisso are most often cooked in savory sauces that are considered natural accompaniments to polenta, whether soft polenta or slices of firm polenta toasted on the grill or fried in olive oil. Either of the next two recipes will go well with polenta cooked as described on pages 105 and 107.

1 medium yellow onion, finely chopped

1 medium carrot, scraped and finely chopped

2 cloves garlic, finely chopped

$1/2$ cup finely chopped flat-leaf parsley

1 stalk celery, finely chopped

$1/3$ cup extra virgin olive oil

2 pounds leeks, washed and thinly sliced (about 4 cups leeks)

About 1 $1/2$ pounds salt cod, soaked at least 2 days

$1/2$ cup slivered basil

Combine the onion, carrot, garlic, parsley, and celery in a large skillet and sweat very gently in the olive oil over low heat for about 20 minutes, or until the vegetables are meltingly soft. Add the leeks and stir to mix well. Continue cooking another 20 minutes or until the leeks are soft, adding a little water if necessary. The vegetables should not brown at all—burned or browned leeks give off a peculiarly acrid flavor that will ruin the sauce.

While the leeks are cooking, prepare the soaked cod. Dry the cod, if necessary, with paper towels and cut in small pieces, not more than an inch or so to the side. When the leeks are very soft, stir the cod pieces into the vegetables, combining thoroughly. Add $1/2$ cup hot water to the pan and stir it in. Bring to a simmer and cook, uncovered, for 20 minutes, adding the basil for the last 5 minutes of cooking.

Serve immediately, with polenta or, if you prefer, over toasted slices of country-style bread.

Note: This takes well to reheating and may be prepared ahead, in the morning, say, for serving in the evening.

Salt Cod with a Tomato Sauce
baccalà alla livornese

There's a strong tradition in the Mediterranean that the use of many New World food products, but especially tomatoes, was spread by Jewish merchants and travelers who were in contact with Jewish communities all over the Inner Sea and thus in a good position to spread novelties like these. So it's interesting that Livorno, which historically had a large and important community of Jews, was also the place in Tuscany where tomatoes are most closely associated with the local cuisine. "Alla livornese" means the same thing in Tuscany that "alla napoletana" means elsewhere—a dense and savory tomato sauce.

About 1 $\frac{1}{2}$ pounds salt cod, soaked for at least 2 days, as described on page 138
1 cup dry white wine
Lots of freshly ground black pepper
2 medium yellow onions, finely chopped
3 cloves garlic, finely chopped
$\frac{1}{3}$ cup finely chopped flat-leaf parsley
1 $\frac{1}{4}$ cups extra virgin olive oil
3 cups peeled, seeded, and chopped very ripe, red tomatoes
$\frac{1}{4}$ cup finely chopped or slivered fresh basil
Flour to dredge the cod
2 cloves garlic, crushed with the flat blade of a knife
1 tablespoon finely minced flat-leaf parsley, for garnish
Zest of $\frac{1}{2}$ lemon, minced or julienned, for garnish

Pat the salt cod dry with paper towels and cut in serving pieces, about 3 inches to a side. Put the cod pieces in a bowl and cover with the white wine and an abundance of black pepper. Set aside to marinate for at least 30 minutes, or up to 2 hours.

While the cod marinates, make the tomato sauce. In a saucepan over low heat, gently sauté the onions, chopped garlic, and parsley in $\frac{1}{4}$ cup of the olive oil for about 20 minutes, or until very soft but not brown. Add the tomatoes, raise the heat to medium, and cook rapidly until the tomatoes have reduced to a dense, thick, chunky sauce. If necessary, add a little more white wine or some plain water to keep the tomatoes from burning. Stir in the basil for the last 5 minutes of cooking. Set aside but keep warm until ready to use.

Remove the pieces of cod from the marinade and pat dry with paper towels. Spread the flour on a plate and lightly dredge the pieces of cod. Put the remaining 1 cup oil in a deep frying pan and heat to frying temperature—about 350° to 360°F. When the oil is hot enough, add the crushed garlic cloves and let brown thoroughly, then remove. Fry the pieces of cod, a few at a time, in the garlic-scented oil until golden on all sides. Drain on a rack covered with paper towels.

Arrange the pieces of fish on a serving platter, heat the tomato sauce to a simmer, and spoon the sauce over and around the fish. Garnish with minced parsley and lemon zest and serve immediately.

Chicken and Meat
pollame e carne

Chickens, ducks, rabbits, guinea fowl, sometimes geese as well, are all classed as *animali da cortile,* farmyard animals, that traditionally come under the strict care of the farmwife. Fed from table scraps occasionally enriched with a little cracked corn or gruel, and, in the case of fowl, whatever grubs and insects they can scavenge, they are in the truest sense free-ranging and naturally raised. Rabbits on Tuscan farms are kept in hutches and it's a duty of old grannies to collect wild grasses and greens to fatten them for the cooking pot. Years ago, when she was still alive but very old, I used to come across Diamante, the Antolini grandmother, hunched with age but merry nonetheless, with an awkward shawlful of wild grasses slung over her back. She'd collected them in the abandoned fields below my house, and the flesh of the rabbits she fed was perfumed with the aromas of wild meadows.

A plump fowl or rabbit is convenience food at the ready, quickly dispatched, plucked or skinned, and cut into pieces for frying when unexpected guests arrive. The chicken run and the rabbit hutch keep food a good deal fresher than the freezer, and produce a far tastier dish. Farmhouse cooks might occasionally buy a piece of beef or lamb from the butcher in town, but it would never occur to them to purchase a chicken or a duck. In fact, many of my neighbors raise these animals to sell to town butchers—in Fernanda's butcher shop on the steep via Dardano in Cortona, you'll find, as you will in other Tuscan towns, chickens, rabbits, and guinea fowl on display from farmyards she knows well, her mother's or her sister's or a neighbor's in the hill country behind the walled Etruscan town.

In Tuscan restaurants, grilled meat can achieve a high degree of gastronomy, and a Tuscan mixed grill, most often composed of a lamb chop, a pork chop, a sausage, a piece of pork liver wrapped in a net of caul fat, and perhaps other meaty delights, is an excellent way to show off the quality of fine meats, especially when these are grilled over the live embers of a wood fire. The summa cum laude of this technique is *bistecca toscana* or *bistecca fiorentina,* a sumptuous thick T-bone or porterhouse cut from the region's prized Chianina beef, sprinkled with nothing but salt and pepper and grilled over the embers. Served with a little dollop of extra virgin olive oil and a spritz of lemon juice, it's elegant beyond belief, albeit in a primitive fashion, and could quickly put beefsteak back in your diet.

In the farmhouse kitchen, however, meat is far more often braised or simmered for hours in a small amount of aromatic liquid, a technique that's called *in umido.* Traditionally, meat often came from older animals, ones that had outlived their usefulness in other ways (wool, eggs, drawing the plow), and this method was a way of rendering the flesh tender enough for even elderly teeth to tackle. While the meat cooks on the stove top or in the oven it absorbs the flavors of wine, tomato concentrate, and a whole host of *odori,* aromatic herbs and vegetables like carrots, onions, and garlic, that are finely chopped and sweated in oil at the beginning of the cooking process. Then the meat is added and browned before the liquid goes in, a little at a time, to be reduced over hours of slow cooking until it becomes a rich and syrupy sauce, a spoonful of which goes with each slice of the meat.

Of course, such simple techniques require ingredients that are in themselves full of flavor, which means, on the whole, that meat, like vegetables and fruits, should be raised as naturally as possible with no added elements to prolong the creature's life or make its flesh more tender. Fortunately, it's increasingly easy to find meat like this in American markets, whether beef, lamb, or chicken. Pork is another matter: It may take some searching to find a supplier of naturally raised pork, but it's well worth the effort. Whole-foods stores, natural-foods stores, and food co-ops are good places to begin the search; farmers' markets, even those primarily made up of vegetable growers, often include people who also raise pork or who know other farmers who do.

Peppery Grilled Chicken
pollo al mattone o pollo alla diavolo

6 SERVINGS

This is called *pollo al mattone* because the bird is flattened with a brick for ease of grilling, or *pollo alla diavolo* (deviled chicken) because the peppery seasoning of crushed black peppercorns and crumbled dried hot red chile peppers is torrid as the dickens.

 1 cup extra virgin olive oil
 1 tablespoon crushed black peppercorns, or to taste
 1 tablespoon crumbled hot red chile pepper or crushed red pepper flakes, or to taste
 1 tablespoon chopped fresh rosemary
 3 or 4 sage leaves, coarsely chopped
 1 teaspoon salt
 3 small chickens, split in half
 Juice of 1 lemon
 Lemon wedges, for garnish

Mix the oil with the black and red peppers, rosemary, sage, and salt and set aside, covered, for several hours or overnight.

Prepare the chicken halves by cutting away and discarding excess yellow fat from the insides of the birds. Flatten them by laying each half, skin side up, on a board and pounding it smartly with the flat side of a cleaver. This should crack the breast bone so that the birds will lie flat on the grill and cook more evenly.

Put the chicken halves on a platter or in an oven dish and cover with the peppery olive oil. Leave to marinate, turning occasionally, for at least 1 hour. Or refrigerate, covered, for several hours or overnight.

When ready to cook, prepare the grill, leaving plenty of time for it to heat up if you're using charcoal or wood. When the coals are hot, place the chicken halves, skin side down, on the grill and set the grill a good 8 inches from the source of the heat. Stir the lemon juice into the savory oil remaining in the platter and use this to brush over the chickens as they cook. Grill for 15 minutes on each side, turning once, brushing frequently with the oil and lemon juice. Test for doneness: The juices should run clear yellow when the chicken is thoroughly cooked.

Serve immediately, piled on a platter garnished with lemon wedges.

Country-style Chicken
pollo alla campagnola

4 TO 6 SERVINGS

U se a vin santo that is on the dry side for basting the fowl, or, lacking vin santo, use a dryish sherry. Butter doesn't appear often in the Tuscan country kitchen; it was made, if at all, in the summertime after the calves had been weaned. It lends extra richness to this dish but, if you prefer, it may be omitted.

1 (4-pound) roasting chicken, free-range or naturally raised
Salt and freshly ground black pepper to taste
2 tablespoons sweet butter
1/2 cup extra virgin olive oil
1 pound white onions, very thinly sliced
1/3 cup dry vin santo or dry oloroso sherry
1/4 cup chicken stock, preferably homemade, if necessary

Preheat the oven to 400°F.

Pull the fat out of the chicken cavity. Rinse the bird in cool water and dry well, inside and out, with paper towels. Sprinkle the chicken inside and out with salt and pepper.

In a roasting pan large enough to hold the chicken, melt the butter in the olive oil over medium-low heat. Add the onions, stir into the fat, and sweat gently, lowering the heat if necessary to keep the onions from browning. Cook for about 20 minutes or until they are very soft.

Push the onions out to the sides of the pan and set the chicken in the middle. Place in the preheated oven and roast for 30 minutes, basting every 10 minutes or so with the vin santo or sherry. Then lower the heat to 325°F. and continue roasting another 30 minutes, continuing to baste with the vin santo or with the juices in the pan. If the pan juices reduce too much, baste with chicken stock or hot water.

The chicken is done when a leg moves loosely on its joint or when the juices run clear yellow when pricked with a fork.

Remove the chicken from the oven and set aside to rest for 10 minutes or so before carving. If the pan juices are too liquid, boil them rapidly over high heat, taking care not to fry the onions. The onions should be quite brown, but roasted rather than fried, and very soft.

Lemon Chicken
pollo al limone

This was a favorite recipe of my friend and neighbor, the late Nika Hazelton, whose crusty wit could not conceal a love of Tuscany that was as strong as her love for almost anything made with lemons. Use any fresh herbs that are available—even plain parsley is delicious, and in summer fresh basil gives the dish an entirely new perspective.

2 fresh lemons, preferably organically raised

1 cup dry white wine

$1/4$ cup plus 2 tablespoons extra virgin olive oil

5 tablespoons minced fresh herbs: sage, thyme, rosemary, parsley, or others according to what's available

2 cloves garlic, peeled and minced

3 to 4 pounds chicken, preferably free-range, cut in serving pieces (a whole bird, cut up, or chicken parts, according to your preference)

Salt and freshly ground black pepper to taste

Grate the zest of the lemons into a bowl large enough to hold all the chicken pieces, then squeeze in all the lemon juice, holding back the seeds. Whisk in the wine, $1/4$ cup of the olive oil, the herbs, and the garlic. Add the chicken pieces, turning them to coat well with the marinade. Set aside, covered, in a cool place to marinate for several hours. (Or prepare the chickens in the morning and refrigerate them until time to start dinner.)

When ready to cook, preheat the oven to 350°F.

Heat the remaining 2 tablespoons of olive oil in a large frying pan. Drain the chicken pieces, reserving the marinade, and sauté them over medium heat until they are golden and crisp on all sides, about 5 to 7 minutes to a side. Place the chicken in an oven dish large enough to hold all the pieces in one layer. Pour the remaining marinade into the frying pan and bring to a boil, scraping up any brown bits remaining in the pan. Pour the marinade over the chicken pieces and set the dish in the oven. Bake for 25 to 30 minutes, or until the chicken pieces are done (juices will run clear yellow when you prick a piece with a fork). Taste for seasoning, adding salt and pepper if desired.

Serve immediately in the dish in which the chicken was baked, or remove to a heated platter and pour the pan juices over.

Braised Chicken with Celery "Rocks"
pollo in umido con rocchi di sedano

Sometimes I think a person could spend every day in Italy for the rest of her life and never stop discovering new things in the kitchen—*rocchi di sedano,* for instance, simple little croquettes of steamed celery that are served with chicken that's been gently braised in wine and aromatics. It's a specialty of the Valdarno, or at least of that part of the Arno valley that's in Arezzo province. This is familiar territory, but I'd never heard of this dish until just a few months ago. And now I wonder how I ever lived without it.

The chicken may be cooked in the oven or on top of the stove. (For stove-top directions, see the end of the recipe.)

1 (4- to 5-pound) roasting chicken
Salt and freshly ground black pepper to taste
1 medium red onion, finely chopped (about $\frac{1}{2}$ cup)
1 stalk celery, finely chopped (about $\frac{1}{3}$ cup)
2 tablespoons finely chopped flat-leaf parsley
1 medium carrot, finely chopped (about $\frac{1}{3}$ cup)
1 clove garlic, finely chopped
2 tablespoons finely chopped fresh thyme
2 tablespoons extra virgin olive oil
$\frac{3}{4}$ cup dry red wine
2 tablespoons tomato conserve diluted with $\frac{1}{2}$ cup warm water
For the rocchi:
6 stalks celery, including the green tops, preferably the more flavorful outside stalks
Salt and freshly ground black pepper to taste
1 extra-large egg, lightly beaten
3 tablespoons freshly grated Parmigiano-Reggiano
2 to 3 tablespoons unbleached all-purpose flour
Oil for deep-fat frying

Pull any excess fat out of the chicken cavity. Rinse the bird in cool water and dry well, inside and out, with paper towels. Sprinkle the chicken inside and out with salt and pepper. Preheat the oven to 425°F.

Make a battuto by chopping together the onion, celery, parsley, carrot, garlic, and thyme until minced. In a heavy oven dish or casserole large enough to hold the chicken, gently sweat the battuto in the oil over medium-low heat until soft. Push the battuto out to the sides of the pan and place the chicken in the center. Spoon some of the pan juices over the bird and set in the oven to brown for 10 minutes, then turn, baste the bird again, and continue browning an additional 10 minutes. Remove from the oven and turn the heat down to 325°F.

Add the red wine to the casserole and set it on a burner over medium-low to medium heat. When it has reduced by about one-third, add the tomato conserve and water. Boil for 1 or 2 minutes to combine the flavors, then add salt and pepper to taste, cover the pot, and return the chicken to the oven to cook very gently for about $1^1/_4$ hours. The chicken is done when a leg moves loosely on its joint or when the juices run clear yellow when the bird is pricked with a fork.

When the chicken is done, remove from the oven and set aside to rest for 10 minutes or so before carving. If the pan juices seem too liquid, boil them down rapidly over high heat until you have a rather syrupy liquid in the pan.

While the chicken is cooking, make the rocchi: Cut the celery in 2-inch-long pieces and place in a saucepan. Cover with water, add a little salt, and bring to a boil. Simmer, uncovered, until the celery is very soft—about 20 to 25 minutes. Drain the celery and chop coarsely on a board. Turn the chopped celery into a colander and press handfuls of it between your palms to get rid of excess liquid. Now turn the thoroughly drained chopped celery into a bowl and mix with the beaten egg, the cheese, and enough flour just to hold it together. Taste the mixture and add a little salt and pepper if necessary.

Add oil to a frying pan to a depth of about $^3/_4$ inch. Heat over medium heat until it has reached frying temperature (360-375°F). When the oil is hot, form the celery mixture into fat little patties about 2 inches across. The mixture is loose, and it helps to shape the patties with wet hands. Slip them into the hot oil and fry, turning once, until brown on both sides.

Remove to a rack covered with paper towels to drain.

Serve the carved chicken, with a few spoonfuls of sauce for each serving, accompanied by the celery patties.

To cook the chicken on top of the stove: After sweating the battuto, raise the heat to medium and brown the chicken on all sides, turning frequently until it is thoroughly browned. Add the wine and tomato paste as directed and cook, covered, over medium-low to medium heat for 1 hour. The chicken should cook more quickly on top of the stove than in the oven, but if it is still a little underdone for your taste, cook another 15 minutes, or until the juices run yellow when the bird is pierced with a fork.

Oven-roasted Guinea Fowl with Pancetta and Herbs
faraona arrosto

4 SERVINGS

Guinea fowl, or guinea hens, are not as well known or widely used in America as they once were, and no one seems to be able to tell me why. The flesh is as tender as that of a naturally raised chicken, but with a slight but pleasantly gamy flavor that reminds me of pheasant. They're small birds, rarely weighing as much as four pounds, ideal for dinner for four, especially if there's a rather substantial first course like pasta. Because they tend to be dry, guinea fowl are best cooked with a slice of prosciutto (or pancetta, or blanched bacon) draped over to baste the bird with its fat.

2 ounces pancetta, chopped
1 clove garlic, chopped
3 sage leaves
1 sprig rosemary
Salt and freshly ground black pepper to taste
2 to 3 tablespoons extra virgin olive oil
1 (2 ½-pound) guinea fowl, split in half
2 slices prosciutto
¼ cup vin santo or dry sherry

Preheat the oven to 425°F.

Combine the pancetta, garlic, sage, and the leaves of the rosemary and chop until the mixture is very fine. Add a little salt and pepper and combine with 1 tablespoon of the oil. Rub the inside of each half bird with this mixture and lay the halves, skin side up, in a roasting pan that will just hold them. Drape a prosciutto slice over the top of each breast and sprinkle with a little more salt and pepper.

Roast in the preheated oven for 20 minutes, basting with 2 tablespoons of vin santo every 10 minutes. Then turn the heat down to 350°F. and continue roasting an additional 30 minutes, basting frequently with the juices in the pan. If the juices run clear when the meat is pierced with a fork, the bird is done.

Roasted Game Hens
pollastrini arrosti

6 SERVINGS

Once some friends of mine, dining in a country trattoria, were served exquisite little game birds that had been roasted on a spit—the birds so small that a single plump olive had been tucked inside each tiny bird as a stuffing. "Wonderful," they exclaimed to the proprietor, "but what are they?" *"Pettirossi,"* he replied proudly, "robin red-breasts."

Now, the consumption of robins is as illegal in Italy as it is in America, but there's no getting around the Tuscan predilection for little birds. I prefer to stay on the right side of the law and roast Cornish game hens. They may lack that frisson of the forbidden that robins have, but I'd rather have the robins singing under my windows.

Spit-roasting small birds like game hens is tricky, so I do these in the oven instead.

1 thick slice pancetta or prosciutto
6 Rock Cornish game hens, each about ³/₄ pound
6 fresh sage leaves
6 bay leaves, preferably fresh
12 black olives (preferably small Gaeta or niçoise)
Salt and freshly ground black pepper
2 tablespoons extra virgin olive oil
6 thin slices pancetta or prosciutto

Preheat the oven to 400°F.

Cut the thick slice of pancetta or prosciutto in 6 equal portions. Tuck a piece of pancetta inside each bird, along with a sage leaf, a bay leaf, and 2 of the olives, pitted if you prefer. Sprinkle salt and pepper all over the outsides of the birds and rub into the skin, rubbing with some of the olive oil at the same time. Wrap a thin slice of pancetta or prosciutto around each bird, stretching the meat to cover the bird well. Set the birds in a baking dish in which they will all fit comfortably.

Roast for 15 minutes, then turn down the oven to 325°F. and continue roasting 30 to 45 minutes longer, or until the birds are done and the juices run clear when the bird is pierced with a fork.

Serve immediately, with the pan juices as a sauce.

Roast Duck with Black Olives
anatra con olive nere

The bitterness of black olives is a splendid foil for the rich meat of duck. Ideally, this is a winter dish, made with fresh, uncured olives that have ripened on the trees. The long, slow cooking process converts their acrid nature into something tantalizing and delicious. Unless you live under a California olive tree, you will probably not have access to fresh olives, so make this with wrinkled, dried, salt-cured olives for the most authentic flavor. If you do have access to fresh olives, however, I'm told you should drop a handful in rapidly boiling water, leave for about 20 minutes, then drain and use in the recipe.

The thick layer of fat that ducks carry beneath their skin, a protection against the cold of their watery natural environment, makes them unappealing to some people. Cutting the duck in pieces and browning it extracts much of that fat. But don't discard it—it's a magnificent medium for sautéing potatoes to go with the duck.

1 teaspoon fennel seeds
1 clove garlic, crushed with the flat blade of a knife
Salt and freshly ground black pepper to taste
1 (5-pound) duck, cut in serving pieces
$1/4$ cup extra virgin olive oil
5 whole cloves garlic
12 small onions, preferably small flat yellow ones, peeled but left whole
$1/2$ cup pitted black olives
4 or 5 sage leaves, slivered
$1/2$ cup red wine
$1/2$ cup light chicken broth

If you have a spice grinder, grind the fennel seeds to a coarse powder, then pound them in a mortar with the crushed garlic and about 1 tablespoon of salt, or to taste. When the mixture is reduced to a paste, add plenty of black pepper. Rub this spice mixture all over the duck pieces and set aside, lightly covered, for about 30 minutes, or longer if necessary. Refrigerate the duck if you're not going to cook it within an hour.

When ready to cook, preheat the oven to 350°F. In the bottom of an oval roasting dish, preferably one that has a lid, add the olive oil and gently brown the whole garlic cloves and onions lightly but thoroughly on all sides. Remove from the pan and set aside.

Add the duck pieces to the oil remaining in the pan. Raise the heat to medium-high and brown the duck pieces, turning at least once, on all sides, about 10 minutes to a side. When all the duck has been browned, tilt the pan and remove most of the oil, leaving about 2 tablespoons in the bottom of the pan. Add the black olives and sage slivers, stirring to mix all the ingredients together, then add the wine. Let the wine bubble and reduce for about 5 minutes, until all the alcohol has been thrown off and the wine has been reduced by about half. Stir in the broth, add the onions and garlic cloves, and cover the pan.

Set in the preheated oven to bake until the duck is done and the sauce is reduced to a syrupy liquid that coats the onions and olives—about 2 hours in all. To further brown the duck, remove the pan lid for the last 15 minutes of cooking.

Remove the duck to a warm serving platter and surround it with the onions, garlic cloves, and black olives. If the juices in the pan are very liquid, boil over high heat for a few minutes to reduce. If, on the other hand, they've boiled down too much, add another ½ cup red wine and cook, scraping up the brown bits in the bottom of the pan. Serve the sauce poured over the duck and its garnishes.

Fried Rabbit
coniglio fritto

Very low in fat and cholesterol, lean, flavorful rabbit should be more greatly appreciated than it is in this country. In Tuscany rabbit is on every menu and part of every farmhouse feast. Perhaps it's the Thumper factor that makes us so reluctant to embrace this meat, but we eat veal and baby lamb, so. . . . If you're not a rabbit lover, this quick and easy recipe may convert you. It reminds me of southern-fried chicken, the rabbit pieces lightly crumbed and deep-fried in olive oil.

3/4 cup unbleached all-purpose flour
2 large eggs
2 tablespoons dry white wine
3 or 4 sage leaves, finely chopped
1 sprig rosemary, leaves only, finely chopped
2 tablespoons finely chopped flat-leaf parsley
2 cups fine soft bread crumbs
Salt and freshly ground black pepper to taste
1 (2 1/2-pound) rabbit, cut in 6 to 8 pieces
Extra virgin olive oil for deep-fat frying

Spread the flour out on a deep plate.

In another deep plate, combine the eggs with the wine and beat with a fork to mix thoroughly.

Mix the herbs together and chop again to make a very fine mixture. Combine with the bread crumbs and salt and pepper to taste and toss with a fork to mix well. Spread on a plate or a sheet of wax paper.

Dip the rabbit pieces in the flour, shaking off the excess. Dip in the egg mixture to coat lightly but thoroughly. Then roll each rabbit piece in the herbed bread crumbs. Set aside.

Put a good inch of oil in the bottom of a frying pan large enough to hold all the rabbit pieces in one layer, and heat to frying temperature, 350°F. (If you don't have a thermometer, heat it until a small cube of bread quickly sizzles and browns.) Drop the rabbit pieces in the hot oil. The temperature will drop immediately and then start to climb again. Adjust the heat source so that the temperature stays fairly constant between 325°F. and 350°F. Fry the rabbit pieces for 15 to 20 minutes to a side, turning once and adjusting the heat so the rabbit doesn't get too brown.

Remove the rabbit pieces and drain briefly on a rack covered with paper towels. Serve immediately.

Rabbit in Its Own Sauce
coniglio in umido

4 TO 6 SERVINGS

In this recipe, the rabbit makes its own sauce, with the addition of a very little wine, some wild mushrooms, a few tomatoes. This is a variation on *coniglio alla cacciatora,* rabbit huntsman's style. Note the technique of scorching the rabbit until it gives off liquid, then discarding the liquid before continuing with the cooking process. This is an old-fashioned method, considered absolutely essential by some Tuscan home cooks, who say it gets rid of a wild flavor in the meat; other cooks say the technique is unnecessary and without merit.

1 (2½- to 3-pound) rabbit, cut in 6 to 8 pieces

½ cup dry white wine

¼ cup extra virgin olive oil

1 clove garlic, finely chopped

1 or 2 sprigs rosemary, leaves only, finely chopped

Salt and freshly ground black pepper

2 medium yellow onions, very thinly sliced

½ ounce dried porcini mushrooms, soaked in warm water to cover, or ½ cup pitted
   black olives (Gaeta or niçoise)

½ cup chopped canned tomatoes

Place the rabbit pieces in a deep skillet and set the pan over high heat. Cook the rabbit, stirring constantly with a wooden spoon and turning frequently, until the pieces have given off a quantity of liquid. Discard the liquid and add wine to the pot. Return to heat and continue turning the rabbit pieces in the wine until most of the wine has evaporated and there are only a few tablespoons left.

Turn the heat down to medium-low. Add olive oil, garlic, rosemary, and salt and pepper to taste. Stir the rabbit pieces with the oil and herbs and sauté gently for about 5 minutes to a side. Add the sliced onions and the mushrooms or olives. Strain the mushroom soaking liquid through a sieve into the pan. (If you're using black olives instead of mushrooms, add a few tablespoons of water or dry white wine to the pan.) Simmer gently for an additional 5 to 10 minutes, or until the liquid has reduced slightly and the onions are softening. Now stir in the tomatoes, raise the heat to medium-high, and when the tomatoes are bubbling vigorously, cover the pan and cook for 20 to 30 minutes, or until the rabbit is cooked through. Serve immediately.

Oven-braised Rabbit
coniglio al forno

4 TO 6 SERVINGS

Fresh rabbit is preferable to frozen, but it's often very difficult to come by. If you can only get frozen rabbit, plan to thaw it slowly in the refrigerator, in a covered dish, for at least 24 hours.

> 1 (3-pound) rabbit, cut in 6 pieces
> 3 sprigs rosemary, leaves only, finely chopped, or a big pinch of crushed wild fennel,
>   or 3 or 4 sage leaves
> 4 cloves garlic, peeled and crushed with the flat blade of a knife
> $1/4$ cup olive oil
> Salt and freshly ground black pepper to taste
> About $1/4$ cup light chicken stock or dry white wine, if necessary

Rinse the rabbit pieces under running water, pat dry with paper towels, and set aside.

Mince the aromatics with the garlic and combine in a small bowl with the olive oil, salt, and pepper. Rub the mixture all over the rabbit pieces, then set aside for at least 30 minutes. This step may be done ahead but the rabbit should be covered and refrigerated if it is to be held for more than 1 hour.

When ready to cook, preheat the oven to 375°F.

Place the rabbit pieces, together with any bits of the marinade, in a covered terracotta or other oven dish. Cover and bake for 1 hour, checking from time to time: The rabbit should yield some liquid, but if it gets too dry, add a little stock or wine. At the end of this time, raise the oven heat to 450°F., remove the lid, and continue cooking for another 15 minutes, turning once. This will brown the rabbit nicely and evaporate some of the juices. Serve immediately.

Note: During the final 15 minutes of cooking, the rabbit pieces may be basted with about $1/4$ cup vin santo, or with dry white wine. Vegetables may be added to roast with the rabbit: Potatoes, carrots, onions, or small cabbages, cut in chunks and sprinkled with salt and a little olive oil, should be put in for the full cooking time, but mushrooms will cook in the last 15 minutes. Some cooks add about $1/2$ cup crushed canned tomatoes before putting the rabbit in the oven. You may also substitute a small chicken for the rabbit, adjusting the cooking time accordingly (the chicken is done when the leg juices, pierced with a skewer, run clear yellow without a trace of pink).

Christmas Gifts of Food

Tuscans do not as a rule give gifts at Christmas, especially among adults, except for gifts of food, although the custom, like many traditions, is changing. But food is given in abundance—elaborate sweets in fancy packages, like traditional Tuscan panforte and panpepato and the sweet yeast cakes, panettone and pandoro, that are Italian standards, unavoidable wherever you travel in Italy at Christmastime, but also old-fashioned local delicacies like Siena's soft almond-paste ricciarelli and rock-hard anise-flavored cavallucci.

Our first Christmas in Italy, some twenty years ago, we were living in Rome but planning to spend Christmas in Teverina. I went dutifully to Piazza Navona, Rome's hustling Christmas fairground, to purchase fruitcakes for my Tuscan neighbors. The Roman fruitcake, called *pangiallo,* typically contains an abundance of gummy dried fruits that characterize fruitcakes all over the world, and, for reasons best known to Roman bakers, it is so undercooked that the interior oozes with wet dough. Not to my taste, but it seemed to be the thing to do so I purchased enough pangialli to go around all the neighboring farmhouses. What I received in return was startling.

The first was a quart of fresh pig's blood, presented to me in the Italian equivalent of a Mason jar by Mario Rossi, who had just slaughtered a pig. "What will I do with it?" I asked. "Mita will know," he said. And she did. I carried the container carefully down the mountainside from Mario's, the dark and viscous liquid sloshing alarmingly, then across the little stream that divides us, and another mile or so up the opposite hill to the stone farmhouse we were then rehabilitating. I set the Mason jar on the kitchen table.

The second gift was a brace of live white turtle doves, the kind that ornament particularly sentimental valentines, with pretty rose wattles over their beaks and fluorescent pink legs that seemed far too thin to support their weight. Their little breasts throbbed with warmth and life.

The third was yet another live animal, a chicken. She came in what a friend aptly calls the ubiquitous Mediterranean plastic bag. She was plump and befeathered and she murmured contentedly in her unlikely nest.

The chicken seemed easiest to dispose of. I drank half a bottle of spumante for courage and, imitating a gesture I had seen but never anticipated I would be called on to perform, I invoked the ghosts of all the chickens I had held while my father chopped their heads off during the stalwart years of World War II, and wrung her neck. "If 'twere done, 'twere better it were done quickly," said the father of my children. In fact, the execution itself, once decided, was easier than plucking the bird, but when all the feathers were removed and she (I did keep thinking of her this way) was nestled snug in a roasting pan, stuffed with thyme and rosemary, basted with garlicky olive oil, and thrust into the oven of the woodstove, she became a pleasure for us all.

Of the second gift, the brace of doves, the children said: "Kill them and we'll divorce you." There was no way around that, and frankly, after the first experience, I lacked heart and will. The recycling principle, learned from years of recycling American fruitcake, prevailed. We gave the doves to a friend in a distant town, a friend with a farm and a dovecote that seemed just the ticket. I never saw them again.

But what to do with a quart of fresh, rich, dark, ruby red pig's blood? Mita came to my rescue, as she has done many times before and since. We would, she announced, make *sanguinaccio*. A blood pudding with antecedents as Renaissance-dark and mysteriously troubling as the color of the stuff itself, sanguinaccio is made throughout Italy (indeed, throughout rural Europe), the style varying slightly from village to village, wherever and whenever the family pig is slaughtered, usually at Christmastime, when the pig provides meat for the festive table. In case you ever slaughter a pig, or are given its blood, this is how Mita made sanguinaccio.

She took fresh lard, pure white rendered fat from her own recently butchered family pig. In a long-handled frying pan over the embers in the kitchen fireplace, she melted the lard and sizzled in it a good handful of finely chopped onions. Then she added a handful of raisins and an equal number of pignoli, or pine nuts. When these were toasted golden brown in the clear fat, she stirred in the quart of blood and as it bubbled and began to thicken she crushed a dozen or so cavallucci biscuits, sweet, anise-flavored jaw-breakers from Siena that are impenetrable without being soaked in a glass of white wine, and added the crumbs to the pan of blood. A little sugar to sweeten the mixture, a little grated lemon zest to offset the sweetness, and then the unlikely concoction cooked down until it was as thick as Christmas pudding, or Christmas fruitcake.

It was quite possibly the most unlikely Christmas gift we had ever consumed—and we consumed, I will admit it now, the entire delicious thing, sliced in wedges like a pie. It permanently redefined the words *rich* and *strange*. I have not regarded fruitcake in the same way since.

Roast Pig
porchetta

6 TO 8 SERVINGS

At the weekly markets in rural towns, at the annual agricultural fairs, at country weddings and baptisms, at every kind of large, public celebration in Tuscany, there's bound to be *porchetta,* a whole young pig (but not a baby, not a suckling). If you go to a country market, like the Thursday market in Camucia on the road between Arezzo and Chiusi, you may smell it before you see it. Smell, that is, the extraordinary fragrance of garlic and rosemary, warm fennel and bay leaves, with which the pig has been stuffed, along with liberal quantities of salt and pepper and the pig's own liver, chopped and mixed with the aromatics, before it's slowly roasted overnight in a wood-fired oven and brought to market.

And then you see it, the whole pig, literally head to tail (sometimes the head displayed apart, a guarantee of quality), skewered on a thick stake called a *palo,* its crisp skin roasted to a deep oak red color, its flesh oozing with the white fat beneath the skin. You can buy it by the *etto,* 100 grams, and take it home for lunch. Or you can buy a panino, a sandwich, made of slabs of sliced roasted pork layered inside crisp rolls and wrapped in wax paper, to munch as you proceed through the market. Ask for it *"senza grasso,"* if you want less fat, *"con la crosta,"* if you want the satisfying crunch of that nut brown, crackling skin. In the province of Arezzo, it's an institution.

This recipe, alas, is not for a whole porchetta, since I think few among us would be able to produce the delicious thing. Certainly not in your average kitchen, in Tuscany or in the United States. But in butcher shops in Asian neighborhoods, you can buy a piece of pork belly—not, I assure you, the pig's stomach, but rather the paunch or flank, the under cut of the animal from which pancetta, and some bacon, is made. As the Chinese know, this is a delicious cut of meat, at least in part because its thin layers of fat and lean, like the layers of puff pastry, lend considerable flavor and fragrance to the meat. Chinese butchers also share with Tuscans the knowledge that the skin (sometimes called the rind) of the pork is an essential feature, without which this just doesn't work. If the belly comes with rib bones attached, ask to have them removed or remove them yourself, an easy chore, at home.

My young neighbor Maura Antolini is an expert cook and a working mother, who sells clothing from a stall in the market that travels from Camucia to Cortona to Castiglion Fiorentino. For her daughter's second birthday, a party that involved both sets of grandparents, three sets of aunts and uncles, assorted cousins, and a few family friends—but curiously, to an American, no other two-year-olds—Maura made, among other dishes, this absolutely delicious variant on the traditional porchetta.

1 (3- to 4-pound) fresh pork belly, with the skin or rind
3 cloves garlic, finely chopped
1 tablespoon salt, or more or less to taste
Freshly ground black pepper to taste
1 tablespoon ground fennel seeds, preferably freshly ground
4 or 5 bay leaves, coarsely chopped
2 sprigs rosemary, leaves only
4 ounces pork liver, if desired
1 cup wine, either red or white

The pork belly is a long, thin piece of meat that must be seasoned before rolling and tying. Remove the rib bones, if necessary. (Don't discard them—these are spareribs and make a flavorful addition to a soup or stock. Freeze them until ready to use.) Spread the pork belly out, skin side down, on a work surface.

Preheat the oven to 375°F.

Combine the garlic, salt, pepper, fennel, bay leaves, and rosemary, and chop or work in a mortar to make a coarse but aromatic mixture. If using the liver, chop it fine and mix with the spices. Rub the mixture over the pork belly, forcing the aromatics into the meat. When all the spice mixture has been rubbed in, roll the belly up, jelly-roll fashion, in a compact roll and tie with butcher's twine every inch or so. Rub more salt and pepper into the outside skin.

Set the rolled and tied pork belly on a rack in a roasting pan and place in the oven. Roast for 15 minutes, then baste with half the wine. Baste again after another 15 minutes, and continue basting with the pan juices, adding a little water if necessary, until the pork is done, about 2 hours. After the first hour, if the pork is well browned, lower the heat to 325°F.

Remove from the oven and set the pork aside to rest. Transfer the pan juices to a small saucepan and let rest, then skim the fat off the top. Boil down the remaining juices, if necessary, to make about 1/2 cup of syrupy sauce.

The pork may be served, thinly sliced, after resting for half an hour or so, but like many pork dishes, it is even better left to cool to room temperature or just above, when it is easier to slice thinly.

Spit-roasted Pork Loin
arista di maiale

8 SERVINGS

At home in Teverina, any winter holiday meal, be it Thanksgiving, Christmas, or a friend's birthday or anniversary, calls for *arista*, a magnificent boned and rolled loin of pork studded with rosemary and garlic, that is balanced on a spit and roasted in front of the fire in the big living room fireplace. It turns slowly on the *girarrosto toscano*, a Tuscan clockwork turnspit that goes off like an alarm clock every 20 minutes to tell the cook it's time to wind it up again. Basted periodically with red wine over the hours that it cooks, the meat, when done, is nearly caramelized on the surface with the combination of heat, fat, and wine, while the inside remains succulent and tender without being dry.

Not everyone is lucky enough to have a fireplace big enough for cooking, much less a girarrosto toscano, but the dish is almost as good baked in a modern electric or gas oven. In any case, the procedure is similar. If you want to cook it in front of a live fire, see the note at the end of the recipe.

4 pounds pork loin, boned, rolled, tied or not (see recipe)
2 cloves garlic
2 sprigs rosemary, leaves only
1 tablespoon salt
$^1/_4$ cup extra virgin olive oil
1 $^1/_2$ cups red wine

If the roast has not been tied, spread it out on a work counter. Chop together the garlic and rosemary leaves and mix with the salt and 2 tablespoons of the olive oil. Use half this mixture to rub over the inside of the pork, then roll up and tie securely in several places with butcher's twine. Rub the remaining garlic-rosemary mixture all over the outside of the roast.

If the roast has already been tied, thinly slice one of the garlic cloves and strip the leaves from one of the rosemary sprigs. Stick the point of a sharp knife all over the pork to a depth of about $^1/_2$ inch, inserting a garlic slice or a pinch of rosemary leaves in each little opening. Chop the remaining garlic clove with the leaves of the remaining rosemary and mix with the salt and 2 tablespoons of the oil. Rub this all over the outside of the roast.

The roast may be prepared several hours ahead, or the night before you're planning to cook it. Refrigerate if you're not going to cook with an hour or so.

When ready to cook, preheat the oven to 350°F.

Set a large frying pan over medium-high heat and add the remaining 2 tablespoons of olive oil. When the oil is very hot, add the pork loin and sear it on all sides to brown it. As soon as it is brown, remove from the heat and place on a rack in a roasting pan. Add a little of the wine to the frying pan and return to the heat to deglaze. Scrape the pan juices over the pork.

Place the pork in the oven and cook for about 1½ hours, basting every 20 minutes or so, first with the wine, then when that's gone, with the juices in the pan. Reduce the heat to 325°F and continue roasting an additional 1½ to 2 hours, more or less, depending on how well done you like your pork.

When done, remove the pork from the oven and set aside for 10 minutes or longer before slicing. Strain the pan juices through a fine sieve and set aside to let the fat rise. Use the fat to sauté potatoes to accompany the pork; boil the juices down to thicken them considerably, then spoon them over the thinly sliced pork.

To spit-roast: If you have a large fireplace and a spit, you can roast the arista in a true Tuscan manner, but it will take longer than oven roasting. For a 4-pound roast, I count on a minimum of 4½ hours with the pork turning slowly before the fire, basting religiously every 20 minutes. Do note that you may skip the browning in the recipe above if you are going to spit-roast the meat. Be sure to set a roasting pan beneath the spit to catch the drippings.

A boneless loin like this is easy to spit-roast because it balances well on the spit and seldom needs any other attachment; the prongs that come with the spit hold it in place.

The most important factor in roasting any meat is the fire. Be sure to start the fire at least 2 to 3 hours in advance in order to build up a good bed of coals—a little pure wood charcoal (not briquettes) added to the embers helps give a steady heat. Set the spit roaster as close to the coals as is convenient; you may have to adjust this during the roasting process. To test for doneness, insert a meat thermometer so it reaches the center of the loin—it should register 170°F.

Note: Thinly sliced arista is as good cold as it is hot, some say even better. It makes a sensational sandwich on thin slices of Tuscan bread with a little mustard or mayonnaise or plain unsalted butter.

Family Pig

When I first went to live in Tuscany a good quarter of a century ago, our neighbors on the adjoining farm kept a stock of half a dozen pigs, big robust animals of a standard European breed called, even in Italian, "large white." It was a common sight most afternoons to see Mita Antolini, stout stick in one hand and spindle in the other, spinning wool as she walked her pigs down past our house and into the forest where they would graze placidly on acorns, chestnuts, beech mast, and the roots of wild plants, all of which gave succulence to their increasing girth. Pigs, the Tuscans said, helped to keep down vipers by rooting out the eggs of these poisonous reptiles and eating their young.

But pigs represented a good deal more than rooters of reptiles. A pig, either on the hoof or in the larder, always meant security for Tuscan families. Pigs are superefficient animals, rapidly converting slops, leftovers, garden rubbish, and forage into a source of highly nutritious meat, meat moreover that can itself be transformed through salting and drying into a long-lasting supply of sausages, hams, pancetta, and jars of creamy white lard to see Tuscan families through the lean months of winter.

Nowadays the Antolini pig stock is reduced to a pair of beasts, and Mita no longer herds the swine, which are kept instead in their own enclosure a good distance from the house. But the pig slaughter, sometime in the weeks leading up to Christmas, is still an annual affair of great importance. The butcher comes out from town to perform the deed, first stunning the animal with a blow from a special gun, then hoisting it and slitting its throat to let the blood run quickly out. The blood goes into sanguinaccio, described on page 159. Then, once the carcass has been flayed, the real work begins.

The organ meats, especially the prized liver, are set aside for immediate consumption, and nowadays, with a freezer in the house, the most valued parts of the animal, chops, roasts, and such, are cut up, wrapped, and frozen. The four legs—two *spalle,* or shoulders, and two prosciutti, or haunches—are thickly coated with salt and set to drain for a week or more, turned daily, often with more salt added as the first coat dissolves. When they are judged ready, all this salt is carefully washed away and the hams are rubbed with pepper and a paste of thick white lard mixed with more pepper and sometimes crushed garlic. Then they are hung, suspended from rafters under the roof in the dry upper story of the house, and left for six months to a year or longer, to cure and dry and transform themselves into the dark red, fat-marbled, aromatic miracle we call prosciutto. (Only in the Casentino, the valley north of Arezzo, is prosciutto sometimes cured by a light smoking, and that too is a habit that's dying out.) The belly and back are also cut into slabs like bacon and salted to make pancetta or rigatino, and the fat is melted down into lard, used throughout the year for deep-fat frying, especially for fried sweet pastries at Carnival and other feasting periods.

Meanwhile, the rest of the pig is turned into fresh pork sausages (buried in wheat chaff in a terra-cotta crock, they keep for long weeks in a cool place), and various types of salumi, or dry-cured sausages, including the Tuscan favorite finocchiona, so-called because it's flavored with the fragrant seeds and mustard yellow flowers of wild fennel. Then Mita makes head cheese, boiling the pig's head and other parts until the bones have fallen away, then chopping all the gristly bits of meat and fat, seasoning them, and pressing them into a linen sack.

Finally, when the day's work is ended, the liver is turned into fegatelli for the evening meal: Chunks of fresh pork liver, liberally sprinkled with salt and pepper, are wrapped in lacy caul fat, skewered along with bay leaves, and set on a grill to cook over the embers of the fire, the fat sputtering, its fragrance mingling with that of crackling bay leaves and that of roasting meat, a fitting dish—and by all accounts an extraordinarily ancient dish—to commemorate the sacrifice of the family pig.

Pork Sausages with Greens
rape o pulezze con salsiccie

6 TO 8 SERVINGS

The Tuscan love of sausages means that they're served with just about everything—with beans, of course, but also opened up, mixed with lard, and smeared on a fresh crust of bread, or cooked with various vegetables, especially with bitter cabbage-type greens like the turnip greens that put out fresh shoots and yellow blossoms in late winter and spring.

Coming over a hilltop in the mountains above the Val di Chiana in the early Tuscan spring, you may be dazzled by an extravagant vision in the valley below, freshly plowed fields, rich and brown, checkered with patches of brilliant green young grain and the acute mustard yellow of flowering *rape,* turnip greens, under a stormy spring sky. The tender shoots that the greens put out as they flower are called *pulezze*—the part of the plant with flower buds still tightly furled. Pier Francesco Greci, an Arezzo food historian, says pulezze are the only proper greens to cook with sausage, but in fact any of the deliciously pungent greens of winter and early spring—turnip, mustard, or collard greens, kale or cavolo nero (black cabbage), broccoli di rape or rapini, or even sharp greens like Chinese flowering broccoli, available in Asian markets—are delicious treated this way.

This is another of the dishes traditionally carried out to men working in the fields, along with a loaf of bread and a jug of wine, to be consumed on the spot. Rita Magli, who grows beautifully tender greens in her garden below the magnificent Calcinaia church in Cortona, serves this piled on slices of lightly toasted Tuscan bread.

> 8 fresh pork sausages (1½ to 2 pounds), preferably Tuscan-style, or the kind American butchers call "sweet Italian"
>
> 2 tablespoons extra virgin olive oil, or more if necessary
>
> 3 to 4 pounds greens, selected from those mentioned in the headnote
>
> 2 cloves garlic, finely chopped
>
> Salt and freshly ground black pepper, if necessary

Cut the sausages in half lengthwise and sauté them in 2 tablespoons of the olive oil in a large skillet over medium-high heat until brown on both sides. Remove them from the pan and cut them in inch-long chunks. Return the sausage chunks to the pan in which they cooked and set aside.

Rinse the greens in several changes of water, discarding any wilted or yellow leaves. Cut away and discard any tough stems. Put the greens, with the water clinging to them, into a large kettle, adding a little more water if it seems necessary, and set over medium-high heat. Boil quickly, stirring frequently, until the greens are thoroughly wilted and settled into the pan. Then cover the pan, turn the heat down to medium-low and cook for 15 to 25 minutes, or until the greens are tender. (Turnip and collard greens take quite a long time to cook; if you're using broccoli rape, or rapini, or Chinese broccoli, they will be done in 15 minutes or less.)

Add the garlic to the sausages in the pan and set over medium-low heat. Gently sauté until the garlic is tender but not brown. As soon as the greens are tender, turn them, with their cooking liquid, into the sausage pan and chop them coarsely while you cook over medium-low heat, stirring occasionally, for about 10 minutes, just long enough to meld the flavors and boil down any remaining liquid from the greens. Taste and add salt and pepper if necessary—the sausages may have sufficient seasoning for the dish.

Serve immediately, over lightly toasted slices of Tuscan-style bread if you wish. They're often accompanied with beans cooked as in the recipe for Tuscan Beans (page 67).

Variation: Tuscans don't normally do this, but I've found that pulezze con salsiccie makes a wonderful sauce for pasta. Using a short stubby pasta form, such as penne, cook as usual in plenty of lightly salted water, drain when the pasta is still a little resistant to the bite, and stir into the greens and sausage. Let the pasta finish cooking in the liquid in the pan.

Tuscan Meat Loaf
polpettone

Tuscan meat loaf is one way to describe this, although *polpettone* translates literally as "one big meatball." This is just about as far from the typical American lunch-counter meat loaf as you can get, and, in its simplicity and delicacy of flavors, as suitable for a dinner party as it is for family meals. Tuscans are not finicky about food being served piping hot from the stove; in fact, like most Mediterranean people, they believe that many dishes actually taste better when the intensity of cooking heat has gone out of them. Because polpettone is often served at room temperature or a little warmer, it can be prepared ahead of time, in the cool of the morning, for instance, for a late lunch or for dinner. It is never chilled in the refrigerator—it would lose its unctuous texture.

1½ ounces dried porcini mushrooms
2 thick slices stale country-style bread, crusts removed
½ cup whole milk
1 pound ground lean beef
½ pound ground pork
2 ounces prosciutto, fat and lean together, chopped
2 eggs
Freshly grated nutmeg to taste
Salt and freshly ground black pepper to taste
2 cloves garlic, minced
⅓ cup minced flat-leaf parsley
1 medium yellow onion, halved and thinly sliced
3 tablespoons extra virgin olive oil
About ⅓ cup unbleached all-purpose flour
About ½ cup dry white wine
½ cup freshly made tomato sauce

Put the dried mushrooms to soak for at least 15 minutes in very warm water to cover. Tear the bread into chunks and cover with the milk in a small bowl. Set aside to soak.

When the mushrooms are soft, set aside the mushroom pieces and strain the soaking liquid through a fine sieve to remove any grit. Rinse the soaked mushrooms under running water to get rid of any earth still clinging to them. Add the soaked mushrooms to the strained liquid and set aside.

Lightly squeeze the bread pieces between your hands and tear into small bits. Put in a large mixing bowl and combine with the meats, including the prosciutto. Break in the eggs and mix with the meats, adding the nutmeg, salt and pepper, minced garlic, and parsley. Mix with a wooden spoon or your hands to make a smooth amalgam. Form into a compact, firm shape, round or oval, like a loaf of country bread. Work it well to be sure there are no air holes. Set aside.

In a heavy saucepan or casserole large enough to hold the polpettone, gently sweat the onion slices in the oil over medium-low heat until the onion is very soft but not brown, about 10 minutes. Remove the onion slices and set aside.

Spread the flour on a plate and roll the meat loaf in it to coat the outside lightly. Add the loaf to the casserole, raise the heat to medium, and lightly brown on all sides, turning the polpettone carefully and adding a little more oil if necessary. When it is thoroughly brown, return the sliced onions to the pan and add the mushrooms with their soaking liquid. Lower the heat to medium-low, cover the pan, and cook gently for 1½ hours. As the liquid starts to cook away, add, a little at a time, up to ½ cup wine. (If the liquid continues to cook away, add a little more wine or plain water.)

At the end of the cooking time, pour the tomato sauce over the top of the meat loaf. Cook, uncovered, an additional 15 to 20 minutes, stirring occasionally, or until the sauce is thickened. Remove from the heat and let cool. (Do not chill.) When the polpettone is cool enough to handle, remove from the pan and slice in serving slices, about ½ inch thick (less is better if you can manage it). Arrange the slices on a serving platter and spoon the remaining sauce over them.

Grilled Beef Steak
bistecca ai ferri

It's sometimes called *bistecca alla fiorentina* but it isn't really Florentine. In fact, the people of Cortona claim it as their own, and with considerable justification. Each year in early August, Cortona holds a *sagra della bistecca,* or steak fair, when thousands of these steaks are cooked on grills set up in the main park to feed the hungry multitudes. The modern sagra is but a pale reflection of the annual agricultural fair that used to be held in Cortona. The old fairs were great institutions, where animals of all kinds, along with other agricultural products and machinery, were bought and sold. The country folk came from miles around, so it was a great time for socializing and for young people to look over the current crop of mates. It was also the time when new work contracts were drawn up for the coming year, so there was considerable jockeying for better working conditions. Nowadays the only thing left is the sagra della bistecca but it's a glorious celebration in itself and a splendid time for meat-lovers to get together and feast.

A proper Tuscan bistecca is a porterhouse or T-bone steak cut from Chianina beef, named for the Val di Chiana, where these cattle were once predominant. A handsome race of majestic white cattle, the docile Chianina, even as late as the 1960s, were all-purpose beasts of burden, the engines of Tuscan agriculture. In old photographs of Tuscan country life, it's a matched pair of Chianina oxen that draws the plow through the fields and pulls the wagons loaded with grain, grapes, or olives. A similar pair, their horns gilded and twined with red ribbons, still draws the Palio cart in the magnificent spectacle that precedes the Siena horse race twice each summer around the Piazza del Campo in the beautiful heart of the city, and archeologists speculate that white teams of Chianina cattle were also used to draw the carts in triumphal processions and sacrificial rites in ancient times.

Chianina beef is a tender, flavorful meat, lean and close-grained, with a good balance between lean and fat that makes it superb for grilling. Since you will probably not be able to get it in the United States, use a steak from a naturally raised animal, something like Coleman beef from Colorado, widely available in fine supermarkets and food shops. You can, of course, simply grill the steak and enjoy it, but I like this garnish of arugula and shaved Parmigiano-Reggiano, especially if the cheese is on the young, fresh side.

1 bunch fresh arugula, washed and dried

¼ pound Parmigiano-Reggiano

Salt and freshly ground black pepper to taste

2 porterhouse or T-bone steaks, cut about 1½ inches thick

2 tablespoons extra virgin olive oil

Lemon wedges, for garnish

A steak this good deserves only the best treatment, which means grilling it over wood embers or good charcoal made from natural wood, not briquettes. You could, I suppose, do it on one of those gas grills that have become so omnipresent in American suburban life, but I have to confess that I don't quite see the point of it. To me, it's a little like moving the kitchen stove outdoors and quite misses the point of outdoor cooking, which really should be done only with wood or charcoal. Whatever your fuel choice, this is not something for an oven broiler.

Build up a good fire of wood or charcoal to establish a bed of coals at least 3 inches thick. Chris Schlesinger, one of the great grillmasters of this country, says you should be able to hold your palm over the coals for a count of 5 and no more before it's too hot to handle. That's when the fire is ready.

Have ready the well rinsed and dried arugula. Shave the Parmigiano-Reggiano, using a vegetable parer or a small knife, into regular curls of cheese. Set aside.

Sprinkle a small amount of salt and pepper on both sides of the steaks and drop the steaks on the grill. Cook for 5 to 7 minutes, or to taste, and turn the steaks. Cook for another 7 to 10 minutes, by which time the steaks should be on the rare side of medium-rare, the ideal, but if you want them more well done, cook to taste.

Have the arugula arranged on a warm serving platter and as soon as the steaks are done, immediately drop them on the warm arugula, drizzle the olive oil over them, and top with the shavings of Parmigiano-Reggiano.

Serve immediately, with lemon wedges.

A Tuscan Butcher

At first glance, the macelleria in Panzano looks no different from any other Tuscan butcher shop—a small, gleaming, white-tiled space on a side street in this village that sits athwart the main road cresting the Chianti hills south of Greve. Inside the shop door is the usual pair of chairs for waiting customers; beyond is a raised platform from which the macellaio himself looks over his domain. It is all quite scrupulously clean—Maurizia, the macellaio's tiny, sharp-eyed assistant, bustles in his wake, scrubbing surfaces, knives, cutting boards, trays, just as soon as they are used. Sausages and hams hang from hooks over the counter, and behind a window carcasses of slaughtered animals hang dormant in the cooler, awaiting the swift slash of the macellaio's well-honed knife, a visible assurance to fastidious customers that the butcher's meat is freshly carved.

And the customers are very fastidious on the whole. Tuscans take their meat seriously. Whether it's a slice of rigatino or pancetta to lend savor to a sauce, or a thick and handsome T-bone or porterhouse steak from the famous Chianina beef cattle, Dario Cecchini provides nothing but the best, personally selected and, in the case of lamb, personally raised as well on his nearby farm, a rare Tuscan breed called Toscana Massese. The glass cases behind which he presides glow with a colorful array—rosy brown sausages, green-flecked vegetable and pork pâtés, burnished ruby chunks of pork and chicken livers, and pale pork chops, dark cuts of beef, creamy golden chickens with their crested heads and yellow legs attached.

But this is more than a first-rate butcher shop. You sense that the minute you step inside and hear the music. It might be Billie Holiday singing "God Bless the Child," or a Mozart sonata played by Claudio Abbado. You notice the decor, bright red loops of chile peppers, artful clusters of dried thistle flowers, baskets of dried garlic and dried chickpeas, a sense of order and of style. And then you see the books stacked up on library shelves, volumes and volumes, in English, French, and Italian, cookbooks, books about Tuscan folk traditions, books about butchering and the raising of veal calves, even an antique volume on the geography of the Gran' Ducato of Toscana. This, you sense quickly, is no ordinary butcher.

Indeed. Ask Dario, handsome enough to be a film actor if he weren't so devoted to his chosen profession, how he perfected his impressive skills. For answer he offers a Taoist tale (a photocopy to take away, so you know he's been asked the question many times). It concerns Prince Wen-hui's butcher, who wielded his knife "with a rhythm so musical it recalled the celebrated melodies of dance." A normal butcher uses up his knife in a month, a good butcher has his for a year, but for nineteen years Wen-hui's butcher used the same knife, its edge as sharp as the day he first honed it. How come, asks the prince. "Slowly, with great gentleness, the knife moves through empty spaces," the butcher replies.

A Taoist butcher who listens to Billie Holiday as he carves, delicately and with great precision, a pork roast to serve a dozen or so exemplary Tuscan gourmands? This is rare indeed.

"I'm not a Taoist," Dario objects with gentle irony. "I just like that story." He's been at this since the age of twelve, following in the footsteps of his father, grandfather, and great-grandfather with a little time off for university and veterinary studies. He is passionate about a sense of continuity and of community. The ninety-two-year-old lady who first directed me to his shop comes on Saturdays for her weekly steak, cut from the carcass of a Chianina beef hanging in the cooler. A Tuscan porterhouse usually weighs between 800 grams and a kilo (2.2 pounds) but for *l'anziana,* and for her alone, Dario cuts a little filetto, just big enough for her Sunday treat. "She can't eat much anymore," he explains, "so, you know, I make an exception." Any Saturday of the year you might find a miniparty taking place, with wine from the butcher's own grapes and a few slices of prosciutto or salami, made and cured by the butcher himself, offered to customers who drop by for a piece of meat and a chat.

On the question of Chianina, Dario is eloquent and exasperated. Using this meat for steak alone is stupid, he says. The whole animal is stupendous. What he admires most is the old tradition of consuming every part of the beast, including the *pancia,* the belly meat. "Roll it around lots of garlic," he says, "and tie it and braise it." "In broth?" "In water! Good meat doesn't need to be cooked in broth."

"Maybe we have to shut up about Chianina," he says after a while. "People come in with lots of money and they take out their money and say, okay, give me a bistecca Chianina." But money can't buy what's most precious, what Dario calls "the culture of food," and in any case it's not possible, he says, to live on steak alone. He's constantly researching, talking, reading, experimenting, looking for evidence of quality whether it's in the field or in the kitchen. One week he makes salsiccie *ebraiche,* Jewish sausages, minced beef flavored with wild marjoram, intensely peppery in flavor, based on his own research into the venerable traditions of the Tuscan Jewish kitchen. Another week he makes *tonno del Chianti,* sort of rillettes of boned marinated rabbit, torn to shreds and embedded in olive oil like preserved tuna. He makes a special trip to Irpinia in the Avellino near Naples for his chile peppers, his lemons come from Sorrento, his pistachios from Sicily. Nothing but the best. Despite the hip surroundings, the cheflike attention to detail, Dario Cecchini is not a modern man, nor does he really want to be. "I want to be a macellaio as they used to be for centuries," he says, with an engaging, half-apologetic smile. He sees himself, it seems, as the end-point of a funnel that stretches back over the centuries, a funnel through which the venerable traditions of the past flow into the future.

Slow-cooked Peppery Beef Stew
peposo

4 SERVINGS

Dario's recipe for peposo creates a meltingly tender stew, made more interesting by the quantities of black pepper that season it. This simple but very tasty dish, the butcher says, was prepared by the masons who worked on Brunelleschi's landmark dome for Santa Maria del Fiore, the great duomo of Florence, but if so, they surely didn't use tomatoes, which didn't come into general use in Tuscany until the nineteenth century. (The dome was erected in 1436, long before tomatoes came from the New World to Europe.) Tuscan food authority Leo Codacci says peposo originated in Impruneta south of Florence on the Arno, a famous center for terra-cotta production. During the long nights of tending the Impruneta kilns in which the huge *orci,* terra-cotta jars for storing oil and grain, were fired, Codacci says, the kiln-burners would prepare the dish to stave off hunger pangs. Others claim it comes from the Pistoiese, north of the Arno, and even from the Versilia, over on the coast south of La Spezia.

Whichever version is right (possibly all, possibly none), it's the kind of simple, meaty dish one would expect from a bunch of guys cooking together while they pursue their craft. It requires long (very long), slow (very slow) baking in an oven or atop the stove on the lowest possible fire—just barely simmering is the idea. If you must add water during the cooking, make sure it is boiling water in order not to reduce the temperature too much. An electric slowcooker might make an ideal replacement for an old-fashioned wood-fired oven. Traditionally, peposo is served over crusts of slightly stale country bread to absorb the meat juices, but it's also very good with steamed new potatoes, another New World import. You could even serve it with pasta, to yield twice as many portions. This is called peposo because of the pepper, which should be used with great generosity.

> 2 pounds very lean beef stew meat, preferably from the shank, cut in large pieces
> 10 whole cloves garlic, peeled
> An abundance of freshly crushed (not ground) black pepper—at least 2 tablespoons, or more if you wish
> 1¼ pounds drained canned whole tomatoes, coarsely chopped
> ½ cup robust red wine, preferably Chianti
> Salt to taste

Put all the ingredients except the salt in a heavy pot, preferably one made of earthenware, cover the pot, and set it over very low heat or in an oven preheated to 275°F. Cook for 12 hours or so very, very gently, so that the liquid in the pot just barely simmers. If the liquid starts to boil away, add a little boiling water and turn the heat down even lower. At the end of the cooking time, the meat should have almost dissolved into a rich and creamy sauce. Toward the end, taste and add salt if you wish.

Variation: Some cooks suggest marinating the meat in all the other ingredients (except the salt) for 6 hours, then cooking over slow heat for 6 hours, an interesting but not terribly different change.

Tuscan Pot Roast
stracotto

8 TO 10 SERVINGS

With the exception of the glorious bistecca Chianina, Tuscans don't eat a lot of beef. Once the T-bones have been removed from a Chianina carcass, however, something has to be done with the rest of the meat, and *stracotto* is one thing to do with it. This kind of pot roast exists all over Italy, a real Sunday dish, elegant, flavorful, and practical for the cook, since the sauce for the pasta and the meat cook all at once and together. Americans may find it odd to serve two courses with the same fundamental flavors, but to Italians it's perfectly normal. What makes this particular treatment Tuscan is the presence of a robust Chianti wine in the sauce. Any flavorful red wine with a good acidic balance will do.

3 1/2 pounds beef, such as top round, rolled and tied

3 or 4 cloves garlic, thinly sliced

2 medium carrots, scraped and thinly sliced

2 medium yellow onions, thinly sliced

1 thick stalk celery, thinly sliced

3 sprigs rosemary, leaves only, chopped

1/4 cup extra virgin olive oil

1 1/2 cups dry red wine

1 pound very ripe fresh tomatoes, peeled, seeded, and chopped, or 1 cup chopped
     canned tomatoes

1 tablespoon butter

1 tablespoon unbleached all-purpose flour

Salt and freshly ground black pepper to taste

Using a small sharp knife, make incisions all over the meat to a depth of 1/4 to 1/2 inch and insert the garlic slices in them.

In a heavy saucepan over medium-low heat, gently sauté the carrots, onions, celery, and rosemary in the oil until the vegetables are beginning to soften but not brown. Add the garlic-studded beef, raise the heat to medium, and brown the beef on all sides, turning frequently. Add the wine and let it boil until reduced to about 1/2 cup. As soon as it's reduced, stir in the tomatoes. Cover and let simmer for about 1 hour.

Work the butter and flour together to make a paste, then stir thoroughly into the cooking juices. Cover tightly, reduce the heat to low, and let cook at a bare simmer for 2 hours longer, adding a little hot water, wine, or broth if the liquid in the pan reduces too much.

When the meat is done, lift it out of the cooking juices and set aside to rest for about 15 minutes, then slice off three thin slices of meat. Chop them with a knife as finely as possible.

Degrease the juices in the pan, setting aside about $1/2$ cup of the meat juices to garnish the meat. Season with salt and pepper. Add the chopped meat to the remaining juices and serve this as a sauce over pasta for a first course. Serve the meat as a second course with the reserved juices as a garnish. (This is often served with a contorno of puréed potatoes.)

Pot Roast in a Lemon Sauce
manzo al limone

4 TO 6 SERVINGS

Tuscan recipes like this one, with lots of lemon flavor, are often said to be of Jewish origin. I'm not at all sure why. Historically, there have been important Jewish communities in the region, in Florence, of course, as the capital, and in Livorno, which was a major port. But even tiny Pitigliano, perched on a hilltop in southern Tuscany—so southern that it's closer to Rome than to Florence—had a large Jewish community. Like most in Italy, Pitigliano's Jews, a full 10 percent of the total village population of 3,000, disappeared with Fascism and the Nazi imposition of racial laws, although the synagogue still stands and holds occasional services. (Pitigliano's Jewish heritage has been beautifully detailed in *The Classic Cuisine of the Italian Jews* by Edda Servi Machlin, whose father was the rabbi of the community.)

Whether Jewish or not, the use of lemons adds sparkle to this basic Tuscan pot roast.

2 pounds beef round, rolled and tied
6 tablespoons extra virgin olive oil
1 lemon
Salt and freshly ground black pepper
1 cup veal or chicken broth

Pat the meat dry with paper towels. In a heavy saucepan over medium heat, slowly brown the meat on all sides in the oil.

While the meat is browning, grate the lemon and set the grated zest aside.

When the meat is thoroughly browned, sprinkle it with salt and pepper. Squeeze the juice of the grated lemon into the pot and add the broth. Reduce the heat to medium-low, cover the pot, and cook very slowly for 3 hours, checking from time to time and adding a little more broth if necessary. At the end of the cooking time, stir in the grated zest and let cook another 10 to 15 minutes.

Remove the meat from its cooking juices and set aside to rest for 15 minutes. If the juices in the pan seem too thin, raise the heat and boil down to make a sauce. Slice the meat and arrange on a platter, covering the meat slices with the juices in the pan.

Mixed Meat Stews
buglione, scottiglia, e cioncia

IN THE humblest sort of Tuscan country restaurants, the kind with a bar in front where the village men gather on Sunday afternoons for a game of whist or *la morra* (two men throw out one, two, or three fingers, at the same time shouting a guess at what the total will be; loser buys the next round), a glass of wine, or two or three, a smoke, and a gossip, the kind of restaurant that exists principally on traffic from the nearby town because nobody in the village would dream of going to a restaurant to eat a meal, much less pay for it, the kind with a woman in the kitchen producing a strictly local (and delicious) cuisine who may have "heard" that they make focaccia with sage leaves on it in the next valley but doesn't believe any one around here would fancy that sort of embellishment—in this kind of restaurant you may, especially in winter, come across an odd dish that goes by several different names— *buglione* in southern Tuscany, *scottiglia* in the Casentino north of Arezzo, or *la cioncia* in the Val di Nievole west of Florence.

No matter what it's called, this stew, for that's what it is, is made in almost exactly the same way: A battuto of aromatics that might include sage or basil or wild mint (nepitella), with onion, garlic, carrot, celery, and parsley, is toasted in oil; then a variety of meats are added—veal, lamb, pork, chicken, rabbit, a piece of game, a quarter of guinea fowl—along with red wine, sometimes with broth, sometimes with a little wine vinegar, always with a very little hot red chile pepper to spark the sauce, and more often than not with tomatoes. Then the stew cooks for a good many hours—the longer the better, most cooks say—until the meats are falling apart and a nearly miraculous exchange of flavors has occurred.

The only thing that really changes from one place to another is the rationale behind the dish. Buglione, I'm told, is made from scraps left from the landlord's table and given to peasant families, so it might be a mixture of beef, lamb, pork, and chicken, although nowadays you may find buglione d'agnello or buglione di maiale, indicating buglione made solely with lamb or pork (and sometimes *cinghiale,* wild boar). La cioncia has a similar story, only it's made from scraps of meat left on hides brought in for tanning, the Val di Nievole being a notable area for leather work. Scottiglia's explanation gets a little closer to reality, if not to precise truth: Scottiglia, it's said, comes about when groups of men get together of an evening to play cards and pass the bottle. Each man brings a little something to contribute to the common pot, a piece of pork, half a chicken or a rabbit, a couple of pigeons, or the spare ribs from a wild boar. All this is cut in small pieces, browned, and cooked in wine and water. Every now and then a little wine is added and the stew is done when several hours have passed and the meats are falling away from the bone. It's served up, as usual, over slices of toasted bread rubbed with garlic.

Marinated Braised Pork or Boar Stew
buglione di maiale o cinghiale

6 TO 8 SERVINGS

Wild boar are the raccoons of the Tuscan countryside, noisome pests who do tremendous damage to crops, whether garden vegetables, grain in the fields, or grapes in the vineyards. The only thing they don't destroy is tobacco, which is the reason, many people say, for the increase in tobacco culture in recent decades. (Others say it's the result of government subsidies.) From November until March is open season on boar.

So loathed are boar, however, that many Tuscans won't touch them, though the flesh of a young animal can be delicious if properly hung. Instead, they marinate a piece of humble domestic pork and cook it as if it were the wild game. I have to confess, I prefer the tenderness of a farm animal to the tough, often rank flavor of old boar.

2 pounds lean pork shoulder, cut in large stewing pieces

For the marinade:

1 cup red wine

1/2 cup red wine vinegar

1 sprig rosemary

3 or 4 sprigs sage

3 cloves garlic, crushed with the flat blade of a knife

3 tablespoons extra virgin olive oil

2 tablespoons finely chopped pancetta or prosciutto

2 stalks celery, finely chopped

1 medium carrot, scraped and finely chopped

1 medium yellow onion, finely chopped

1/4 cup finely chopped flat-leaf parsley

2 cloves garlic, finely chopped

1 small dried hot red chile pepper

3 sprigs sage, leaves only, coarsely chopped

1 sprig rosemary, leaves only, coarsely chopped

1 1/2 cups fresh, sweet, ripe tomatoes, peeled, seeded, and chopped, or canned whole tomatoes, drained and chopped

8 to 10 (1-inch-thick) slices stale country-style bread (1 per serving)
1 clove garlic, cut in half
Salt and freshly ground black pepper to taste

Place the pork in a bowl and cover with the wine and wine vinegar. Strip the leaves from the rosemary and add to the bowl, along with the sage, torn in pieces, and the garlic. Stir to mix well, cover with plastic wrap, and set aside in a cool place to marinate 6 hours or overnight.

Next day, remove the pork pieces from the marinade and pat dry with paper towels. Reserve the marinade.

In a heavy-duty saucepan, heat the oil over medium-low heat. Add the pancetta and as soon as the fat begins to run, stir in the celery, carrot, onion, parsley, and chopped garlic. Stir to mix well and cook slowly for about 20 minutes, or until the vegetables are very soft and not the least brown. Remove the vegetables with a slotted spoon and set aside. Raise the heat and in the fat remaining in the pan, brown the pork pieces on all sides. When the pork is completely brown, lower the heat again, return the vegetables to the pot, and stir in the hot red chile pepper and the chopped sage and rosemary, mixing well.

Strain the marinade through a sieve or a colander lined with cheesecloth directly into the saucepan. Bring to a simmer and continue simmering while you add the tomatoes and stir them in. When the tomato sauce is simmering, adjust the heat so the stew simmers constantly without really boiling. Cover and cook for 3 to 4 hours, the longer the better. Check the stew every now and then to make sure there's enough liquid in the pot—if it seems dry, add more red wine.

When the meat is very tender, toast the bread slices on both sides and rub on one side with the cut garlic. Place a slice of garlic toast in the bottom of each plate, sprinkle with salt and black pepper, and spoon the sauce over, piling the meat on top.

Variation: For a different but equally delicious flavor, substitute boneless lamb shoulder in cubes for the pork in this recipe. And if you want to make scottiglia, use seven different meats ("seven magic meats," my friend Fabrizia the folklorist says)—veal, beef, turkey, rabbit, guinea fowl, lamb, pork—just a small amount of each. Don't marinate the meats but prepare instead a rich broth, using pig's trotters or a calf's foot to serve as the liquid, along with red wine and chopped tomatoes.

Braised Lamb with Eggs
agnello all'uova

6 TO 8 SERVINGS

This is an old country dish from the southern Valdichiana, a region whose cuisine is beautifully described by Maria Luisa Valeri in her book *Pane, Olio e Sale.* Adding eggs to the sauce, of course, makes it go much farther, which is the point of most of these country dishes. This was more often made with kid than lamb, Maria Luisa told me, but lamb is easier to find in American markets and will do just as well.

> 2 cloves garlic, coarsely chopped
> 2 tablespoons extra virgin olive oil
> Salt and freshly ground black pepper to taste
> 2½ pounds boneless lamb shoulder, cut in 2-inch chunks
> 1 cup dry white wine
> ½ cup light veal or chicken broth
> 6 to 8 eggs (one to a serving)
> ½ cup freshly grated Tuscan Pecorino or Parmigiano-Reggiano

In the bottom of a heavy saucepan, gently sauté the garlic in the oil over medium-low heat until it is just starting to brown. Sprinkle salt and pepper over the lamb pieces and add to the pan. Turn the lamb in the oil until browned on all sides, then add the wine and raise the heat to medium. When the wine has reduced by half, stir in the broth. Let come to a simmer, lower the heat to medium-low or low, cover, and simmer gently until the lamb is done and tender, about 1½ hours.

At the end of the cooking time, preheat the oven to 250°F. Remove the lamb to a terra-cotta casserole and place it in the preheated oven to keep warm. (The recipe may be prepared ahead to this point.)

In the sauce remaining in the pan, which should be simmering rather than boiling, poach the eggs gently, letting the whites set but keeping the yolks rather loose. Remove the casserole from the oven and slide the eggs over the top of the meat. Pour the sauce over the eggs, dust with the grated cheese, and serve immediately, over lightly toasted slices of country-style bread if you wish.

Lamb with Black Olives
agnello con olive nere

6 TO 8 SERVINGS

As with the recipe for duck with black olives on page 152, the olives used in this traditional recipe are fresh, black, uncured, ripe olives, but wrinkled, salt-cured black olives will do just as well. If you do have ripe black olives from an olive tree in your backyard, drop a handful in rapidly boiling water for about 20 minutes, then drain and use in the recipe.

This is often served with soft polenta (see page 105).

> 2 pounds lamb shoulder or leg, cut in small stewing pieces
> Salt and freshly ground black pepper to taste
> 2 or 3 cloves garlic, finely chopped
> 2 sprigs rosemary, leaves only, finely chopped
> 2 tablespoons extra virgin olive oil
> 1 cup dry white wine
> 1 cup black olives, pitted if you prefer
> 2 tablespoons tomato paste mixed with $1/4$ cup water

Pat the pieces of lamb dry with paper towels and sprinkle generously with salt and pepper.

In a heavy saucepan or casserole, gently sauté the garlic and rosemary in the oil over medium-low heat until the garlic is soft but not brown, about 10 minutes. Add the seasoned lamb, raise the heat to medium, and turn the lamb pieces, stirring constantly, until they have browned thoroughly on all sides. Add the wine, let come to a simmer, and cook until reduced by half.

Stir in the olives and the dissolved tomato paste, mixing everything together, then cover the pan and continue cooking on very low heat for about 1 hour, or until the sauce is very thick and the lamb is cooked through. Check the sauce periodically and add more wine or water if it seems necessary.

When the lamb is done, serve it immediately, accompanied by polenta, if you wish.

Tuscan Easter Lamb or Kid
capretto o agnello pasqualino

8 TO 10 SERVINGS

Roast kid, very young, delicate in flavor and aroma, and exquisitely tender, is often the centerpiece of the Easter menu, although lamb is also frequently served. Lamb is a lot easier to find in America, but do try to purchase the more delicate tasting meat from small, naturally raised animals. The larger sizes, even though conventionally labeled as lamb, would be considered something close to mutton in other parts of the world. This recipe is adapted from one in Righi Parenti's book, *La Cucina Toscana;* he claims it as a dish from Siena, but in fact you can find its like all over Italy at Eastertime.

1 (4-pound) boned shoulder or leg of lamb or kid
3 or 4 slices prosciutto, fat and lean
2 sprigs rosemary
1 cup dry red wine
Salt and freshly ground black pepper
1 medium yellow onion, chopped
6 tablespoons extra virgin olive oil
24 small new potatoes, peeled
1/2 cup light veal or chicken broth
1 cup dry white wine

Prepare the lamb the night before you're planning to cook it, piercing it all over with a little sharp knife, making holes about 1/2 inch deep and inserting bits of prosciutto or sprigs of rosemary in each one. Set the lamb in a bowl and pour on 1/2 cup of the red wine. Leave, covered, in a cool place all night. Next morning, turn the lamb, pour on the remaining 1/2 cup red wine, and sprinkle the lamb with salt and pepper.

Preheat the oven to 400°F.

In a roasting pan just large enough to hold the lamb with all the potatoes, gently sauté the onion in 4 tablespoons (1/4 cup) of the olive oil over medium-low heat until the onions are very soft and golden, but not brown. Remove the lamb from its marinade and pat dry. Add to the roasting pan and spoon some of the onions and oil over it to moisten. Set the pan in the oven and cook for 30 minutes, turning once or twice, to brown the lamb.

Remove the lamb from the oven and turn the heat down to 300°F. Mix the potatoes in a bowl with the remaining 2 tablespoons of olive oil, turning them to coat them well. Add them to the roasting pan, along with any oil left in the bottom of the bowl. Pour the broth and white wine over the roast and return to the oven. Roast for 1½ hours, basting occasionally with the juices in the pan or with the marinade. The lamb is done when it is very tender and the potatoes are brown and crisp on the outside.

Fricassee of Lamb or Veal
agnello o vitello in fricassea

6 TO 8 SERVINGS

Another very old-fashioned recipe that also uses eggs to give more body to the dish. The egg-lemon sauce is reminiscent of Greek avgolemono. The recipe can be adapted to veal, or to chicken.

2 pounds lean lamb shoulder or leg, cut in small stewing pieces
Salt and freshly ground black pepper to taste
2 cloves garlic, minced
1 medium yellow onion, chopped
2 tablespoons extra virgin olive oil
1 sprig rosemary, leaves only, chopped
2 tablespoons finely minced flat-leaf parsley
1 tablespoon unbleached all-purpose flour
$\frac{1}{2}$ cup dry white wine
$\frac{1}{2}$ cup light veal or chicken broth
2 eggs
Freshly squeezed juice of 1 lemon

Pat the lamb pieces dry with paper towels, sprinkle with an abundance of salt and pepper, and set aside.

In a heavy saucepan or casserole, gently sweat the garlic and onion in the oil over medium-low heat until the vegetables are very soft but not brown, about 10 to 15 minutes. Add the pieces of lamb and continue cooking over medium-low, turning the lamb frequently until all of the pieces have lost their rosy color. Add the rosemary and parsley and stir to mix well, then stir in the flour and cook, stirring continuously, until the flour has lost its raw aroma and blended into the sauce.

Stir in the wine and raise the heat to medium. Let bubble and reduce by about half, then add the broth and stir once more. Cover the pan, lower the heat again, and barely simmer the lamb in its sauce until the meat is very tender, about 1 hour, checking from time to time and adding a little more broth or wine if it seems necessary.

When the lamb is done, remove the pan from the heat and set aside to cool slightly. Meanwhile, beat the eggs very well with the lemon juice. Add the sauce from the stew to the egg-lemon mixture, beating well. Then, stirring constantly, mix it into the juices remaining in the pan. It's important to keep the mixture moving so the eggs don't have a chance to scramble. The heat of the lamb should be sufficient to thicken the eggs slightly to make a velvety sauce that envelops the pieces of lamb. If it's still too liquid, return the pan to *very* low heat, or set in a pan of simmering water, and cook, stirring without cease until the sauce has reached the desired consistency.

Note: If fresh wild mushrooms are available, a little handful may be added to the stew with the herbs. Chanterelles are particularly good with lamb, or, if you're making a fricassea of veal, morels are delightful. Neither of these mushrooms is much used in traditional Tuscan cooking, which relies instead on porcini, but the flavors in this dish should be kept soft and gentle, rather nurserylike, and porcini are just too aggressive for the job.

Angelo Pellegrini's Florentine Baked Tripe
trippa alla fiorentina

8 TO 10 SERVINGS

This is a book about the cooking of the Tuscan countryside and not about that of the very cosmopolitan city of Florence. Nonetheless, *trippa alla fiorentina* is so special that it deserves a place herein. Florence may be the only city in the world where the most popular street food is tripe, and you can buy tripe almost as easily as you can buy a hot dog in New York. Indeed, you can buy two types of tripe in Florence, trippa itself, which is one part of the cow's stomach, and *lampredotto,* which is another part and considered even tastier by Florentines. When you're next in Florence, you'll almost always find, in most of the major markets, a stall selling lampredotto sandwiches—a rich, rare treat. Meanwhile, try this recipe, which, slightly unorthodox, came from the late Angelo Pellegrini, a Tuscan emigrant to America who wrote brilliantly about the food and traditions of his birthplace from a position of eminence in the English department at the University of Washington in Seattle.

Be forewarned, however: The first time I made this, I was made anxious about what I can only describe as the barnyard smells coming from the cooking pot. Those odors dissipated, however, and by the time we sat down to eat they had completely disappeared, leaving something quite delicious in their wake.

1 cup vinegar
4 pounds honeycomb tripe
1 cup white wine or dry white vermouth
4 ounces lean salt pork or pancetta
2 tablespoons extra virgin olive oil
2 tablespoons butter
$\frac{1}{2}$ large onion, peeled and chopped
1 stalk celery, leaves included, chopped
1 small carrot, chopped
1 tablespoon minced flat-leaf parsley
1 tablespoon minced fresh thyme
1 tablespoon roughly chopped capers
4 cloves garlic, peeled and minced

1 teaspoon arrowroot

2 cups chicken stock

2 tablespoons tomato sauce

Dash of Tabasco

Salt and freshly ground black pepper to taste

2 ounces Calvados

½ cup freshly grated Parmigiano-Reggiano

½ cup dried unseasoned bread crumbs

Combine the vinegar with 2 quarts of water and bring to a boil. Add the tripe and when the boiling resumes, let it cook 3 to 4 minutes, then remove the tripe and plunge it into cold water until it cools. Drain the tripe, remove and discard any lumps of fat, and slice the tripe into strips about ¼ inch wide. Place the strips in a heavy nonreactive ovenproof pot. Add the wine or vermouth, bring to a boil, and let boil, uncovered, until most of the wine has evaporated. Set aside in its cooking pot.

Preheat the oven to 350°F.

Dice the salt pork and place in a saucepan over low heat. Cook slowly until the pork bits are brown, then discard the pork fat, leaving the browned bits in the pan. Add the olive oil and butter to the pan and when the butter has melted, add the onion, celery, and carrot. Cook gently until the onion is transparent, then add the parsley, thyme, capers, and garlic. Mix thoroughly, sprinkle the arrowroot over the mixture, and stir to combine well.

Mix the chicken stock with the tomato sauce and Tabasco and add to the vegetables. Simmer 5 minutes to combine the flavors, then pour over the tripe, mix thoroughly, cover, and bake for about 4 hours. Examine the tripe from time to time and add stock as needed. The mixture should be dense but fluid.

When the tripe is done, taste and add salt and pepper if desired. Just before serving, add the Calvados, grated cheese, and bread crumbs. Mix well. Lower the oven temperature to 250°F. and return the tripe to the oven for 5 to 10 minutes before serving.

Vegetables
verdure

In traditional country families, men and women divided their labors in very specific, well-defined, time-honored ways. Women's work was connected to the house, if not precisely in the house, while men went farther afield, literally to the ends of the family property and into the woods, tending flocks or plowing fields. The farmer's responsibility was the *campi,* the big plantings of grain, corn (maize), and field legumes (beans, chickpeas, and black-eyed peas, called *fagioli all'occhio*) that would see the family and its animals through the winter. The responsibility of the farmwife, or *massaia,* on the other hand, was the *orto,* the vegetable garden, an enclosed and carefully delimited space that was usually sited close by the house. In his fields, the man took care of the staples, the core foods of the Tuscan diet, mostly carbohydrates, that belong in the center of the plate, while in her orto the woman tended the embellishments, the tomatoes, onions, garlic, greens, not so important perhaps as the core foods in keeping body and soul together, but adding interest, color, vitamins, and vitality to the basic core and helping it all go down.

Of course, nothing in the real world is as neat and tidy as an anthropologist's dream. Nonetheless, even today housewives don't go into the fields much except when all hands are called to help with the harvest, and men don't go into the garden much except to turn the soil over in the early spring. No one says keep out, mostly because no one needs to. To grow up in a culture like this is to know, almost by instinct, where the boundaries lie.

My teacher in the arts of the vegetable garden over the years has often been my neighbor Mita Antolini who, like most women in this valley, has a superb hand at coaxing good things from the rich soil of her *orto*—actually several *orti*, located in various strategic sites but always close by the house. The planting year for Mita's garden begins before the calendar year has run its course, late in December, after the pig has been slaughtered. The week between Christmas and New Year's, if the weather's not too foul for planting, is when the garlic cloves and broad beans *(fave)* get pushed deep into the moist black earth, well below the frost line, to gather force over the months ahead and be ready to surge out of the ground when the sun starts to strengthen and the earth grows warm again.

Once the garlic and fave are settled in, the ground lies still, often under a light blanket of snow, until March when the potatoes are sown, always at the dark of the March moon, because root vegetables should be sown and harvested when the moon is dark, while leafy vegetables like spinach and lettuce belong to the full moon whose light pulls the sugar up into their leaves and makes them sweeter and sturdier.

Here are some of the vegetables Mita grows in her garden: potatoes, squashes, zucchini, two or three different kinds of onions, garlic, spinach and chard, broad beans, green beans, peas, beans for drying and shelling, chickpeas, lettuces, various bitter salad greens from the chicory family, cucumbers, peppers, eggplant, tomatoes for salads and tomatoes for preserving (the pear-shaped San Marzanos for the latter), cavolo nero (a splendid form of kale, quintessential in Tuscan winter meals), cabbages, cauliflower (a newer addition), bulb fennel, cardoons but not artichokes (too chilly up in these hills), melons (not very successfully), carrots, celery, parsley, basil, turnip greens (broccoli di rape)—and occasionally other vegetables for which she's been given seed by friends or neighbors. But these other vegetables don't usually last more than a season or two because of their unfamiliarity.

In fact, what Mita grows in her garden is probably not too different from what her mother, possibly even her grandmother, grew before her. She saves her seed from year to year, and thus hasn't the need to buy the market seeds that nowadays, in this vast European Community of which Tuscany is an enthusiastic member, come mostly from Dutch greenhouses specializing in vegetables raised for hybrid seed, even seed for vegetables that have never before been grown in Holland. There are a few vegetables that she doesn't grow, such as asparagus, leeks (surprisingly, because she's always looking for produce that will stand through the winter), beets (ditto), and lentils—although lentils are a more or less staple crop just a few dozen miles away in Umbria.

The only new crop adopted and made a part of her family's diet in recent years has been cauliflower, the result of an attempt by an English friend to introduce the Antolinis to market gardening. ("Grow good cauliflower and take it to market.") It didn't work, in part because Mita's cauliflower, although superior, is at its best at the height of the local cauliflower season and can't compete in price, but also because no one in this family, with the exception of the new daughter-in-law, Maura, understands the concept of merchandising. So the cauliflower, instead of going to market, became a valuable adjunct to the Antolinis' own table.

Even though vegetables are generically called contorni, what surrounds the main dish, this is not a meat-and-two-veg world. With some exceptions, most notably potatoes, vegetables are served not as a garnish for meat or fish but mostly as a separate course, not just in Tuscany but throughout Italy, and indeed in much of the Mediterranean. It's a statement of the value with which they are regarded that vegetables should stand on their own without needing to lean on a piece of protein for support or importance. A vegetable can be a primo, replacing pasta or minestra, or a secondo, replacing meat or fish, or it can come between the primo and secondo as an added course.

On the whole, vegetable cookery in the Tuscan countryside is a pretty plain affair. Many vegetables are eaten raw or simply boiled or steamed, then dressed with olive oil and perhaps a chopped clove of garlic. A step toward greater elaboration may be taken with the process called saltare, the same word as the French sauter. Vegetables that are saltate are steamed, drained, sometimes chopped, then sautéed briefly in aromatic olive oil with chopped garlic, a little dried hot red chile pepper, and sometimes a bit of tomato sauce to nap the vegetables.

And then vegetables, either leftover or made up for the occasion, can get turned quickly and easily into main dishes, especially for a light lunch or supper, by the addition of eggs in some form. Sometimes, as in Asparagi alla Fiorentina, it's simply a question of adding cooked eggs, fried or poached, to top the dish. Sometimes it's that old country staple the frittata, basically a substantial omelet with a vegetable filling—a great recourse when you have more mouths to feed than vegetables to feed them. And sometimes it's the most elegant of these transformations, the sformato, literally an unmolded dish, an egg-rich cross between a savory steamed pudding and a soufflé, often served as a main course for lunch or supper. (Restaurant chefs sometimes offer a trio of tiny sformati, one perhaps made with tomatoes, another with a green vegetable, and a third with cheese.) Use the recipes for Sformato di Asparagi or Sformato di Spinaci as models and vary accordingly. Just remember that, for a sformato, a vegetable must have most of its liquid pressed out or drained to prevent the sformato from becoming watery.

Fresh Spring Asparagus with Butter-fried Eggs
asparagi alla fiorentina

6 SERVINGS

This is a curious but appealingly simple preparation, because for once Tuscan cooks use no olive oil but only fresh country butter—which may be why it's called *alla fiorentina,* indicating that it's fancy city food.

This is clearly a dish for special occasions, the most special of all being any time in April or May when there's an abundance of plump green asparagus grown on local farms and rushed into the markets of Florence. Locally grown produce, wherever you are in the world, is always the most flavorful—please don't even think of trying this with out-of-season asparagus imported from Mexico. And if you can find freshly made unsalted country butter, perhaps in the local farmers' market, it will be all the better for it.

About 2 1/2 pounds fresh green asparagus
Salt and freshly ground black pepper to taste
1/4 pound (1 stick) unsalted butter
1/4 cup freshly grated Parmigiano-Reggiano, or more to taste
6 eggs, preferably straight from the farmer

Preheat the oven to 350°F.

Trim the asparagus in the usual manner by breaking away the tough ends and rinsing the flower heads carefully. Bring a large pot of lightly salted water to a rolling boil and cook the asparagus until it's done to taste—for this dish it's best if slightly al dente, that is, with a little remaining crispness to the bite. Count on 5 to 10 minutes, depending on the thickness of the asparagus stalks.

While the asparagus is cooking, place half the butter (1/2 stick) in an oval gratin dish just large enough to hold all the asparagus and melt the butter until it's foaming. Drain the asparagus thoroughly and lay the stalks in the foaming butter in the gratin dish. Sprinkle lightly with salt and freshly ground pepper and then strew the grated cheese over the top. Place in the oven while you cook the eggs, but don't leave the dish in the oven more than about 7 to 10 minutes, or just long enough to melt the cheese and lightly brown the butter.

Meanwhile, add the remaining ½ stick butter to a frying pan and set it over medium-low heat to melt and foam. Gently fry each of the eggs, one at a time. Ideally they should be done sunny side up, the yolks basted with butter until they are slightly but only *slightly* thickened. Serve the asparagus in the gratin dish and pile the eggs on another heated platter. Guests help themselves to the asparagus and slide an egg on top, so that when the yolk is broken, the egg mixes with the cheese and butter to make a sauce for the asparagus.

If you wish, pass more grated cheese at the table.

Asparagus Pudding
sformato di asparagi

4 SERVINGS

Use this as a basic recipe and vary it according to your pleasure. You will need a round mold with a flat bottom, about 3 inches high and 7 to 8 inches in diameter, and a second larger pan into which the mold will fit with a few inches to spare. Tuscan cooks use special metal molds, either individual ones for each serving or a larger one for the full mixture; if you don't have this sort of mold, a small soufflé dish will do just fine.

1/4 cup (1/2 stick) unsalted butter

3/4 pound tender asparagus

Salt and freshly ground black pepper to taste

1 cup whole milk

1 tablespoon all-purpose flour

3 large eggs

1/4 cup freshly grated Parmigiano-Reggiano

3 ripe tomatoes, peeled, seeded, and chopped, or use canned tomatoes, drained and
    seeded, for garnish

Finely minced fresh flat-leaf parsley or basil, for garnish

Preheat the oven to 300°F.

Use a small amount of the butter to grease the bottom and sides of the mold thoroughly. Cut parchment paper to fit the bottom of the mold and fit over the buttered bottom.

Prepare the asparagus as in the preceding recipe and cook it in lightly salted water to cover until it is just barely done. Drain it and cut about 1 inch of each tip away from its stem.

In a frying pan, melt 2 tablespoons of the butter over medium-low heat. Add the tips and stems and gently cook them until thoroughly tender. Remove the tips and set aside.

Now add 1/2 cup of the milk to the pan and continue cooking the stems until they are soft enough to purée, about 10 to 12 minutes. Put the contents of the pan through a vegetable mill or process in the food processor. (If you use a food proces-

sor, you should then push the purée through a fine sieve to get rid of any stringy bits of asparagus.)

Wipe out the same frying pan in which you cooked the asparagus, melt the remaining butter, and slowly stir in the flour to make a roux, letting it cook about 5 minutes, stirring, to get rid of the raw taste of the flour. The roux should not color. Now add the remaining $1/2$ cup milk and stir to combine well, making a besciamella, the Italian version of a béchamel. Cook an additional 3 to 5 minutes or until the besciamella is as thick as heavy cream.

Remove the pan from the heat, stir in the asparagus purée, and set aside to cool slightly before you add the eggs. When the mixture is cool enough to add the eggs without cooking them, beat them one at a time with a wire whisk and add, incorporating each egg well with the whisk before adding another. Finally stir in the grated cheese and fold in the reserved whole asparagus tips. Add salt and pepper as desired. Turn the mixture into the prepared mold and set the mold in a larger pan. Add boiling water to the larger pan to come about 2 inches up the side of the mold and place in the oven.

Bake until the sformato is firm (test it as you would a cake, by inserting a clean broom straw in the center), about 50 to 60 minutes. Remove from the oven, let cool slightly, and turn out on a warm serving platter. Serve immediately, garnished with a very light tomato sauce made by puréeing the tomatoes and cooking them in a saucepan just long enough to thicken them slightly. If you wish, add a tablespoonful of minced parsley or basil to the tomatoes.

Artichokes
carciofi

THE ARTICHOKE season in Italy begins in November, when the first of the southern crop starts to reach Tuscan markets, but it doesn't reach a peak until early spring, when Tuscan violet artichokes *(violetti di Toscana)* are ready, small elegantly formed fruits, green tinged with a beautiful deep purple. These are so tender and flavorful that they're often eaten raw in a salad or as part of a Pinzimonio (page 45). Italian artichokes, for the most part, lack the infernal internal choke that prickles the throats of those who eat it by mistake. Why these small Italian types aren't grown on this side of the Atlantic is a mystery to me, but perhaps even as I write this, some enterprising grower in Castroville, California's artichoke-central, is working on the task.

Deep-fried Artichokes
carciofi fritti

6 SERVINGS

A merican chefs and cooking authorities often advise against using extra virgin olive oil for deep-fat frying, but to my mind there's nothing better. (I don't, of course, use fine estate-bottled oils for this; a standard—and inexpensive—commercial oil, like Colavita or some supermarket proprietary brands, gives very good results.) Thrifty Tuscan cooks are able to reuse frying oil a couple of times by straining it thoroughly to remove any sediment before it has cooled down, then storing it in a cool, dark place before using it again.

The trick to successful deep-frying is to maintain a steady temperature between 360°F. and 380°F. Anything lower than that and the coating will absorb oil and become greasy and indigestible; anything higher and you risk burning the food. A frying thermometer is a cheap and invaluable investment that guarantees excellent results.

> 1½ lemons
> 6 large globe artichokes
> 1 cup all-purpose flour
> 2½ cups olive oil, preferably extra virgin, for deep-fat frying
> Parsley sprigs and lemon quarters, for garnish
> Salt to taste

Have ready a bowl of acidulated water—about 6 cups of water to which the juice of 1 of the lemons has been added—to keep the prepared artichokes from blackening.

Prepare the artichokes by breaking back and discarding the tough outer leaves, exposing the tender, pale insides. Cut away and discard the tough upper part of each artichoke. As you work, rub the exposed surfaces with the remaining lemon half to prevent them from blackening. If the artichokes have prickly inner chokes (Italian artichokes don't but most American ones do), cut the artichokes in half lengthwise and scrape away the choke, using a small paring knife or a serrated grapefruit spoon. Cut each artichoke half lengthwise into 4 to 6 pieces. As you finish each artichoke, toss the pieces into the bowl of acidulated water.

When all the artichokes are ready, drain them in a colander, tossing to drain well, but do not dry them. Place the flour in a clean paper bag, add the drained but still damp artichoke pieces, and toss to coat lightly with flour.

Heat the oil to frying temperature—about 360°F., or when a small cube of bread tossed into the hot oil quickly sizzles and turns golden. Add a few pieces of floured artichoke and fry until they are crisp and golden, about 4 minutes. Remove with a slotted spoon and drain on paper towels. Proceed with the remaining artichoke pieces. When all are done, pile onto a serving platter, garnish with a few sprigs of parsley and some lemon quarters, sprinkle with sea salt, and serve immediately.

Straight-up Artichokes
carciofi ritti

6 SERVINGS

These stuffed artichokes are called *ritti* because they stand up *(diritti)* in the pan. In Italy they're made with big, round, tender globe artichokes called *mamme* (meaning mothers or, more poetically, breasts); American globe artichokes are similar although, as usual, with that pesky problem of the internal choke. Italian chokeless mamme can be stuffed whole without presenting any problems to the eater. In America, I cut globe artichokes in half and remove the choke before stuffing. They should therefore be called *carciofi sdraiati,* or "artichokes lying down."

1 lemon
3 ounces pancetta or imported prosciutto, minced
3 cloves garlic, minced
$\frac{1}{2}$ cup minced flat-leaf parsley
$\frac{1}{3}$ cup toasted unseasoned bread crumbs
$\frac{1}{4}$ cup extra virgin olive oil
6 large globe artichokes
Freshly ground black pepper to taste

Preheat the oven to 350°F.

Using a vegetable peeler or small sharp knife, pare away the zest of the lemon and chop it on a cutting board with the pancetta or prosciutto, garlic, and parsley to make a fine, homogeneous mince. Transfer to a small bowl and mix with the bread crumbs and 2 tablespoons of the olive oil. Set the mixture aside.

Prepare the artichokes: First squeeze the juice of half the lemon into a large bowl of cool water into which you will toss the artichokes as you finish preparing them. Use the other lemon half to rub over the cut edges as you work to keep them from turning black. Trim the stems, leaving about 1 inch exposed, and cut the artichokes in half lengthwise. Pull away and discard the tough outer leaves of each artichoke until you reach the partly tender inside ones. Using scissors or a sharp knife, trim the sharp points off the remaining leaves (this isn't really necessary but Tuscan cooks think it makes a nicer presentation). Using a serrated grapefruit spoon or a small sharp knife, scrape away the prickly choke. Toss each artichoke half into the bowl of acidulated water as it is finished.

When you've finished with all the artichokes, place the halves, cut sides up, in an oven dish and stuff with the reserved stuffing, filling the cavities and pressing a little stuffing between the leaves. Drizzle the remaining oil over the halves and add 1½ to 2 cups of boiling water to the dish. Bake in the preheated oven for 45 minutes to 1 hour, or until the artichoke hearts are very tender and easily pierced with the sharp point of a knife. Check them from time to time, adding a little *boiling* water as they consume the water in the dish. By the end of the cooking time, there should be a very little liquid left in the bottom of the oven dish. Spoon this over the artichokes and serve immediately. Season with pepper.

Green Beans for Saint Anne's Day
fagiolini sant'anna

4 SERVINGS

The beans in question are the green version of fagioli all'occhio, long, skinny, tender beans known to us as yard-long beans, asparagus beans, or Chinese beans, and, in their dried form, as black-eyed peas. The green beans are not exactly overflowing in United States produce markets; nonetheless they can be found and they make a spectacular presentation. Or you can grow your own—equally spectacular are these annuals with their purple flowers climbing over a fence or railing.

You don't need to have yard-long beans for this preparation, however; any type of fresh green bean will do and the recipe can be adapted for small, slender zucchini, or even green peppers, cut in long strips after roasting to blacken and peel the skin (see page 48).

They're called Sant'Anna because the saint's day is July 26, just about the height of green bean season in Tuscany.

2 pounds slender green beans
Salt to taste
1/4 cup extra virgin olive oil
2 cloves garlic, crushed with the flat blade of a knife
1/2 small yellow onion, finely chopped
1 cup chopped ripe red tomatoes, peeled and seeded, or use chopped canned tomatoes
1/4 cup slivered fresh basil
Freshly ground black pepper

Rinse the beans and top and tail them, cutting them if you wish into shorter lengths—3 to 4 inches. Bring a large pot of lightly salted water to a rolling boil over high heat and drop the beans in. Let cook for about 5 minutes, or until the beans are starting to soften but still retain considerable bite. Drain and shock with cold water. Set aside.

Put the oil in a frying pan large enough to hold the beans and over medium-low heat gently sauté the garlic and onion until they are soft but not brown. Add the tomatoes and the blanched beans, turning to mix very well. Stir in 1 cup boiling water and cook until the beans are tender. Add the slivered basil during the last few minutes of cooking, then taste and add more salt, if you wish, and the pepper.

Serve immediately or set aside to serve at room temperature.

Tuscan Beanpot Beans
fagioli al fiasco

6 TO 8 SERVINGS

Beans fit right into the Tuscan larder because they're a) cheap, b) easy to store, c) cheap, d) painlessly easy to prepare, and e) cheap again, and as nourishing as meat, an important consideration for thrifty Tuscan cooks. Like potatoes, beans are one of the few vegetables that are served as a true contorno, an accompaniment to meat, most often pork in some form, whether sausages, chops, or slices of roasted loin. But they are just as often served on their own as a main dish.

The secret, and it's the only secret, to making good beans is to cook them as slowly as possible, just below the simmering point, for hours and hours. The gentlest heat comes from the bread oven after the bread has come out, or from a corner of the hearth where the pot can be left, with ashes and embers heaped around it, from morning till suppertime. Or cook them, as modern Tuscan cooks do, in an earthenware pot on top of the stove over the gentlest possible heat.

The beans used in Tuscany are often the long, fat, white beans called cannellini or *toscanelli,* but in some areas speckled borlotti beans are preferred, while around Pescia, cooks seek out Sorano beans from the Sorano valley. Each bean has its qualities and local cooks swear by local beans and only local beans. If you're ever in Lucca, the Antica Bottega di Prospero, via Santa Lucia 13 in the heart of town, has an excellent selection of beans, including all of the above plus scritti (the name means "written on" and the beans look like smaller versions of borlotti with their hieroglyphic tracings), *piattellini* (small, flat white beans), *alberghini,* and *cicerchie,* old-fashioned chickpeas that look like dried fave. Rarest of all are the creamy yellow, almost round beans called zolfini, from the area around Montevarchi, in the Arno valley south of Florence, and said to be indispensable for a proper Ribollita (page 69). Pale yellow zolfini are similar to what we call sulfur beans in Maine, but Dario Cecchini, who is something of a bean expert, as well as a great butcher (see pages 172–173) assures me that they are ancient Tuscan beans and not from the New World at all.

A Tuscan bean pot is shaped a little like a traditional Chianti wine bottle, a narrow neck swelling to a bulbous base. The ones I buy from a potter in Cortona are particularly handsome, glazed bright yellow and splashed with viridian green. The shape is ideal for cooking beans, the narrow neck helping to retain moisture while the base gives the beans plenty of room for expansion. I have often been puzzled by almost universal instructions in recipe books to cook fagioli al fiasco in a traditional glass Chianti bottle, first removing the woven straw basket that cradles the base. Were beans ever actually cooked in an empty Chianti fiasco? None of the traditional cooks I've asked about this would confirm it and it seems highly unlikely when you stop to think about it—once beans the size of cannellini, for instance, have swelled in the cooking liquid, they're almost impossible to shake out of the bottle. I suspect that some unwitting food writer years ago misinterpreted instructions to cook beans in a fiasco, meaning the kind of fiasco my Cortonese potter makes, and food writers ever since have followed suit.

If you don't have a Tuscan fiasco, use an earthenware bean pot or a high, straight-sided terra-cotta casserole, remembering that clay vessels will crack on an electric ring. A heavy enameled cast-iron pan with a lid is a fine alternative.

1½ cups dried beans, soaked overnight in water to cover
3 tablespoons extra virgin olive oil
2 or 3 sprigs fresh sage
1 small white or yellow onion, quartered
1 or 2 cloves garlic, peeled
Salt to taste

Drain the beans from their soaking liquid and place in the bean pot with fresh water to cover to a depth of 1 inch. Add all the ingredients except the salt to the pot and bring very, very slowly to a simmer. When the liquid is just simmering, cover the pot and continue cooking until the beans are very tender but not falling apart. The liquid should shimmer with the heat and never come to a rolling boil. Check the beans from time to time and if more water is needed, add only *boiling* water to the pot. It is impossible to give an accurate cooking time because so much depends on the age and size of the beans—and age, at least, is nearly impossible to determine unless you've grown them yourself or know the farmer who did so. Count on at least 1½ hours, but it can take up to 3 hours for the beans to soften to that tenderly melting stage. If it takes longer than this, the beans are awfully old indeed and probably should be discarded.

The finished beans should be not at all soupy but rather napped in a velvety cooking liquid in the same way that grains of rice are napped with liquid in a well-made risotto. Add salt only in the last hour or so of cooking.

Serve immediately. Or, when the beans are done, you can, if you wish, turn them into *fagioli all'uccelletto* (recipe follows).

Savory Beans
fagioli all'uccelletto

6 TO 8 SERVINGS

Some people say they're called *all'uccelletto* because they're supposed to be cooked with small birds, while others claim they're simply beans cooked the way you'd cook small birds if you had them.

> 3 to 4 cups cooked beans, prepared as for Tuscan Beanpot Beans
> 2 to 3 ounces pancetta or prosciutto, finely minced
> 2 cloves garlic, minced
> 3 or 4 fresh sage leaves, minced
> 1 tablespoon extra virgin olive oil
> 4 small Tuscan-style or sweet Italian sausages
> 1 ½ cups chopped fresh, sweet, ripe tomatoes, previously peeled, or use canned whole
>   tomatoes, chopped
> Salt and freshly ground black pepper to taste

Have the beans ready and keep warm while you prepare the rest of the dish.

Chop together the pancetta or prosciutto, garlic, and sage to make a very fine mince. Sauté gently in the olive oil over medium heat until the pancetta is giving off fat and the aroma of the garlic and sage starts to rise. While the aromatics are cooking, open the sausages, discarding the skins. Add the sausage meat to the pan, breaking it up with a fork. Cook, stirring occasionally, until the sausage meat has browned, then stir in the tomatoes and continue cooking until the tomatoes have reduced to a thick sauce. Taste and add salt and pepper if necessary.

Stir this sauce into the beans and cook down over medium-low heat until the beans are napped in the thick sauce.

Serve immediately, on their own or as an accompaniment to a pork dish.

Note: To make a vegetarian version, omit the meats and increase the olive oil to ¼ cup. Add a chopped onion to the initial soffritto of garlic and sage.

Broad Beans Cooked with Prosciutto
fave al prosciutto

4 SERVINGS

Fava or broad beans, called *baccelli* in Tuscany, are the first green vegetables to come out of Tuscan gardens after the long cold months. It's true that many vegetables winter over well, especially members of the cabbage family, but even in the most temperate parts of Tuscany there's still a delicious shock of the new with the first earthy tenderness of fava beans, quickly followed by sweet green peas. So loved are the first baccelli that they're often eaten raw as a first course, accompanied by a fresh and creamy Pecorino.

Broad beans, once widely grown in America, have inexplicably fallen into disuse. The broad beans found in our produce markets are, for the most part, unacceptably mature and tough; if you want beans tender enough to eat raw, you'll have to grow your own. Fortunately they're an easy plant, tolerant of cold weather, and a handsome addition to the garden with their erect stalks and pretty black and white flowers.

1 medium white onion, halved and thinly sliced
1/2 clove garlic, flattened with the blade of a knife
2 or 3 thin slices of prosciutto or pancetta, chopped
1/2 cup extra virgin olive oil
3 to 4 pounds tender young fava (broad) beans, shelled
1/2 cup light chicken broth or plain water
Salt and freshly ground black pepper to taste

Put the onion, garlic, and prosciutto or pancetta in a saucepan with the olive oil and set over medium-low heat. Cook, stirring occasionally, until the onion is soft but not beginning to brown, and the prosciutto or pancetta is releasing some of its fat, about 10 to 15 minutes.

Stir in the shelled beans and add the broth, a very little salt (because the prosciutto may be salty), and pepper. Raise the heat to a fast boil and cook the beans quickly, without covering, to retain their bright color and flavor. By the time the beans are tender, there should be just a few tablespoons of syrupy liquid in the bottom of the pan. If necessary, add a little more boiling broth or liquid while cooking the beans.

Serve immediately.

Sautéed Greens with Garlic and Oil
verdure saltate

6 SERVINGS

Tuscan cooks have a whole repertoire of garden-fresh greens just about year-round, except during the hot, dry summer when greens aren't so necessary anyway, there being a plethora of tomatoes, peppers, eggplant, and other hot-weather vegetables. In the deep midwinter, even up in our mountain valley, my neighbors harvest cavolo nero, the magnificently flavorful Tuscan black kale that adds so much to winter soups and stews. Like many old-fashioned members of the *Brassica* family, cavolo nero resists cold well—I've seen it standing through snowstorms. Other members of this family are also relished, most especially turnip greens (broccoli di rape, rapini, or pulezze, page 166), a late green from the end of winter and early spring.

And then there's a raft of wild greens that are harvested and eaten either in salads or cooked, as in this recipe, depending on how young and tender they are. Most of these are just lumped together under the heading of chicory, but older farmwives like Mita Antolini can easily recognize a dozen different types of edible wild greens growing in abandoned fields and along the edges of terraces. As in other parts of the Mediterranean, these are considered a valuable tonic in springtime and, in fact, most of them are good sources of iron for blood that's thinned out and tired from the stresses of winter.

Beyond wild greens and brassicas, spinach and chard are also valued in Tuscan kitchens (years ago, in international hotel cuisine to call a dish "Florentine" was to indicate the presence of spinach). Any of these greens—spinach, chard, turnip and mustard greens, broccoli di rape, kale, cavolo nero (if you can find it), or collards—may be prepared in the following manner. Remove tough stems if necessary, chop the greens if you wish, rinse carefully (very carefully in the case of spinach, which tends to be sandy), and boil in the water clinging to the leaves, adding a little more if they start to stick until the greens are tender. The time will vary enormously, from 10 minutes for fresh young spinach to as much as 45 minutes for collards. Once the greens are tender, drain and chop. Then continue with this very simple procedure.

3 pounds fresh greens, cooked as described earlier

3 cloves garlic, chopped

¼ to ⅓ cup extra virgin olive oil

1 small dried hot red chile pepper

Salt to taste

1 or 2 teaspoons aged red wine vinegar or lemon juice

Have ready the cooked, drained, and chopped greens.

In a saucepan large enough to hold all the greens, sauté the garlic very gently in the oil over medium-low or low heat until the garlic is very soft but not taking color. Add the dried chile pepper, broken in bits (for less heat, discard the seeds and white membrane before adding to the pan), and stir it in.

Add the chopped greens and stir and turn them in the aromatic oil until they have completely absorbed it. As soon as the greens start to sizzle in the heat of the pan, remove from the heat, stir in salt and vinegar or lemon juice to taste, and serve immediately, on their own or poured over lightly toasted slices of Tuscan-style bread that have been rubbed lightly with a cut clove of garlic and drizzled with a small amount of oil.

Spinach Pudding
sformato di spinaci

6 SERVINGS

Spinach, cooked like the greens in the preceding recipe, is a lovely dish on its own, but steamed spinach is also the basis for a sformato that can be a first course or light main course for lunch or supper. A sformato becomes positively elegant when served with a light tomato sauce (see the tomato sauce with Asparagus Pudding, page 196). Sformati are usually thickened with an egg-enriched white sauce, as described in the asparagus recipe. Florentine chef Fabio Picchi of Ristorante Cibrèo makes this spinach pudding with ricotta instead. It makes a lighter pudding, one in which the astringent flavors of spinach ring clear and true. This is an adaptation of his method.

Be sure to drain the spinach very well, squeezing it between the palms of your hands. (In Tuscan alimentari, you can buy spinach already cooked, drained, and squeezed into balls.) Otherwise, the pudding will be watery and not very nice.

3 pounds fresh spinach, carefully rinsed
Unsalted butter for the baking dish
About 3 tablespoons bread crumbs for the baking dish
1 clove garlic, finely chopped
1 small onion, finely chopped
1/4 cup extra virgin olive oil
Salt to taste
3 extra-large eggs, separated
1 pound ricotta, preferably goat's milk ricotta
Freshly grated nutmeg to taste
Freshly ground black pepper to taste
1/2 cup finely grated Parmigiano-Reggiano

Cook the cleaned spinach as in the preceding recipe in the water clinging to its leaves, adding a very little more water if necessary, until it is thoroughly tender. This will take up to 20 minutes for such a large quantity of spinach.

While the spinach is cooking, butter the bottom and sides of a 2-quart mold or soufflé dish (you may also use smaller individual molds, 1 per serving) and sprinkle bread crumbs all over the inside. Combine the oil, garlic, and onion and sauté very gently over low heat in a small skillet until the vegetables are very soft.

When the spinach is done, drain in a colander, then squeeze between your palms to extract even more liquid. Finally, chop on a board and squeeze again to get rid of as much liquid as possible.

Preheat the oven to 375°F.

In a large bowl combine the spinach with the salt and mix in the onion and garlic with their cooking oil. Stir in the lightly beaten egg yolks and ricotta and season with nutmeg and black pepper. Add the grated cheese and stir to mix everything together well.

In a separate bowl, beat the egg whites to stiff peaks. Using a rubber spatula, lightly but thoroughly fold the whites into the spinach mixture. Turn into the prepared mold and set the mold in a larger baking dish or roasting pan. Bring a kettle of water to a boil and add boiling water to the larger dish to come about 1½ inches up the sides of the mold. Place in the preheated oven and bake 15 minutes, then lower the heat to 325°F. and continue baking for a total of 40 minutes to 1 hour, or until the sformato is firm in the middle and pulling away slightly from the sides. (If you use smaller individual molds, they will cook more quickly—start testing after 20 minutes.)

Remove from the oven and invert a plate over the mold. Turn it over and say a quick prayer before removing the mold which, with good fortune, will slide away from the sformato leaving it standing proudly on the plate. Serve with a little light tomato sauce, which will conceal any mishaps in the unmolding.

Mixed Summer Vegetables
misto di verdura dell' orto

4 SERVINGS

Summer days are very long in Tuscany. Florence, after all, is a little farther north than Portland, Maine, and at these latitudes the sun rises early and sets late and the twilight, moreover, lingers in midsummer until past nine o'clock. Mita often uses these late, cool hours to work in her vegetable garden, weeding, watering, and transplanting. When it's time to start supper she strolls back down the rows, picking up a little of this, a little of that, rinses what she's gathered at the outside faucet, and takes it inside to put together with a little olive oil, some fresh herbs, and garlic. The ingredients change from one day to the next, but here's one example.

2 cloves garlic, crushed with the flat blade of a knife

2 fresh white onions, sliced

1/2 cup extra virgin olive oil

3 or 4 tomatoes, not very ripe, still a little streaked with green,
   cut in wedges or thick slices

4 or 5 small zucchini, sliced about 1/4 inch thick

About 1/2 pound slender green beans, topped, tailed, and cut in 1-inch lengths if
   desired

1 small bunch chard, slivered

1 bunch flat-leaf parsley, chopped (about 1/2 cup)

12 zucchini flowers, cut in strips

3 or 4 branches fresh basil, leaves only, slivered (1/4 cup)

Salt and freshly ground black pepper

Rinse and prepare all the vegetables and herbs. In a frying pan large enough to hold all the vegetables (keeping in mind that they will cook down), gently sauté the garlic and onions in the olive oil over medium-low heat until the onions are very soft but not turning brown, about 10 minutes. Add the tomatoes and zucchini, turn the heat up to medium, and stir to mix well. Cover the pan and continue cooking, stirring occasionally, until the zucchini have softened slightly and the tomatoes start to give off some of their juice, another 10 minutes. Now add the green beans, chard, and parsley and stir again. If the mixture seems dry, add 1/2 cup water. Cook quite briskly, covered, until the green beans are tender, occasionally adding a little more water if necessary. This will take another 10 minutes.

Finally, stir in the zucchini flowers and basil. Stir and taste, adding salt and pepper. Let cook 5 minutes more, then serve immediately. Or let cool to room temperature and serve.

This is delicious on its own, as a first course, or you can convert it into a main course for lunch or supper by poaching 1 egg per person in a separate pan of gently simmering water, then serving the eggs on top of the vegetables.

Eggplant in a Sauce of Peppers and Tomatoes
soffritto di melanzane e peperoni

4 TO 6 SERVINGS

Eggplant are not used a great deal in the Tuscan country kitchen, but when they are they're almost always combined with sweet bell peppers and tomatoes in a preparation that shows up, in one form or another, all over the Mediterranean. This is the Tuscan farmwife's very simple version.

About 1 pound eggplant (2 small or 1 large)

Salt to taste

2 large sweet bell peppers, preferably green and red

¼ cup extra virgin olive oil

1 medium yellow onion, chopped

1 clove garlic, chopped

3 large, very ripe tomatoes, peeled, seeded, and chopped

½ cup slivered fresh basil

1 tablespoon large salt-cured capers, rinsed and chopped

Freshly ground black pepper

Rinse the eggplant and cut in 1-inch cubes. Place in a colander, sprinkle liberally with salt, and put a plate over the eggplant with a weight (a can of tomatoes is fine) on top. Set the colander in the sink or over a bowl to drain. Leave for about 1 hour, then rinse the salt off the eggplant and dry the cubes with paper towels, pressing well to extract most of the moisture.

Core the peppers and remove and discard the seeds and white inner membrane. Chop the peppers into big pieces.

In a large frying pan over medium heat sauté the eggplant cubes in the olive oil until they are brown. (The eggplant must be very dry to brown.) As the cubes brown, remove them from the oil and set aside. When all the eggplant has browned, lower the heat to medium-low or low and add the peppers, onion, and garlic to the pan. Cook gently until the peppers and onion are soft. Do not let the onion or garlic brown.

Return the eggplant to the pan along with the chopped tomatoes, stirring to mix everything together well. Cook for about 20 to 30 minutes, or until the tomatoes are reduced to a thick sauce that naps the eggplant and peppers. Stir in the slivered basil and capers, mixing well. Add pepper and, if necessary, salt (there may be sufficient from the salting of the eggplant).

You may serve this immediately, but it's customary to serve it at room temperature.

Braised Sweet Pepper Stew
peperonata

6 TO 8 SERVINGS

Embarrassingly simple preparations like this one illustrate the Tuscan principle that good food only comes from good ingredients. A summertime mixture composed of red, green, and yellow sweet peppers, fresh from the garden and thickly sliced, stewed in olive oil with onion, tomatoes, and a fragment of garlic—that's all.

6 sweet (bell) peppers, red, yellow, and green
2 medium yellow onions, halved and thinly sliced
3 tablespoons extra virgin olive oil
Salt and freshly ground black pepper to taste
3 ripe medium tomatoes, peeled, seeded, and chopped

Cut the peppers in lengthwise strips about ³/₄ inch wide, discarding cores, seeds, and white membranes.

In a saucepan large enough to hold all the ingredients, gently sauté the onion slices in the oil over medium-low heat until the onion is soft and golden but not brown, about 10 minutes. Add the pepper slices with a little salt and pepper to taste, cover the pan, and cook for about 20 minutes, or until the peppers are soft and just starting to brown. Remove the cover and raise the heat slightly to medium or medium-high. Stir in the chopped tomatoes and continue cooking, stirring frequently, an additional 10 minutes, or until the tomatoes are just starting to break down into a sauce. If the tomatoes release a great deal of water, raise the heat to high and cook rapidly, stirring constantly, until the juices are reduced.

Serve immediately or allow to cool to room temperature.

Porcini Mushrooms
funghi porcini

THERE'S A certain point, late in August, when the Tuscan summer seems to turn and settle on itself like a yellow country cat seeking a warm spot in the sun. Even though the days are still warm and the resinous fragrance of the macchia, the forest scrub, still perfumes the air, you wake one morning sensing that autumn is only a few weeks away. Then late one afternoon, dark purple thunder clouds build up in the western sky and a drenching rainstorm sweeps across the hilltops. Mita, stopping by for a morning chat, is ecstatic: *"Si fanno funghi,"* she sings; soon there'll be mushrooms.

It takes exactly this combination of soaking rain followed by hot sunny weather to bring out the *Boletus* mushrooms. Porcini, or little pigs, are one of the glories of the Tuscan late summer, especially welcome because for a change they're free, costing nothing but the pleasurable effort of combing the forest floor to seek them out. Most of my neighbors have special secret places, treasure troves of mushrooms that they, and they alone, have discovered. Some people claim they can grow their own: Mario Rossi, on the farm across the valley, used to hose the ground beneath a certain oak tree in the field below his house whenever he wanted porcini. Ten days later, he said, he'd have a feast.

Porcini are widely available in parts of America and Canada and, like Tuscan ones, free for the picking, although you should not consume any foraged mushroom without being sure that it's edible. Still, once you know what to look for, these are unmistakable. If you find some big healthy specimens, free of worm holes, try them in the favorite Tuscan fashion, simply bathed liberally with olive oil, salt, and pepper and grilled over wood or charcoal. In Tuscany, cooks pierce the caps with stiff sprigs of wild mint (nepitella) for flavoring.

The next two recipes are best of all with wild mushrooms you've harvested yourself, whether porcini or orange chanterelles or other edible varieties. Often wild mushrooms are sold in specialty stores and farmers' markets. But if you don't have a supply of truly wild mushrooms, try these preparations with the more unusual mushrooms that are increasingly found in good produce markets—portobello, shiitake, or oyster mushrooms. The recipe for Braised Wild Mushrooms (page 216) can be prepared from wild mushrooms or from a combination of ordinary commercial mushrooms and dried wild porcini, little packets of which are widely available in specialty stores.

Fricassee of Mushrooms
funghi in fricassea

About 4 pounds fresh mushrooms, preferably wild

1 medium yellow onion, chopped fine

$^1\!/_2$ cup extra virgin olive oil

Salt and freshly ground black pepper

2 eggs

2 tablespoons freshly squeezed lemon juice

4 to 6 thin slices country-style bread, lightly toasted

If you're using wild mushrooms, clean them very well, brushing them with a soft brush to remove any earth or forest detritus and cutting away any spoiled or wormy areas. Do not clean with running water, as the mushrooms will become soggy; if necessary, use a damp paper towel. Cut the cleaned mushrooms in chunks.

In a frying pan over medium-low heat gently sauté the onion in the oil until it is very soft but not brown. Add the mushrooms and stir to mix. Raise the heat to medium and cook the mushrooms, stirring frequently. They will first absorb most of the oil, then release it again. When they do, add salt and pepper to taste.

Beat together the eggs and lemon juice. Remove the mushrooms from the heat and quickly stir in the egg mixture, stirring fast so that the eggs form a thick cream rather than scrambled eggs. Serve immediately over the toasted bread slices.

Note: This recipe is easily adapted to the quantity of mushrooms you find. Just use good judgment about how much egg and lemon juice to add.

Braised Wild Mushrooms
funghi in tegame

4 SERVINGS

2 ounces dried wild porcini mushrooms

1½ pounds fresh mushrooms (see Note)

¼ cup extra virgin olive oil

2 cloves garlic, crushed

2 sprigs mint plus 3 tablespoons finely chopped mint

Salt and freshly ground black pepper to taste

Place the dried mushrooms in a bowl and add a cup or more of hot water, enough to cover the mushrooms completely. Set aside to soak for at least 30 minutes. Then strain through a fine mesh sieve lined with cheesecloth. *Do not discard the soaking liquid.* Rinse the mushrooms under running water to rid them of any soil still clinging to them. Pat them dry and chop coarsely.

Clean and slice the fresh mushrooms (see directions in preceding recipe). In the olive oil in a deep frying pan, sauté the fresh mushrooms, garlic, and mint sprigs over medium or medium-low heat until the mushrooms have softened and thrown off considerable liquid.

Add the soaked dried mushrooms to the pan along with their strained soaking liquid. Mix well, then cover the pan and cook for about 20 minutes on medium-low heat, so that the mushrooms simmer together and exchange flavors. Stir in the chopped mint, raise the heat to medium-high, and cook, uncovered, an additional 5 to 10 minutes, or until most of the liquid has boiled away, leaving just a few spoonfuls to garnish the dish. Taste and add salt and pepper as desired.

Note: If a good supply of fresh wild mushrooms is available, omit the dried mushrooms. Add a little water or stock to make up for the lack of mushroom soaking liquid.

Poverty Potatoes—Potatoes with Tomato
patate povere—patate al pomodoro

4 TO 6 SERVINGS

I was amused to find a very similar dish in Spain called *patatas pobres,* only given a rosy color with sweet paprika instead of tomato. Potatoes have an inevitable association with poverty wherever you go in the world, but there's probably no more versatile member of the vegetable kingdom.

> 2 pounds waxy red-skinned potatoes, peeled and cut in chunks
>
> 1 pound red onions, halved and sliced about $1/4$ inch thick
>
> 1 dried hot red chile pepper, broken in two
>
> $1/4$ cup extra virgin olive oil
>
> Salt and freshly ground black pepper to taste
>
> 3 tablespoons finely minced flat-leaf parsley
>
> 3 or 4 drained canned tomatoes, chopped, or garden-ripened tomatoes
>
> $1/4$ cup slivered fresh basil

In a frying pan over medium-low heat, combine the potatoes, onions, hot red chile pepper, and olive oil and stir to mix well. When the potatoes start to sizzle in the oil, add salt and pepper, cover the pan, and cook about 20 minutes, stirring and turning the potatoes with a spatula from time to time. If they seem in danger of burning, add a very small amount of water to the pan—not more than a couple of tablespoons.

After 20 minutes, the potatoes and onions should be softened considerably. Add the parsley and chopped tomatoes and continue cooking, covered—another 20 minutes if using raw tomatoes, 10 to 15 minutes if using cooked canned tomatoes. At the end of this time, remove the lid, raise the heat, and rapidly boil away the remaining liquid, leaving the potatoes and onions napped in a sauce of tomatoes. Stir the basil into the potatoes and serve immediately.

Mashed Potato Pie
torta di patate

This is the kind of dish served at supper when just the family is gathered. The old folks sit on benches next to (sometimes actually inside) the hearth, while around the big table under a dangling central ceiling light, the younger family members arrange themselves—always, however, with the *capo di casa,* literally head of the house, at the head of the table. From this vantage he (and it's always a he, the title passing usually from father to eldest son) slices the bread and distributes it to the other members of the family in a gesture whose ritual nature really is not lost on anyone present. It's a time for the simplest kind of dishes, ones you'd never dream of serving to invited guests—more's the pity, because, as this recipe shows, often the food is interesting as well as satisfying.

3 tablespoons extra virgin olive oil plus more to grease the pan

¼ cup finely ground toasted bread crumbs

1 medium yellow onion, finely chopped

3 fresh pork sausages, preferably Tuscan-style flavored with fennel, or use "sweet
  Italian" sausages

2 pounds russet potatoes, peeled and cut in chunks

Salt to taste

3 eggs, lightly beaten

3 tablespoons freshly grated Parmigiano-Reggiano

Preheat the oven to 375°F. Prepare a round tart pan or a low, straight-sided oven dish about 8 or 9 inches in diameter by greasing the bottom and sides with a little of the olive oil, then shaking 2 to 3 tablespoons of the bread crumbs all over the inside.

In a frying pan over medium-low heat, gently sauté the onion in 1 tablespoon of the oil until it is very soft and golden but not brown. While the onion is cooking, open the sausages and discard their skins. When the onion is very soft, add the sausage meat to the pan and raise the heat to medium. Cook, stirring frequently, until the meat has completely lost any trace of pink color.

Meanwhile, bring a large pan of lightly salted water to a rolling boil, add the potatoes, and cook until they are tender enough to mash. Drain the potatoes as soon as they are done and transfer them to a large bowl. Mash them immediately (it's important to do this while they're still hot), mashing in an additional 2 tablespoons of olive oil and salt to taste as you do so. As soon as the oil is thoroughly incorporated, add the onion-sausage mixture, along with all the pan juices, and fold it in. Add the eggs and cheese and mix well. Taste the mixture and adjust the seasoning.

Transfer the potato mixture to the prepared baking dish, smoothing the top. Sprinkle the top with the remaining bread crumbs, drizzle with a thread of olive oil, and bake for 20 to 30 minutes, or until the pie is firm in the middle.

Sara's Potatoes with Garlic and Rosemary
patate saltate all'aglio e rosmarino

4 TO 6 SERVINGS

This is the dish my daughter turns to whenever she gets homesick for Tuscany—which she does almost any time she's not actually there. It's probably the first thing she ever learned to cook on her own—one of those little nothing recipes that parents can use to encourage self-sufficiency in their offspring.

> 2 pounds waxy red-skinned potatoes
> Salt to taste
> 1/4 cup extra virgin olive oil
> 3 or 4 cloves garlic, crushed with the flat blade of a knife
> 2 sprigs fresh rosemary
> Freshly ground black pepper to taste

Boil the potatoes in lightly salted water until they are tender enough just to be pierced with a sharp knife. Remove from the heat and drain. As soon as the potatoes are cool enough to handle, peel them and slice about 1/4 inch thick.

Heat the oil in a large frying pan over medium heat and add the sliced potatoes, garlic cloves, and the leaves stripped from the rosemary branches. Turn frequently with a spatula to keep the starchy potatoes from sticking to the bottom of the pan. (Once they start to brown this is less of a problem.)

Sprinkle the potatoes with salt and pepper and continue cooking, stirring and turning frequently, until they are thoroughly brown and tender. Serve immediately.

Stuffed Cabbage with Ricotta
còi pién

8 SERVINGS

Don't be alarmed at the apparent complexity of this recipe. You can steam the cabbage leaves and mix the stuffing ahead, then refrigerate until ready to stuff the leaves and cook them.

16 to 18 large cabbage leaves (2 per serving)

Salt to taste

1 ½ pounds mixed greens (chard, spinach, dandelion greens, escarole, or other, or a combination of any of these)

1 pound ricotta, preferably made from goat's or sheep's milk

½ cup grated Parmigiano-Reggiano

½ cup bread crumbs

2 eggs

½ pound lean ground veal

Salt and freshly ground black pepper to taste

1 clove garlic, minced

2 tablespoons minced flat-leaf parsley

1 tablespoon unsalted butter

2 tablespoons extra virgin olive oil

3 cups canned whole tomatoes, chopped, with their juice

Discard the outer leaves of the cabbage to expose the tender, greener inside ones. Carefully remove 16 to 18 large, perfect cabbage leaves and cut away the tough base of the stem of each one with a sharp knife. Bring a large pot of salted water to a rolling boil and immerse the cabbage leaves in it until they are pliable, about 3 to 4 minutes. Drain in a colander and set aside. (May be prepared ahead and refrigerated until ready to use.)

Wash the greens very well in several changes of water until they are perfectly free of sand. Steam them in the water clinging to their leaves just until tender, then drain well. Chop the greens rather fine and place in a large bowl. Combine the greens with the ricotta, grated Parmigiano-Reggiano, bread crumbs, and eggs. If you are making this for immediate use, add the ground veal. Otherwise, save the veal and add just before you stuff the cabbage leaves. Add pepper and salt and mix well.

When ready to cook, gently sauté the garlic and parsley in the butter and oil over medium-low heat in a casserole or heavy saucepan. When the garlic is soft but not brown, stir in the chopped tomatoes with their juice and let cook gently for about 10 minutes. Stir the ground veal into the greens and cheese mixture if you haven't already added it.

Spread a leaf on a counter or worktop, with its shiny outer side down. Working from the base to the tip of the leaf, spread on a couple of tablespoons of stuffing, wrap the base of the leaf over the stuffing and start to roll toward the top, tucking in the sides of the leaf as you go along. Continue with the remaining cabbage leaves until all the stuffing is used up. Immerse the cabbage rolls, seam side down, in the tomato sauce, spooning the sauce over them. Cook, covered, over medium heat for about 30 minutes, or until the sauce has thickened and been partially absorbed by the cabbage rolls.

Butternut Squash in a Sweet and Sour Sauce
zucca in agrodolce

In Tuscany, Halloween is not a children's festival, and the pumpkin plays a greater role on the table than as a jack-o'-lantern. When bred for flavor rather than size, pumpkins are a delicious vegetable. In America, however, this treatment works better with squash. I've used butternut, but any hard, orange-colored winter squash would be acceptable. The squash should be cut in $3/4$-inch cubes, but you need not be compulsive about this—there's a discreet charm to irregularity in most presentations.

> 2 pounds butternut squash, peeled and cut in cubes
> About $1/4$ cup unbleached all-purpose flour
> 1 cup extra virgin olive oil
> Salt and freshly ground black pepper
> 3 tablespoons aged red wine vinegar
> $1^1/2$ tablespoons sugar

Put the squash cubes in a colander or sieve and toss with the flour to coat them lightly.

Bring the olive oil to frying temperature (375°F.) over medium-high heat. Drop the dusted cubes of squash into the hot oil to fry—you may find it easier to do this in two batches. As they crisp and brown along the edges, remove them to a rack covered with paper towel.

When all the squash has been fried, remove all but about 1 tablespoon of the cooking oil from the pan. (The oil may be carefully strained of impurities and reused.) Sprinkle the squash lightly with salt and abundantly with black pepper and return the cubes to the pan in which they cooked. Return to medium-high heat and add the vinegar and sugar. Cook, stirring constantly to turn the squash cubes in the heat, until the vinegar-sugar mixture has reduced to a thick syrup that naps the squash cubes.

Serve immediately.

Fried Zucchini Blossoms
fiori di zucchine fritti

6 SERVINGS

Use only the masculine blossoms, the rule books say, for the feminine ones will develop into full-fledged zucchini. Well, I have to admit that I can't tell the difference. In any case, as most gardeners know, one rarely suffers a dearth of zucchini. I pick whatever flowers look ready, and since I only make these delectable things once or twice a summer, there are always plenty left behind to grow into zucchini. Or not, as the case may be.

Many Tuscan cooks tuck a little piece of anchovy or mozzarella, sometimes both, inside the zucchini blossom, but I really prefer the unadulterated simplicity of these on their own. These things are addictive—I could eat the entire batch, I think, all by myself.

> 24 just-picked zucchini blossoms with stems attached
> 1 ½ to 2 cups extra virgin olive oil (or mix oil and lard, or, for economy's sake, olive oil and vegetable oil)
> 1 cup unbleached all-purpose flour
> Salt to taste

Pick over the blossoms, discarding any that look spoiled or buggy. Rinse them very lightly and quickly and drain in a colander.

In a large skillet, heat the oil slowly over medium-high heat to frying temperature—about 360°F.

While the oil is heating, gradually whisk the flour into 1 cup water to obtain a thin cream. Add a pinch of salt and whisk it in.

When ready to fry, take a blossom by its stem, dip it in the flour-and-water batter or pastella, let the greater part of the batter drip back into the bowl, and drop the coated blossom in the hot oil to sizzle and fry till crisp and golden. Proceed with the rest of the blossoms, frying them in batches, and removing them, when crisp, with a slotted spoon to drain on a rack covered with paper towels. When all the blossoms are done, sprinkle with more salt and serve immediately.

Sweets and Desserts
dolci

Via Nazionale, paved with broad dressed stones, is the ambling main street of Cortona. The only flat thoroughfare in this town built on the side of a mountain, it probably dates back to the original Etruscan settlement. Most of the time it's closed to anything but foot traffic, which makes it a perfect route for leisurely observation at close hand of the inhabitants of one of the oldest towns in Tuscany. The locals call it the Ruga Piana or the Lungapiana, and it's here that they conduct the *passeggiata,* the highly ritualized social stroll that takes place every day in the late afternoon or early evening for an hour or so before everyone goes home to dine. Back and forth they go, turn, and back and forth again, between Piazza Signorelli at one end of the street and Piazza Garibaldi at the other, the squares named in modern times to honor Cortona's great native-son painter and the national hero and founder of modern Italy.

But if anyone thinks of Garibaldi and Luca Signorelli during the evening passeggiata, they are few in number. There are weightier and more important things to ponder, all the intricate, busy, often incredibly political, frequently scandalous matters of provincial small-town life, matters that, it's safe to say, also go back to Etruscan origins.

One difficult decision each evening is whether to pause at the Bar Signorelli at one end of the passeggiata or Bar Banchelli at the other, for a ritual coffee or a syrupy-sweet drink lightened with acqua minerale and a little *boccone,* a mouthful of a snack, to go with it. There are advantages to both: Bar Signorelli is larger, more brightly lit, more populated, somewhat jollier perhaps, but Bar Banchelli has an extraordinary advantage in the sweet and savory pastries, the ice creams and sherbets, the cakes, cookies, and candies prepared by Emilio Banchelli and his son Gianni and sold in the shop that's presided over most of the time by Emilio's wife Maria.

I used to think there was nothing special about the Bar Banchelli, but that was when I thought every old Tuscan hill town had a pastry shop as fine as this, glass cases filled with an array of little iced lemony cakes and crisp flaky breakfast *cornetti* (the Italian equivalent of a sweet croissant) and jam-filled tarts and custard-filled cream puffs and nutty jaw-breaking *cantucci* or biscotti to soften in a glass of vin santo, pastries with walnuts or hazelnuts or almonds, with fig jam or orange glaze or a thin coating of rich, dark, black chocolate, not to mention the *ossi de' morti,* crisp meringues, for All Souls', and the panforte and panpepato, dense and spicy ancestors of the fruitcake, for Christmas, and the *frittelle di riso,* deep-fried sweetened rice fritters, for San Giuseppe, and the colomba and agnello, crushed-almond Easter confections made in the shape of a dove or a lamb, and throughout the summer months, a glorious spread of pastel-colored ice creams and sorbetti. Though all this was admittedly quite fabulous, still I thought, in my ignorance, that every hill town had the equivalent.

That was before I met Emilio Banchelli. You will rarely find Emilio in the bar, but at the top of a steep alley, a vicolo that climbs up the hill above the Ruga Piana, is his *laboratorio*—the word means workplace in Italian but it really is a laboratory where Emilio, a slight, shy man with a beatific smile, conducts his alchemical experiments into the sources of gustatory pleasure. His father Giovanni was a pastry maker who moved down here from Florence in 1932, and his son Gianni, named for his grandfather, is also a pastry maker; he specializes in sugar sculpture and, with Emilio, has won international awards for this most esoteric and ephemeral art. Most recently, Gianni has earned applause for some fairly incredible cakes made at Christmastime in the shapes of Babbo Natale (Father Christmas) and La Befana (the old witch who brings gifts to good children on January 6th), witty caricatures iced in colorful and painstaking detail that are sold in the shop on via Nazionale.

Emilio still has his father's book of recipes, a little spiral-bound notebook, each page devoted to a different sort of sweet delight. Only the quantities are noted, no directions, and only a professional would find the quantities useful—2 kilos (4.4 pounds) of toasted almonds, 4 kilos of candied fruit, for a Christmas panpepato, for instance. He doesn't refer to the recipe book very often these days, keeping it more as a treasured memento of the past. This is partly because, after nearly half a century of doing this work, he has no need for an aide-mémoire, and partly because he has it all computerized anyway.

Some of the sweet recipes that follow are based, as noted, on conversations with Emilio Banchelli, although I've adapted them to American kitchens. Others are simpler sweets from farmhouse kitchens. I should note, however, that most of the Banchelli production is meant to be consumed outside of regular mealtimes, as morning or late-afternoon pick-me-ups.

Meals in Tuscany rarely end with an elaborate sweet course, like the rich cakes of American tradition. Much more likely, for those who are not sated by the meal itself, is a plate (or a piece) of fresh, seasonal fruit—oranges in winter, and then successively strawberries, cherries, peaches and plums, apples and pears, and back to oranges and other sweet citrus again. Only for celebrations is there a sweet course offered, and more often than not it will be one of the simpler sweets purchased at the Banchellis' shop (at least in Cortona it will be) and brought to the meal by invited guests. Other sweets are associated with specific holidays or they're simple things a farmwife whips together from what's on hand to present to a friend who drops in late in the afternoon.

Pepper Cake for Christmas
panpepato

1 THICK CAKE 10 INCHES IN DIAMETER

Panpepato is a peppery version of panforte, the Christmas cake that is traditional to Siena, where there are bakeries producing nothing but panforte, not just for Christmas but all year, since it's sold in great numbers these days to tourists and other visitors. The cake has ancient origins (Sienese food historian Giovanni Righi Parenti finds a reference to *panes pepatos et melatos*—pepper and honey breads—in the early thirteenth century and it probably goes back much, much earlier) and is related to other rich Christmas spice cakes like German lebkuchen and honigkuchen. Symbols of abundance and prosperity, these cakes were consumed by the clergy and the nobility, who could afford them, and not by the peasantry, who most decidedly could not. Honey, sugar, and spices were liberally used in monastic kitchens, the first because it was a by-product of the beeswax produced for church candles, the other two because of the monastery's role in producing medicines—both spices and sugar were pharmaceuticals.

There are other versions of panforte, including panforte al cioccolato, with a glaze of melted bitter chocolate, and panforte bianco (also called Margherita), made with almond paste, which gives it a softer dough. But this is my adaptation of the panpepato made by Emilio Banchelli and sold in his shop in Cortona at Christmastime.

To toast the nuts, preheat the oven to 375°F. Spread the nuts in one layer on a baking sheet and toast in the oven for 15 minutes or so, stirring frequently, until the nuts are golden brown. Watch carefully toward the end of the cooking time, as they can go quickly from golden to burnt. Rub toasted hazelnuts in a clean dish towel to rid the nuts of their brown skins.

Freshly grinding the cinnamon, or any other spices used, in a spice mill will make a big difference in flavor. If you don't have a spice mill, wipe out your coffee mill with paper towels, grind a handful of bread crumbs to get rid of lingering coffee odors, then add a few broken sticks of cinnamon to grind to a powder. Crush the peppercorns in a mortar rather than grinding them with a pepper mill or put them on a hard surface and smack them lightly with a heavy cast-iron frying pan, taking care that they don't fly all over the kitchen.

1 cup blanched toasted almonds

1 ½ cups toasted hazelnuts

½ cup unbleached pastry flour

4 ½ cups candied fruit, including citron and citrus peel

½ cup Dutch-process cocoa

1 tablespoon freshly crushed (*not* ground) black pepper

1 teaspoon freshly ground cinnamon

1 teaspoon pure vanilla extract

Butter and flour for the pan

½ cup sugar

1 cup honey

Powdered sugar to sprinkle over the cake

When the toasted nuts are cool enough to handle (the toasting may be done several days in advance if it's more convenient), chop them coarsely and combine in a large mixing bowl. In another bowl, toss the flour with the candied fruit to coat the sticky pieces lightly and keep them from clumping together. Add the flour-coated fruits to the nuts and mix everything well so that fruits and nuts are distributed evenly. Sprinkle with the cocoa, pepper, and cinnamon, and toss to mix well. Stir in the vanilla and set aside.

Preheat the oven to 300°F. Butter and lightly flour a 10-inch springform pan, and line the bottom with wax paper or parchment.

In a saucepan over medium-low heat, bring the sugar and honey to a boil. Cook until the syrup reaches 250°F. on a candy thermometer—this is the beginning of the hard-ball stage at which a drop of syrup becomes a hard but still pliable ball when dropped in cold water. As soon as that stage is reached, remove the syrup from the heat and immediately pour it over the nut-fruit mixture in the bowl, stirring with a wooden spoon to mix everything together very well. Turn into the prepared pan and bake in the preheated oven for 1½ hours, or until the cake is dry and firm.

Remove and cool thoroughly on a rack, then release from the pan and sprinkle liberally with powdered sugar.

Note: Some people add ½ cup vin santo to the mixture, and some use more and different spices, especially freshly ground coriander seeds and cloves. Another spice mixture I came across included powdered bitter-orange peel. I have no idea where to find it, but if you ever discover it, it sounds quite sensational.

Chestnut Flour Cake
castagnaccio

2 THIN CAKES 8 INCHES IN DIAMETER

From the sublime to the rustic, from the exotic and expensive ingredients of panpepato to the humble simplicity of castagnaccio, is a leap in understanding. Tuscans call the chestnut tree *l'albero del pane,* the bread tree, because chestnuts, more reliable than wheat, will produce flour even in years of dearth when the wheat crop fails. Indeed, mountain communities in Tuscany until very recently relied wholeheartedly on chestnut flour, alone or in combination with wheat flour or cornmeal, to produce bread and porridge (one of the originals of polenta) throughout the winter months.

Castagnaccio is a very old, deeply traditional cake from the Tuscan countryside—not very sweet either, with most of the sweetness coming from sweet chestnuts and probably honey back in the days when sugar was an unimaginable luxury. I would be the first to admit that it's not to everyone's liking, being very plain and, when not well executed, rather heavy and gummy, but a book about Tuscan country traditions would not be complete without a recipe for castagnaccio.

This is not exactly a dessert, but the kind of thing to be served at a veglia, an evening gathering around the winter fire when country grannies would scare and scandalize the younger members of the family with tales, both real and imagined. (For those who are interested, the anthropologist Alessandro Falassi's *Folklore by the Fireside* is a wonderful book about la veglia.) Today's Tuscan countryfolk are more apt to be scared and scandalized by what's on the television set. But they still drink the new red wine, roast chestnuts over the fire, and finish the evening off with a bit of castagnaccio.

In the Casentino valley north of Arezzo, chestnuts are dried over smoldering wood fires before being sent to a water mill like Molino Grifoni to be ground into flour. The method gives Casentino chestnut flour a smoky quality that's very pleasing, but, truth to tell, *every* Tuscan mountain valley claims a chestnut flour of nearly miraculous characteristics, simply because it's one of those incredibly antique foods, like farro (page 76), whose reputation has been burnished by a combination of folklore, nostalgia, and the modern chic for anything rustic and recherché. For American sources for chestnut flour, see page 276.

Years ago, my mountain village celebrated an annual *sagra della castagna,* a chestnut fair, in October when the nuts are at their peak. All the ladies in the village made castagnaccio to be sold to benefit the local church, and of course there was much discussion about whose was best, whose most authentic, and whose spoiled by the easily detected presence of *lievito* in the form of baking soda. This recipe is a compilation of their ideas.

2 ½ cups chestnut flour

2 or 3 tablespoons sugar

Pinch of salt

⅓ cup golden raisins, plumped in ¼ cup warm vin santo, white wine, or plain water

1 cup milk

3 tablespoons extra virgin olive oil, plus a little to grease the baking pans

Grated zest of 1 orange

1 ½ tablespoons fresh rosemary

⅓ cup pine nuts (pignoli), or ½ cup very coarsely chopped fresh walnuts

Sift the chestnut flour into a bowl and stir in the sugar and salt. Drain the raisins, reserving the vin santo or wine if used. Set aside about 1 tablespoon of raisins to go on top and stir the remainder into the flour.

Mix the vin santo or wine, if used, with enough water to make 1 cup, and combine with the milk and oil. Using a wire whisk, stir the liquid into the flour mixture to make a batter with the density of heavy cream. Add the orange zest. Set the batter aside to rest for 30 minutes, during which time it will thicken somewhat.

Preheat the oven to 375°F.

Grease the bottoms and sides of 2 round or square pans with oil and divide the batter between the pans, pouring it in a very thin layer—about ¾ inch deep. Sprinkle the tops liberally with rosemary leaves, the reserved raisins, and either the pignoli or the walnuts. Drizzle about 1 tablespoon of oil over the top of each castagnaccio and bake in the oven for 45 minutes to 1 hour, or until the tops are crisp and lightly crackled. (The inside will still be moist.) Serve hot or at room temperature, in the pan in which it baked, with a little dollop of very fresh ricotta cheese over each slice if you wish.

If there are leftovers, they can be reheated by adding a little dry white wine to the spaces in the pan, covering the pan lightly with a piece of foil, and setting in a 300°F. oven until the wine has been absorbed and the castagnaccio is hot.

Carnival Cream Puffs
bomboloni di carnevale

MAKES 38 BOMBOLONI

While her mother's generation makes Cenci, an old-fashioned country treat for carnival, Maura Antolini makes the slightly more complicated bomboloni. Years ago, bomboloni would only have been made in town pastry shops, but nowadays, as cooking has evolved into a hobby for young Tuscan women (as it did for young American women in the 1960s and 1970s), working mothers like Maura take pride in their ability to master the complexities. But not entirely, for, in a fine example of the new Tuscan cooking, instead of filling her bomboloni with a laborious and rather tricky pastry cream, Maura uses Nutella, a chocolate-hazelnut spread that Italian schoolchildren eat on bread the way American kids eat peanut butter. I've given directions for making a truly delicious chocolate pastry cream, but if you prefer to use Nutella, by all means do so. It's widely available in America, too.

1 packet (about 2 teaspoons) active dry yeast

$^1/_4$ cup sugar, plus some for sprinkling

5 cups Italian-style or unbleached pastry flour

4 tablespoons unsalted butter at room temperature, plus a little more to grease the bowl

$^3/_4$ cup whole milk, warmed to tepid

Pinch of salt

Extra virgin olive oil for deep-fat frying

For the pastry cream (2 to 3 cups):

2 cups milk

6 egg yolks

$^1/_2$ cup sugar

$^1/_2$ cup pastry flour

1 to 2 tablespoons unsalted butter

4 ounces imported semisweet chocolate

1 teaspoon pure vanilla extract

Sprinkle the yeast over $^1/_2$ cup very warm water and set aside to dissolve into a cream.

Toss the sugar with the flour and mound on a board or place in a large mixing bowl. Make a well in the middle and add the butter, cut in small pieces. Draw a little flour over the butter, then pour in the dissolved yeast and warm milk and mix gradually into the surrounding flour, adding a good pinch of salt as you mix. When all the yeast and butter have been incorporated into the flour, knead briefly in the bowl, then on a lightly floured board. The dough should be quite soft.

Lightly grease a bowl and set the dough in it, lightly covered with plastic wrap. Set aside in a warm place to rise.

When the dough has doubled in bulk, punch it down. Roll and spread it on a lightly floured board to make a layer about $1/2$ inch thick. Using a biscuit cutter or an up-ended glass dipped in flour, cut out rounds. Set the rounds on a lightly floured kitchen cloth, cover with another cloth, and set aside to rise again until doubled.

When the bomboloni have risen, heat the oil to frying temperature—360° to 375°F. Drop a few dough circles into the hot oil and fry quickly, turning once, until brown on both sides. Remove with a slotted spoon and set on a rack covered with paper towel to drain. When all the bomboloni have been fried, sprinkle them with sugar on both sides while they're still very hot.

While the bomboloni cool slightly, make the pastry cream: Heat the milk over medium-low heat until very hot but not boiling.

Beat the egg yolks and sugar together in a bowl until the mixture is thick, pale yellow, and forms a ribbon. Sprinkle the flour over the egg mixture and stir it in with a spoon; then return to the beater and beat in the hot milk, a little at a time.

Have a double boiler ready with simmering water in the bottom half. Transfer the cream to the top half of the double boiler and cook, stirring frequently, until it is as thick as custard—15 to 20 minutes. Remove from the heat, beat in the tablespoon of butter and the chocolate, and stir until smooth. Stir in the vanilla extract. If the cream is still too thick, beat in the second tablespoon of butter (do not beat butter into a room-temperature cream as it will not melt properly).

Set aside to cool slightly, then, as soon as the bomboloni are cool enough to handle, use a pastry syringe to fill them with the chocolate cream or Nutella. If you don't have a pastry syringe, simply cut each one in half, spoon in some of the pastry cream, and top with the second half.

Lenten Buns
spolette quaresimali

12 BUNS

These little sweet rolls, which remind me of hot cross buns, are made in Cortona during Lent. Emilio Banchelli, Cortona's master pastry chef, says that spolette were, and perhaps still are, a daily reward provided by the priests for children studying their catechism. "Forty days of Lent," Banchelli said, "and for good children, forty spolette." This is another of the recipes handed down from his father.

$3/4$ teaspoon active dry yeast

4 cups unbleached all-purpose flour

$1/2$ cup plus 2 tablespoons unsalted butter, softened

$3/4$ cup sugar

Good pinch of salt

2 eggs

$1/2$ cup whole milk

$1/4$ cup golden raisins or raisins and candied citrus peel

For the glaze:

1 tablespoon milk, more or less, as needed

$1/2$ cup powdered sugar

Mix the yeast with $1/4$ cup very warm water and set aside to dissolve.

In a large mixing bowl, combine the flour, butter, sugar, and salt. Add the yeast and beat, using a wooden spoon or an electric mixer. Add the eggs one at a time, beating well after each addition. Add enough milk to make a soft, but kneadable dough. Finally add the raisins and/or candied citrus peel and beat in by hand.

Turn the dough out on a lightly floured board and knead about 30 or 40 strokes. Place in a lightly greased bowl, cover with plastic wrap, and set aside in a cool place to rise overnight.

Next morning, punch down the risen dough and shape into small oblong pillows about the size of a deck of cards. Set aside to rise in a warm place for about 30 minutes, or while the oven heats.

Preheat the oven to 350°F.

Lightly grease a baking sheet with oil and set the buns on the sheet, leaving 1 inch between each. Bake for about 20 minutes, or until puffed and brown.

Make a simple white sugar glaze by gradually mixing the milk into the sugar until you have a thick but still liquid glaze. As soon as the buns come out of the oven, remove them to a rack (with a sheet of newspaper beneath it to catch the glaze) and dribble the glaze over the top of each one—in the shape of a cross, if you wish.

Zuppa Inglese/Tiramisù

8 TO 10 SERVINGS

Zuppa inglese was the original tiramisù, the layered pudding that swept across America about ten years ago, when you could find tiramisù on the menu of any restaurant that boasted the "new" Italian cooking or the inspired work of some young chef. Tiramisù is a fine sweet, if you wish, but zuppa inglese is more traditional.

Why English soup? This is so similar to old-fashioned English trifle that I suspect it was brought to Tuscany by the English, who settled here in numbers even in the nineteenth century. (Today there are little pockets of Tuscany, around Greve in Chianti, for instance, where you hear more English spoken than Italian—or Italian with a rigorously British cadence.) English trifle is usually made with raspberry jam as well as custard, and I've seen some recipes for zuppa inglese that include jam too. It used to be made with a liqueur from Florence called alkermes, colored with cochineal, a brilliant, deep red wool dye made from little red bugs, dried and crushed. Alkermes has become very hard to find, even in Tuscany, so the red jam is perhaps a substitute.

You'll need a simple sponge cake, preferably not the freshest, to make this. Use a favorite recipe, or follow the directions below, but note that the sponge cake should be prepared at least a day ahead. Since you can also prepare the pastry cream ahead, the whole thing becomes very easy to assemble a few hours before serving. Then unmold the zuppa inglese and cover with whipped cream, almonds, and chocolate shavings just before you serve it.

For the sponge cakes:

Butter and flour for two 9-inch cake pans

6 eggs, separated

1 cup sugar

1 teaspoon pure vanilla extract, or 2 teaspoons grated lemon zest

1 cup cake flour or pastry flour

Pinch of salt

For the pastry cream (2 to 3 cups):

2 cups milk

1 teaspoon pure vanilla extract

3 eggs

2/3 cup sugar

1/2 cup pastry flour

1 to 2 tablespoons unsalted butter

1/3 cup flavored liqueur or rum

1 cup heavy cream

2 tablespoons sugar

1/4 cup toasted slivered almonds

1/4 cup shaved bitter chocolate

Preheat the oven to 350°F. Butter and flour the cake pans.

To make the cakes: Combine the egg yolks and sugar in the bowl of an electric mixer and beat until thick and pale yellow. Beat in the vanilla, then fold the flour into the eggs.

In a separate bowl with clean beaters, beat the egg whites with a pinch of salt to soft peaks. Stir about a quarter of the egg whites into the egg yolk mixture, then fold in the remaining egg whites. Work quickly, but combine the ingredients thoroughly.

Divide the batter between the two pans and bake for about 25 minutes, or until the tops are golden and springy and the cakes have pulled away slightly from the edges of the pans. Remove and cool on a rack, then turn the cakes out of the pans.

While the cakes are baking, make the pastry cream. Scald the milk by bringing it to the boiling point, remove from the heat, and add the vanilla. Set aside to cool to very warm.

Beat the eggs and sugar together with an electric mixer until the mixture is thick, pale yellow, and forms a ribbon. Sprinkle on the flour and stir it in with a spoon; then return to the beater and beat in the very warm flavored milk, a little at a time.

Have a double boiler ready with simmering water in the bottom half. Transfer the cream to the top half of the double boiler and cook, stirring frequently, over the simmering water until it is as thick as custard—15 to 20 minutes. Remove from the heat and beat in 1 tablespoon of the butter. If the cream is still too thick, beat in the second tablespoon of butter (do not beat butter into a room-temperature cream as it will not melt properly). Set aside or refrigerate to cool thoroughly.

Both the cake and the pastry cream may be prepared a day ahead.

A few hours before you're ready to serve, pour the liqueur into a shallow bowl and cut the cakes into narrow (½ inch or less) strips. Dip the cake strips briefly in the liqueur and use them to line a 1½- to 2-quart round bowl, piecing them together to line the inside of the bowl completely. (Some cooks find it easier to unmold this if the bowl is lined with a single layer of plastic wrap.) Cover the strips with a light coating of pastry cream. Add more strips of liqueur-dipped cake across the bottom layer and cover with pastry cream. Continue in this fashion, layering liqueur-dipped cake strips and pastry cream until you have filled the bowl. (Note that if you wish you may spread a very thin layer of jam on some—but not all—of the cake strips before topping with pastry cream.) The topmost layer should be cake strips. Set a plate on the top and weight it with an 8-ounce can. Refrigerate for several hours.

When ready to serve, carefully unmold the cake on a serving platter. Beat the heavy cream with the sugar until quite stiff. Smooth the cream over the unmolded cake and sprinkle almond and chocolate slivers all over it. Serve immediately.

Sweet Rice Fritters for the Feast of St. Joseph
frittelle di riso per san giuseppe

18 TO 24 FRITTELLE

San Giuseppe, on March 19, is a special day for Italians, including those in America and other parts of the world to which they have emigrated with their culinary heritage. St. Joseph, who so gracefully accepted as his own the child of the Holy Ghost, is an appealing saint, but why his day should be special is puzzling until you realize that it's close enough to the vernal equinox to be a celebration of the first day of spring. Every region of Italy, it seems, has some special dish for the day; in Tuscany it's these little fried puffs of lightly sweetened rice flavored with grated citrus zest and perhaps a shot glass of rum (in more traditional homes it would be alkermes, an old-fashioned red liqueur from Florence).

Emilio Banchelli showed me photos of the Piazza Signorelli in Cortona, not too long ago either, when great cauldrons of boiling fat were set up in the main square and everyone came out for a major fry-up for San Giuseppe. In those days, the fat used was supposed to be olive oil, in keeping with Lenten restrictions, but poorer people often sneaked in *strutto* (melted pork lard) instead. It wasn't just a cheaper alternative—it gave a wonderful flavor to the fritters as well. If you have a source of good quality pure pork lard, try it with these, just to see how brilliantly it works. The frittelle feast may have disappeared from Cortona but the frittelle are still available, as they are in just about every Tuscan town on the days leading up to March 19. Signs in the windows of bars and pasticcerie: *Oggi! Frittelle di San Giuseppe!* are portents, as sure as a robin, that spring is nearly here.

2/3 cup medium-grain rice (do not use risotto rice)

2 cups milk

2 tablespoons sugar

1 teaspoon salt, or to taste

3 tablespoons grated lemon and/or orange zest

1 tablespoon unsalted butter

2 eggs, separated

1 tablespoon rum or strong liqueur

1/4 cup flour

Extra virgin olive oil, or vegetable oil, for deep-fat frying.

Powdered sugar

Mix the rice and milk in a saucepan and bring slowly to a simmer over low heat, stirring very frequently to keep the rice from sticking to the bottom of the pan. As the rice starts to cook, add 1 tablespoon of the sugar, the salt, and grated zest. When the liquid is simmering, cover the pan and continue cooking for about 20 minutes, stirring occasionally, until the rice has absorbed almost all the liquid and is reduced to a soft pudding. Stir in the butter and set aside, covered, to cool (do not refrigerate).

When the rice reaches room temperature, add the egg yolks, rum or liqueur, and flour, beating with a wooden spoon after each addition.

Heat the oil to frying temperature—360°F. to 375°F. While the oil is heating, beat the egg whites with a pinch of salt until they form soft peaks. Sprinkle 1 tablespoon of sugar over them and continue beating until they are stiff. Gently fold the egg whites into the rice mixture. Drop the batter by the tablespoonful into the boiling oil and fry, turning once, until the frittelle are crisp and brown. Remove with a skimmer and set on a rack covered with paper towels to drain. When all the frittelle are done, sprinkle them with powdered sugar and serve immediately.

Rustic Torte
torta rustica

For those who know it, this will be reminiscent of Huguenot torte, an old favorite in South Carolina kitchens. I make no claim for a link between Tuscany and Charleston except that both are regions noted for care in the kitchen. This is my adaptation of a recipe in *Dolci di Siena e della Toscana,* a collection of traditional Tuscan sweets compiled by Giovanni Righi Parenti, who says that the cake was covered in days of yore with crushed dried figs and nuts mixed with honey. This plainer version is more in keeping with today's tastes.

Butter and flour for the pans
1 cup whole hazelnuts
1 ½ cups whole blanched almonds
1 ½ cups unbleached pastry flour
1 ½ cups cornmeal
12 tablespoons (1 ½ sticks) butter, softened
½ cup sugar
4 eggs, separated
½ cup milk
Pinch of salt

Preheat the oven to 300°F. Lightly butter and flour two 9-inch round cake pans.

Spread the hazelnuts on a flat sheet pan and place in the oven for 15 to 20 minutes, or until they are toasted golden brown (watch carefully lest they darken too much). Remove and transfer to a kitchen towel. Put the almonds on the sheet pan and toast them the same way. While the almonds are baking, rub the hazelnuts vigorously in the towel to rid them of most of their skins. When the almonds are done, combine them with the hazelnuts and chop them on a board as finely as possible, or use a food processor to process them, working in short bursts, ½ cup at a time, to a fine granular texture. (Be careful not to overprocess to a paste.) Combine the ground nuts with the flour and cornmeal in a large bowl, tossing to mix well.

Raise the oven temperature to 375°F.

In a smaller bowl, cream together the butter and sugar. Add the egg yolks, one at a time, beating after each addition. Beat in the milk, then combine with the dry mixture and fold to mix well.

In a separate bowl with clean beaters, beat the egg whites with a pinch of salt until stiff. Stir ⅓ of the egg whites into the batter, then fold in the remaining egg whites and turn the batter into the prepared pans. Bake 45 minutes, or until the tops are golden brown and the cakes pull away from the sides of the pans. Remove and let cool on a rack, then loosen the sides of the cakes with a palette knife and turn them out on the rack.

Note: Some cooks spread a little jam or marmalade as a glaze over the tops of the still warm cakes before serving with a dollop of whipped cream, but it's also very good on its own, a dry, crunchy, barely sweetened cake to serve with vin santo or a sweet dessert wine.

Cooked Cream
panna cotta

MAKES 10 TO 12 SERVINGS

Mirella Settori makes this delicate cream at her restaurant, La Casa di Caccia, on a hill overlooking the Mugello valley north of Florence, but it's a dessert that you'll find all over Tuscany. It is splendid with a sauce of wild berries, or with melted chocolate.

4 cups heavy cream
1 envelope unflavored gelatin
½ cup sugar
1 teaspoon pure vanilla extract
5 egg whites

Combine 1 cup of the cream with the gelatin in a small bowl and set aside to soften and dissolve the gelatin. In a small pan, bring the remaining cream to a slow boil with the sugar and vanilla and boil for precisely 3 minutes. Remove from the heat and set aside for 1½ minutes, then add the gelatin-cream mixture and stir until it is fully combined. Transfer to a bowl and cool at room temperature for 3 hours.

At the end of this time, beat the egg whites until very stiff. Gently whisk about half the beaten egg whites into the cream, then fold in the remaining whites. Transfer the panna cotta to individual molds, or small bowls. Refrigerate for at least 3 hours before serving.

Serve with chocolate sauce or with a sauce made from fresh berries, crushed and sweetened with a very little sugar.

Ricotta Cheese Cake from the Mugello
torta di ricotta

MAKES ONE 9- TO 10-INCH TART, ENOUGH FOR 8 TO 10 SERVINGS

Sheep and their wool were always a basis of Tuscan wealth, going back to the days when the great Florentine wool traders established early banking houses that were fundamental to the development of European capitalism. Up until very recently, every farmer kept at least a small flock of sheep, and it was customary to see farm women walking out in pairs along country roads twisting a spindle of wool as they walked and talked—idle hands, as we know, make work for the devil.

Sheep don't just give wool, of course, they also give milk. Tuscan ewe's milk Pecorino was always as important in local markets as Tuscan wool was on the international exchange. Today wool has lost its economic importance, but Tuscan Pecorino is still made and valued, although the huge flocks of sheep that you see in springtime and autumn drifting like clouds across the gleaned fields of the Crete Senese south and east of Siena are mostly owned by Sardinians. (They may have been in Tuscany for three generations or more, but they are still considered, and consider themselves, Sardinian.)

Giovanna Bacciotti is not Sardinian but her 450-odd white sheep are. Like most of the sheep in Tuscany, they're of the breed called *sardo*, good milkers (up to one and a half liters of milk a day) and tough animals who don't mind winter's chilly rains up in the Mugello, where Giovanna farms with her grown children Sandra and Roberto. The Bacciottis make cheeses with that special tang that ewe's milk has, whether a Pecorino fresco (up to one month old), semi-stagionato (five to six months), or an older stagionato or even stravecchio (very old), the traditional grating cheese of Tuscany before Parmigiano-Reggiano dominated the national market.

Like most Tuscan ewe's milk dairies, the Bacciotti farm also makes two special products. Raviggiolo is a barely curdled and thickened whole milk cheese eaten very fresh before the cheese is salted—no more than a day old, maximum. The texture of runny sour cream or mascarpone, sweet yet tangy, raviggiolo is delicious with honey for breakfast or as a dessert; chefs often use it as a garnish in place of cream. (A hot and basil-fragrant tomato soup with a swirl of creamy chilled raviggiolo is an extraordinary combination.)

Raviggiolo, so far as I've been able to determine, is unknown in America but the other special product, ewe's milk ricotta, can occasionally be obtained from sheep dairies like Hollow Road Farms in the Hudson Valley. Made from whey drained when the cheeses are made each morning, *ricotta* means, literally, "re-cooked." When the whey is boiled, which in Tuscan dairies like Giovanna Bacciotti's takes place over a smoky fire that adds good flavor, it rapidly coagulates into the curds of ricotta. The cow's milk ricotta that is commercially available in this country is bland and chalky, with little to recommend it, but goat's milk ricotta, more widely available here than sheep's milk, may be substituted in this recipe. If the ricotta is very damp, it should be drained for two hours before using.

This is the recipe for a torta di ricotta, a lightly sweetened cheesecake or cheese pie, that Sandra Bacciotti gave us one day when we stopped by after the morning milking.

For the pastry:

4 ounces ($\frac{1}{2}$ cup, 1 stick) unsweetened butter

$\frac{1}{4}$ cup sugar

1 egg

1 $\frac{1}{2}$ to 2 cups unbleached all-purpose flour

Pinch of salt

$\frac{1}{2}$ teaspoon ground cinnamon

For the filling:

2 cups milk

Zest of 1 lemon

4 eggs

$\frac{2}{3}$ cup sugar

Pinch of salt

3 tablespoons flour

1 pound ewe's or goat's milk ricotta, drained if necessary

1 teaspoon vanilla extract

Make the pastry: Cream the butter and sugar in a bowl, add the egg, and beat until very light and fluffy. Mix 1 cup of the flour with the salt and cinnamon, sift over the bowl, and stir until just combined. Add another $\frac{1}{2}$ cup flour and stir in. Spread the remaining flour on a board and turn the dough out onto the board. Knead briefly, no more than half a dozen strokes, incorporating some of the flour on the board as necessary. The dough will be very soft. Shape it into a round disk, cover with plastic wrap (or place in a plastic bag), and refrigerate for at least 1 hour or overnight.

Roll the dough out to fit a 9- or 10-inch tart or quiche pan with sides that are 2 inches high—a springform pan is ideal. (A soft dough like this is often easier to roll between two pieces of wax paper.) Line the pan with the dough and set in the freezer, lightly wrapped in plastic so that the dough doesn't dry out, while you preheat the oven to 350°F. Prick the bottom of the dough in the pan with a fork and bake for 15 to 20 minutes, or until the dough is lightly golden and dry. Set aside while you make the ricotta filling.

Put the milk in a small pan with the lemon zest, and heat just to the boiling point; do not let it boil. Set aside to cool slightly and steep while you beat the eggs.

Combine 3 of the eggs with the sugar in a bowl and beat to a thick ribbon. Add a pinch of salt. Sprinkle the flour over and beat into the mixture. Strain the hot milk. Beating constantly, slowly beat the milk into the egg mixture. When all the milk has been added, transfer the *crema pasticciera* (pastry cream) to the upper half of a double boiler and cook over simmering water for 5 to 10 minutes, or until the cream is thick—thicker than heavy cream but not so thick as sour cream. Remove from the heat and let cool to tepid.

Push the drained ricotta through a sieve or food mill into the tepid pastry cream and stir to mix well. Then stir in the remaining egg and the vanilla. Mix thoroughly and set aside.

Reheat the oven to 350°F., if necessary. Pour the ricotta mixture into the prepared pastry shell and bake for 25 to 35 minutes, or until the cream is firmly set but not tough and rubbery.

Variations: Sandra's torta di ricotta was appealing in its simple purity; other cooks might elaborate the ricotta mixture by stirring in a handful of golden raisins, plumped in grappa; lightly toasted slivered almonds or pine nuts; a tablespoon of grated lemon or orange zest; or, if a source of top-quality candied peel is available, some slivers of candied citron.

Ring Cake
ciambella

Make this in a bundt or round tube pan for a nice effect. After turning the cake out, sift powdered sugar over it and fill the center with fresh seasonal fruits cut in small pieces and mixed with a little sugar.

Butter and flour for the cake pan

1½ cups unbleached all-purpose flour and 1 cup unbleached pastry flour, or 2½ cups
    Italian-style flour

1½ teaspoons baking powder

Pinch of salt

½ cup whole milk

6 tablespoons (¾ stick) unsalted butter, melted

¼ cup vin santo or light rum

½ teaspoon pure vanilla extract

1 tablespoon grated lemon zest

3 large eggs

1 cup sugar

Preheat the oven to 425°F. Butter and flour an 8- or 9-inch cake pan.

Mix the flour with the baking powder and salt. Combine the milk with the melted butter, vin santo, vanilla, and lemon zest.

Beat the eggs with an electric mixer, gradually beating in the sugar until the mixture is thick and pale. When the sugar is thoroughly combined, use a spatula to fold in ⅓ of the flour mixture, followed by ½ the liquid, then another ⅓ of the flour, the remaining liquid, and, finally, the remaining flour mixture. Fold to blend thoroughly, but do not overmix.

Pour the batter into the prepared pan and bake 15 minutes, then lower the heat to 350°F. and continue baking another 15 to 20 minutes, or until the cake pulls away from the sides of the pan and the top is golden and springy. Remove from the oven, invert on a cake rack, and leave to cool and settle.

This cake may be served as is with a glass of dessert wine, or with sliced summer fruits, or with a dollop of whipped cream or ice cream. Or, before baking the cake, peel and slice very thinly a firm apple or pear and arrange the slices over the batter.

Cantucci—Biscotti di Prato

ABOUT 36 BISCOTTI

These crisp thick cookies are meant to be dipped in a glass of vin santo or other sweet wine, or coffee, to soften them for eating. The town of Prato, north of Florence, claims them, but in fact they can be found all over Tuscany—and all over America these days. Biscotti, like biscuit, means twice-cooked; these are among the few biscuits that still reflect that original meaning.

A little butter for the cookie sheet

2 cups unbleached all-purpose flour and 2 cups pastry flour, or 4 cups Italian-style flour, plus a little more for the board and the cookie sheet

2 cups sugar

1 teaspoon baking soda

Pinch of salt

4 eggs

1 teaspoon pure vanilla extract

1 cup coarsely chopped toasted almonds

1 cup coarsely chopped toasted hazelnuts

1 egg white beaten with 1 teaspoon water

Preheat the oven to 375°F. Lightly grease and flour a cookie sheet.

In a mixing bowl, toss the flour, sugar, baking soda, and salt with a fork to mix well.

In a separate bowl, beat the eggs with the vanilla just enough to mix yolks and whites. Stir the eggs into the dry mixture, kneading with your hands in the bowl until you have a homogeneous mixture. Turn the dough out on a very lightly floured board. Sprinkle the nuts over the dough and continue kneading for a few minutes to distribute the nuts evenly throughout the dough. Set the dough aside to rest for 10 minutes or so.

Now divide the dough into 6 equal pieces and, using your hands, shape each piece into a long, thin log no more than 2 inches in diameter. As each log is finished, set it on the cookie sheet, keeping them a few inches apart; they expand while baking. Press the top of each log with your palm to flatten it slightly and give it an oval rather than a round section when sliced.

Paint each log with the egg white wash, then bake the logs for 20 to 30 minutes, or until they are dry and lightly colored. Remove from the oven and set aside, on the cookie sheet, until cool enough to handle. Lower the oven temperature to 300°F.

When the logs are cool enough to handle, slice them on the diagonal no more than $1/2$ inch thick, using a long sharp knife. Lay the biscotti, flat side down, on the cookie sheet and return them to the oven for 15 to 20 minutes.

Transfer the biscotti to a rack to dry, cool, and harden for several hours. They can be kept in a cookie tin for 6 weeks or more.

Vin Santo

Vin santo: holy wine. The name alone gives an idea of its unique character, a wine made from grapes carefully selected and laid to dry for months on cane mats or hung in clusters from the rafters of a farmhouse kitchen until the grapes have shriveled and the small amount of juice inside is concentrated with sugars. Then the grapes are gently pressed into wine, mixed with a small amount of *madre* or mother from previous vin santi, and the wine is sealed into small barrels called *caratelli*. The caratelli are stored in airy attics or barns where fluctuations of temperature and humidity over a period of several years produce a liquorous wine of extraordinary complexity and concentration, up to 16.5 percent alcohol, at the same time both dry and sweet on the palate, with intense flavors of dried fruit (prunes, raisins, apricots) and hints of the bitter-sweetness of almonds. The color of the finished wine, poured from the caratello in a ceremony called the *svinatura,* ranges from pale straw to deep golden amber with flashes of brilliant orange.

But what does the name mean? I've been told many stories, among them, that the name derives from the fact that the grapes are dried all winter and pressed during Holy Week right before Easter; that the wine was traditionally used for Communion and other religious rituals; that the wine was named by an enthusiastic Greek bishop (a category in which Tuscan folklore seems particularly abundant) who dubbed it after the wine of Thracian Xantos, which was also made from dried grapes. Any, or all, of these stories may be true. Perhaps. . . . chissà.

Individual farmers might make one caratello of vin santo each harvest, and set the caratello in the attic of the farmhouse to age for three years or so, then bring it out for family occasions, a wedding or christening, or simply to mark the arrival of an honored guest. Larger wineries, like Avignonesi in Montepulciano, which produces one of the most elegant and prestigious vin santi, may make as many as sixty or seventy caratelli, aging the wine for as much as eight to ten years—during which time the wine reduces by half. And it's never enough: If you come across a bottle of Avignonesi's vin santo, by all means snatch it up. The wine, whoever the producer, is in very short supply, and rarely does a quality bottle reach American markets.

I've never happened to be in Tuscany when the vin santo barrels are opened, but my friend Gaia Anderson, who works for Avignonesi, described the svinatura one year when she was "the one girl in a group of hot shots, all connoisseurs and critics of wine. . . . We all tasted from the same glass, a circle of active palates, sniffing, moving, and chewing the vin santo to its soul. Words of comment flew above our heads, and most dropped like dead birds as soon as a new glass was put into circulation. Some dared to find defects, others tried to contemplate, all distractions were a good excuse to take another sip from the glass. . . ."

Vin santo is an exquisite dessert wine and that's when Tuscans tend to serve it, though I have occasionally come across a very dry vin santo served, like sherry, as an aperitivo. It is the only proper accompaniment for the kind of dry, barely sweetened cakes and cookies beloved of Tuscans of all classes and generations, biscotti di Prato, also called *cantucci,* or the peppery spiciness of panpepato and panforte. Should you dip biscotti in vin santo? Ettore Falvo, the anxious guardian of the Avignonesi vinsantaia, would probably faint to hear me say it, but dipping does make a biscotto more palatable, though I also believe, like many Tuscans, that a fine vin santo all on its own is the most superb treat with which to end a meal.

the wines of tuscany

Chianti, it almost goes without saying, is the best known Tuscan wine, but it is not by any means the *only* Tuscan wine. Indeed, in a recent guide to Italy's top wines and wineries, the editors of *Gambero Rosso,* the country's most respected food magazine, list thirty individual Tuscan wine-makers, from Antinori to Vallocaia, that qualify as among Italy's best, giving Tuscany the lead over all other regions, including prestigious Piemonte and prolific Friuli-Venezia Giulia. Many of these are makers of Chianti, but others produce equally noble reds like Vino Nobile di Montepulciano, Morellino di Scansano, Carmignano, and Brunello di Montalcino, as well as the white Vernaccia di San Gimignano.

Faced with such a selection, it would be presumptuous of me to try to compress a complete discussion of Tuscan wines into these few paragraphs. For those who are interested in following this absorbing subject further, I recommend the books and articles of Italian wine experts like Burton Anderson, Nicholas Belfrage, and Victor Hazan, to mention only those best known to English-speaking readers.

Any discussion of Tuscan wines must begin with the caution that Italian wine-making in general, and Tuscan wine-making in particular, have undergone enormous changes in the last few decades with the introduction of new and improved varieties in vineyards and new and more rigorous methods in wineries. As with good olive oil, cleanliness is probably the single most important factor in producing good wine, a fact that vintners themselves—and not just in Italy—have sometimes been curiously slow to recognize. Nowadays, however, good Tuscan producers—and they are in abundance as the *Gambero Rosso* guide indicates—are among the most scrupulous in the world. The rotgut Chianti in a straw-covered flask that I drank (illegally) as an undergraduate in the North End of Boston is a thing of the past, its demise unregretted. There is still bad wine made in Tuscany, as there is in all the world's wine regions, but there is more good wine than ever before—and a revivalist crafts movement in Florence may even succeed in bringing back the straw-covered fiasco.

For all the other wines that are produced in Tuscany, however, Chianti is still the most truly Tuscan wine, made primarily from sangiovese, the most truly Tuscan of grapes. Having said this, I must add that sangiovese is widely planted from Central Italy right down into the south and, in fact, the variety, in one clonal form or another, goes into a number of other distinctive non-Chianti Tuscan wines, among them Brunello di Montalcino, Carmignano, and Vino Nobile di Montepulciano, as well as many of the newer style barrique-aged vini da tavola, or table wines—an Italian designation for any wine, however noble it may be, that does not have a Denominazione di Origine Controllata (DOC).

Whether or not the variety is a Tuscan original, as some experts claim, sangiovese, in any of a number of clonal variations, is the most traditional, most widely grown grape in Tuscany, the foundation of the Chianti blend and of the wine that every peasant farmer makes each year in late September from old vines that stretch along the edges of his *greppe* or terraced fields and form a shady pergola outside his kitchen door.

A well-made Chianti is a fine wine, dry, fruity but a little austere, medium-bodied and with a well-balanced structure, meant to be drunk for the most part within two to three years, though a fine *riserva* may not reach its peak until it's eight years or older. But what makes it Chianti? And why is Chianti peculiarly Tuscan?

Those questions were easier to answer back in the days when DOC regulations for Chianti imposed a strict blend or *uvaggio* of sangiovese grapes mixed with a small amount of canaiolo, another red variety, and either trebbiano, a sort of all-purpose and undistinguished white, or malvasia for freshness. The formula was laid down by Baron Ricasoli back in the nineteenth century, and it was fundamentally not very different from the formula used by farmers all over Tuscany. The cultivation of the grapes and the methods of making and aging the wines were prescribed, as they still are, and Chianti was simply red wine made according to these rules in one of the seven zones of production that stretch from Arezzo in the east, westward to Pisa, south to Siena, and north to just above Florence at Rùfina on the Sieve River.

Chianti Classico is but one of the production zones and, although it's probably the one best known to wine connoisseurs, it's not necessarily the standard by which all other Chiantis should be measured. Indeed, the term *classico* refers less to the "classic" nature of the wine and more to the fact that this hilly, often deeply forested region stretching along the Chianti mountain range between Florence and Siena, was the original zone of Chianti production and home of the Lega del Chianti, a thirteenth-century political consortium. But a Chianti Colli Senesi, from the hills around Siena, or a Chianti Rùfina, from the region east of Florence, can be every bit as good as and often even better than a Chianti Classico. (The other Chianti zones are Colli Aretini, Colli Fiorentini, Colline Pisane, and Montalbano.)

Traveling through this region along the Chiantigiana, the road that leads from Florence to Siena by way of charming towns like Greve and Castellina, the traveler may still see traditional vineyards with vines trained up trees in a manner that goes back to Etruscan methods of cultivation. And he or she may still see fields with *coltivazione promiscua* (promiscuous cultivation), the old-fashioned terraced interplanting of grain, vines, and olives—like a living icon of the ancient Mediterranean triad of crops. But these old ways are increasingly rare, as is the Tuscan tradition of adding a *governo,* in the form of dried grapes, or the must of dried grapes, to induce a secondary fermentation in the wine. In peasant farmhouses you may still see bunches of grapes drying on the rafters to be added to the wine in December or January, but the practice has almost died out among commercial wineries, and vineyards themselves have become broad, monocropped fields of vines that sweep across the landscape without reference to terraces, often without reference to the landscape itself.

One could mourn the loss of these traditions but at the same time one would have to admit that the wine, on the whole, is better today than it was back in the days of *mezzadria,* the Tuscan system of sharecropping which lasted until the late 1960s. (Future historians may well draw a connection between the end of mezzadria and the imposition of a DOC for Chianti and other Tuscan wines, but this is not the place for such speculation.) It was then that many traditional peasant families began to leave the land, or at least the younger, more vital members of those families left for city jobs with guaranteed salaries, paid vacations, and other benefits. Abandoned farms were bought up by outside investors, whether Milanese, English, or American, often with the goal of gaining prestige and not a little money from making wine—

sometimes aiming to have a little fun with it too.* It was a gradual process but over the decades enormous changes have taken place.

Although the rules for Chianti called for a small amount of white trebbiano or malvasia in the blend, the requisite addition of white wine was all too often honored in the breach, and, in recognition of what is really going on, the Chianti Classico zone has recently been given its own separate DOCG (Denominazione di Origine Controllata e Garantita), allowing growers there to make Chianti wines from sangiovese, pure and simple. This means that fine wines such as Sangioveto from Badia a Coltibuono, Riecine's La Gioia, and Le Pergole Torte from Monte Vertine, classified as vini da tavola or table wines despite their outstanding quality, may now be marketed as DOCG Chianti Classico.

The roster of DOC and DOCG wines from Tuscany expands a little each year—Bolgheri, in the coastal Maremma district, is the most recent addition to the list, which also includes robust Morellino di Scansano from the high Maremma region east of Grosseto, elegant Carmignano from the banks of the Arno west of Florence, aristocratic Vino Nobile from Montepulciano, and Brunello from Montalcino, just to mention the reds for which Tuscany is justifiably famous.

But DOCG and DOC do not necessarily signify the best or most interesting wines. Many Tuscan wines, in fact some of the very best, fall outside the DOC or DOCG classifications and must, under law, be marketed as table wines. Some of these are what have come to be called "super-Tuscans," often made from international varietals like cabernet sauvignon, cabernet franc, pinot nero, and merlot, that were not part of Tuscany's traditional grape varieties—though they are fast becoming Tuscan traditions. An outstanding example of this is the peerless Sassicaia, made entirely from cabernet sauvignon grapes at the estate of the Marchese Incisa della Rochetta very near the seacoast in Bolgheri, and marketed as a table wine until the recent decision to create a DOC Sassicaia. Even with sangiovese, experimentation has led to newer, more interesting wines—Piermario Meletti Cavallari's Grattamacco Rosso, for instance, a blend of sangiovese and cabernet sauvignon, is a happy synthesis of the flowery softness of Tuscan sangiovese and the strength and acid balance of cabernet sauvignon. One way or another, Meletti Cavallari might have been speaking for all conscientious Tuscan wine-makers when he said recently: "Marrying the Tuscan tradition of sangiovese with the Burgundian formula of cabernet sauvignon and merlot, we have developed a new way of wine-making."

With the exception of Vernaccia di San Gimignano, a pale, straw-colored wine with flowery accents made from the vernaccia grape, Tuscany is not noted for white wines. Poorly made Vernaccia often tastes resinated, but at its best, as in the products of the San Gimignano winery Terruzi and Puthod, it can be quite remarkable.

---

* One of the largest Tuscan wineries is Castello Banfi, headquartered in Montalcino but with extensive holdings in Chianti and even in Piemonte. It is wholly owned by Americans, the Mariani brothers, John and Harry.

Excessive quantities of the undistinguished trebbiano grape have led producers in recent years to develop Galestro, a very light white wine, sometimes with a little spritz to it, that is popular as a summertime refresher. Other producers have experimented with sauvignon blanc and even chardonnay to produce white wines of varying character, varying, that is, between more or less Californian in style. The best of these, and it is exceptional, is Piermario Meletti Cavallari's Grattamacco Bianco, made from a blend of vermentino, trebbiano, and sauvignon blanc, a wine with fine acidity and a distinctive herbal fragrance, like a freshly mown meadow.

tuscan olive oil

I'm standing near the top of a long wooden ladder, one that's been used so many seasons and repaired with so much baling wire that it's no longer, shall we say, in optimum condition for getting up and down. I have one foot balanced on a slickly oiled rung of this ladder while the other is braced against the supple, yielding branch of an olive tree. My left hand grasps another branch and with my right, I reach out for an elusive cluster of ripening olives, darkly outlined against the brilliant blue of a November Tuscan sky. It is nearing the end of a perfect autumn day, my arms ache, my neck is stiff from constantly arching in search of yet more olives to strip from the branches in a gesture Tuscans liken to milking a cow. I am harvesting olives and I am supremely happy, even when a pepper of shot rattles the leathery leaves of the olive trees and I and my fellow harvesters bellow in concert at a rabbit hunter who has ventured too close to our work site, a terraced grove of trees that are bowed under the weight of ripening fruit.

The olive harvest, which begins early in November and lasts through the weeks leading up to Christmas, is, I think, the finest time to be in Tuscany. It's a merry time, even in alternating years when the harvest is less than what we'd like it to be, even when the sky is not blue and the sun is not there to heal tired bodies with its warmth. Too many afternoons are spent rapidly stripping the trees under leaden skies before threatening clouds spill their burden of rain. Too many times bruised fingers ache with the penetrating cold—my friend Deborah finds old kidskin opera gloves in thrift shops in Paris and New York, cuts off the ends of the fingers, and uses them as slim protection against the bitter cold. But even on cold, gray days, there's a joy to this, the last harvest of the year, and you sense it in the happy shouts and bits of song that echo from one grove to another as workers compare the harvest.

There's happiness in the *frantoio,* the olive mill, too, even when, as often happens, your olives are the ones that get scheduled for pressing at three o'clock in the morning. It's worth staying up all night just to smell and taste that first surge of rich, greeny gold unguent, *olio turbo* it's called, turbulent oil, as it issues from the press. Even in the most modern mill, there's a fire on a hearth in a corner of the room, usually tended by an old man who remembers when blindfolded horses drove the crusher round and round, turning the big granite wheel with infinite patience, and the press itself was operated by manpower, slowly cranking a wooden balance weight while the oil oozed and trickled down over esparto-grass mats.

Nowadays, in big modern cooperative mills that are rapidly replacing the old-fashioned frantoi, the oil is produced by stainless-steel, continuous-cycle machines, the olives tumbling in one end and, in a matter of minutes rather than hours, clean fresh oil coming out the other. But still the old man by the fire toasts slices of saltless Tuscan bread, rubs each slice with a cut clove of garlic, and dips it in a cruet of olio turbo for the ritual of the first tasting.

Modern mills may have robbed the process of much of its color and drama, but they also mean more and better oil for everyone. No longer must loads of olives back up at the mill, two, three, or many more days, waiting for their turn at the press and developing musty, rancid flavors while they wait. And no longer must conscientious growers risk the tainting of their hard-won harvest when a sloppy producer adds bad olives to the mix.

Tuscans produce some of the finest extra virgin olive oil in all the Mediterranean, the only oil-producing region in the world of any consequence. Some people, not just Tuscans, say Tuscan oil is without question the best and sets the standard to which all other oils should aspire. I'm so opposed philosophically to the idea of rating food and wine like this that I can't go along with this judgment. Besides, I've met too many producers of murky, musty, dark, and questionable oil in Tuscany and elsewhere to be quite so categorical.

Still, Tuscan oil is exceptionally good on the whole and getting better all the time. Part of this has to do with cleaner pressing and modern machinery, but much of it has to do with soil and climate, factors that determine quality in almost all foodstuffs. You might not believe this on an August afternoon in the middle of downtown Florence, but Tuscany is cool for an olive-producing region and the varieties grown—principally frantoio but also leccino, pendolino, moraiolo, and a few others—ripen slowly. Moreover, most Tuscan groves are too high for the dreaded olive fly, the *mosca olearia,* that wreaks havoc in regions closer to sea level.

The best oil, producers all over the Mediterranean agree, comes from under-ripe olives, still green or just starting to turn reddish black. Olives in this state must be harvested by hand—it's the only way to collect fruit that is not mature enough to fall from the tree—and rushed to the press within a maximum of forty-eight hours from harvest. The fruit, full of esters and polyphenols, produces the kind of oil for which Tuscany has become renowned, aromatic and full of intense green flavors, with a bitter finish and a peppery kick in the back of the throat as it goes down.

This is Tuscan extra virgin olive oil, and a note about grades of olive oil is in order here. Commercially available olive oil, no matter where it comes from, is almost always either extra virgin oil or pure oil, the latter sometimes marketed as just plain olive oil. These are grades developed by the International Olive Oil Council, a group headquartered in Madrid and made up of oil-producing countries. Extra virgin olive oil is oil produced by mechanical means, without resort to chemical refinements, that has "perfect" flavor and aroma and a free oleic acid content of less than 1 percent. (Free oleic acid content is the result of a laboratory test of rancidity and has nothing at all to do with relative acidity or sourness in oil. In fact, oil that's high in free oleic acid tastes sweet or soapy, rather than acidic.) Pure oil, or just plain olive oil, on the other hand, is oil that failed to make the extra virgin grade and has therefore been chemically refined to strip undesirable flavors and aromas, yielding a tasteless, colorless oil to which a small amount of extra virgin oil has been added to give it some flavor and character. It's an industrial product that is useful but not very exciting, unlike extra virgin oil. It's a little like comparing jug wines with carefully made estate-bottled wines.

I'm often asked which oil is my favorite, or what is the best Tuscan oil. It's a question I don't like to answer, for a variety of reasons, one being that many Tuscan oils are imported in small quantities and sold only in limited markets. Estate-bottled oils, too, are often sold at prices that exceed, ounce for ounce, the price of gold, a price that's justified by the extraordinary hand labor and care taken in hand-harvesting and quick-pressing. Cost alone determines that these are not for general all-purpose cooking, any more than traditional balsamic vinegar is something to toss on an everyday salad. Moreover, you can't always be certain that the oil has been properly handled en route to the purchase point—it may have been exposed to light or heat, or it may be an oil that's already two or three years old, still perfectly useful if it's been handled properly but no longer worth the price of fresh oil from the year's harvest. More and more of the best producers are dating their product, although this is not a legal requirement. Above all, if you buy an expensive oil and you find that it's rancid, return it immediately to the shop where you purchased it and make sure it gets tasted by the person in charge.

I often advise people who are going to Tuscany to do as I do and buy in a hardware store a ten-liter plastic container (or two five-liter ones) called a *bidone,* rinse it out and let it dry, then take it to a frantoio or a growers' cooperative where you know, from tasting it, that the oil is good. Fill it up and bring it back. It's a little awkward, and requires hand-carrying on a plane, but it's completely legitimate to bring through customs. Once you've got it home and have transferred the oil to glass bottles to be stored in a cool, dark pantry or cellar, you'll bless yourself (and perhaps me too) five or ten times over as you use that good Tuscan oil through the course of the next year.

Estate-bottled Oils

The following are a few of the many Tuscan estate-bottled oils. Those listed are generally, if not always widely, available in this country. Here in America, the best time to look for limited production oils like these is in the early spring, when the previous year's harvest starts to arrive on our shores. All these oils are first-class, but you may find many others, both in American specialty food shops and while traveling in Tuscany, that are not listed here.

BADIA A COLTIBUONO

CASTELLO DE AMA

GRAPPOLINI

IL POGGIONE

LE BONCIE

QUERCIABELLA

TENUTA SAN GUIDO

CAPEZZANA

CASTELLO VOLPAIA

GRATTAMACCO

LAUDEMIO

PODERE SAN GIUSEPPE

TENUTA DEL NUMERO UNO

when you go to tuscany

What's the best time to be in Tuscany, people always ask. That depends on what you're looking for. Winter in the countryside is a blissfully quiet time, peaceful and reflective. Vineyards and orchards lie mute, often beneath a light carpet of snow; the tourists have left, and the Tuscans themselves seem somehow more essentially Tuscan. But the days are very short, night falls by late afternoon, and it's hard to get out and do the things one ought to do, such as visit hill towns, museums, churches, and monuments. In springtime, on the other hand, the weather can be glorious but also freakish and changeable, veering from bitter to fresh with alarming unpredictability. In summer Tuscany is crowded with tourists, both Italians and foreigners, many of whom consider themselves honorary Tuscans because they own a little piece of Tuscan land, though it takes more than that to make a real Tuscan.

For me, then, autumn is the time when Tuscany is at its best, especially October into early November when most of the tourists and many of the foreigners have departed, but when the air is still warm and filled with the honey-dripping sweetness of sunshine and blue skies and the ripening fruits of summer's labor. Keats was writing of England not Tuscany, but "season of mists and mellow fruitfulness" never seems more apt a description than here in these fertile hills when the rich brown earth has been turned for next season's crops while the grace of the current harvest is still abundant.

The food of the Tuscan countryside is always at its best in autumn too, from the last of the tomatoes, ripe and heavy on the vine, to the first porcini mushrooms, with their plump, velvety crowns colored like vivid terra-cotta and their bosky fragrance penetrating markets where country folk bring them in baskets to sell. The bacchic intensity of the vendemmia in early October, when the purple grapes are picked, crushed, and pressed into wine, leads into the white truffle harvest in the Mugello and the Crete Senese (San Giovanni d'Asso, east of Siena near the magnificent monastery of Monte Oliveto Maggiore with its splendid frescoes by Luca Signorelli, has a famous white truffle festival in early November). Then comes the joy of the olive harvest, when country roads are blocked by tractors hauling loads of red, green, and purple olives to the frantoi, the olive mills. Every town of substance has a weekly market, overflowing with lush autumnal fruits and vegetables, wild game (hare, pheasants, and boar), fresh walnuts and almonds still milky in their shells, and the sheep's milk cheeses made from herbal spring and summer milk, which ripen to their finest, fullest flavor in the fall.

Tuscany is without doubt the region of Italy best known to Americans, but there are still many parts that are little known even to Italians. I think of the great hidden valleys such as the Casentino in the upper Arno north of Arezzo; the Mugello, birthplace of Giotto and Fra Angelico, northeast of Florence; and the twin valleys of the Lunigiana, north of the Ligurian coast, and the Garfagnana north of Lucca. These, like the splendid heights of the Alta Maremma above the southern coast and the adjacent region around Monte Amiata, Tuscany's highest peak, which stands in isolation like a pyramid marking the southern border, are places where time often seems to have stepped back a bit from the frenetic pace of cities such as Florence. They are places where housewives still bake bread each week and farmers make their own wine and cheese, where restaurants, humble trattorie often tucked behind the local bar, still serve the kind of hearty, country fare that I hope this book goes some way to describe—dishes like buglione in Chiusi and acquacotta in the Casentino and the villages on the slopes of Monte Amiata, testaroli with pesto in the Lunigiana, farro soups in the Garfagnana, potato-stuffed tortelli in the Mugello, cacciucco, rich with seafood, from the coast, and ribollita, that hearty soup by which Tuscans define themselves just about everywhere.

As well as dishes, there are also the food products of the Tuscan countryside to experience in their place of origin—olive oils from Chianti, from Cortona, from Lucca and the Alta Maremma, and elsewhere throughout the region; fresh chickens and little yellow zolfini beans from Montevarchi in the Valdarno; almond and hazelnut biscotti from Prato and spicy panforte and sweet ricciarelli from Siena; fresh ricotta and raviggiolo from the milk of flocks that graze across the Crete Senese; lardo, fat back of pork, cured in marble boxes called *conce* in Colonnata, perched high up in the Carrara marble quarries; the famous bread from Altopascio, crusty and unsalted; artichokes from Pisa and frutti di bosco, woodsy berries, from Pistoia.

The best way to experience all this is in a car, meandering down country lanes that aren't on any map, pausing to sample the offerings of local markets or to view the unattributed magnificence of an altarpiece in a tiny chapel, then stopping for lunch in a small village where the only eating place doubles as gas station, bottega for local needs, and bar where the gentlemen of the village gather on Sunday afternoons. In places like this you'll find it best to put yourself in the hands of the woman (it's almost always a woman) in charge and let her serve you from the pots she has simmering on the stove in the back. Start with some good prosciutto nostrale, the locally cured ham, or dry-cured sausages, go on to whatever pasta and secondo the signora proposes for the day, and finish with a crumbly Pecorino, a handful of figs and fresh walnuts, and a glass of vin santo. You can't ask for much better than that.

Far better than a hotel where you're too often at the mercy of internationally trained chefs, I've always thought the best way to absorb the sense of Tuscany is by renting a house—a villa, it's called, even when quite humble, though some of these rental places are extravagantly sited on aristocratic estates complete with swimming pools and daily maid service. The most important thing, however, for those of us who love food, is the kitchen. With a kitchen you'll be able to take advantage of all that provender that calls out to you, yearning to be yours, in local shops and markets. Nothing will introduce you to the delights of the Tuscan kitchen more than shopping in towns like Cortona, Montepulciano, Massa Maritima, Pontremoli, or Gaiole during the weekly market, then carrying your gastronomic treasures home to turn into stews, soups, salads, and grills. Rental agencies for Tuscan, and other, properties advertise widely in magazines like *The New Yorker* and in the travel sections of big city newspapers. Just be sure to ask for photographs and a physical description of the property with its appurtenances (exactly what kind of stove is in that kitchen? is there indeed a refrigerator?) before you sign on the dotted line or send money.

Restaurants

MANY TUSCAN restaurants are internationally famous, and with good reason. Others are barely known even to the writers of guidebooks. Here are a few where I've enjoyed the food, but this is by no means an exhaustive list. Do call ahead to be sure the restaurant is open when you want to go. And note that some of these places also have a few rooms, usually quite delightful, by the night or the week.

IN AREZZO PROVINCE:

ANGHIARI: *Castello dei Sorci,* tel. 0575/789-066. The walled town of Anghiari sits conveniently between Sansepolcro and Monterchi, two imperative stops for admirers of Piero della Francesca. Castello dei Sorci, outside the town, is a fine place for lunch, offering a copious set menu of rustic food for a fixed price each day. Very inexpensive and crowded on Sundays.

CASTELFRANCO DI SOPRA: *Vicolo del Contento,* loc. Mandri 38, tel. 055-914-9277; fax 914-9906. Mandri is a hamlet just outside Castelfranco, one of the main towns in the Pratomagno north of Arezzo. Angelo Redditi is the chef, and his wife, Lina, runs the comfortable dining room. The menu is a fine example of how country dishes can become elegant in the hands of a gifted cook. Unusually, fish is a specialty. A first-rate wine list completes the attractions. Expensive.

CHIUSI DELLA VERNA: *Corazzesi,* loc. Corezzo, tel. 0575-518-012. Corezzo is a wide place in the road near Chiusi della Verna (not to be confused with Etruscan Chiusi in the south of Tuscany), the monastery founded by St. Francis and where he received the stigmata. Corazzesi specializes in tortelli di patate, big ravioli-like pasta stuffed with potatoes and either fried or toasted on the grill. Inexpensive.

CORTONA: *Il Falconiere,* loc. San Martino, tel. 0575/612-616; fax 617-927. Located in the *limonaia,* the lemon-house, of a handsome seventeenth-century villa, Silvia and Riccardo Barrachi's Il Falconiere provides an elegant menu as well as delightful views of the massive Etruscan walls of Cortona, a hill town south of Arezzo. The cantina offers a good selection of Italian, French, and California wines; there are nine rooms and three suites in the adjacent villa. Moderate to expensive.

PONTE BURIANO: *Trattoria del Pescatore,* tel. 0575/364-096. A famous Roman bridge arches over the Arno, north of Arezzo at Ponte Buriano. The trattoria is one of those workingmen's places that people like me are always hoping to discover, with simple, honest, local cooking. The decor is a curious assemblage of electric heaters, coffeemakers, teapots, and radios, displayed with a carefree hand. Inexpensive.

PRATOVECCHIO: *I 4 Cantoni,* v. Dante Alighieri 31a, tel. 0575-58-26-96. In the heart of the Casentino, this humble truck stop serves fine hand-rolled pasta, ably turned out under the direction of Marta Goretti, who also makes a splendid, thick acquacotta casentinese, with lots of onions and country bread (see recipe, page 60). But call a day ahead to order it if you want to try the acquacotta. Inexpensive.

IN SIENA PROVINCE:

CASTELNUOVO BERARDENGA: *Da Antonio,* via Fiorita 38, tel. 0577/35-53-21. Curiously for Tuscany, where except on the coast, fish is not held in high esteem, this restaurant, in the heart of Castelnuovo at the southern tip of the Chianti hills, specializes in seafood and does an exemplary job. In fact, seafood is all that's served here, and Chef Antonio goes far and wide for the very best offerings, which he prepares simply and with great taste.

CHIUSI: *La Solita Zuppa,* via Porsenna, 21, tel. 0578-21-006. Chiusi is ancient Clusium, an Etruscan capital (whence Lars Porsenna summoned his array for the Etruscan attack on Rome). After a visit to the Museo Nazionale Etrusco and the local Etruscan tombs, a stop for lunch at La Solita Zuppa ("the usual soup") will introduce you to the cooking of southern Tuscany. Hearty soups are a specialty, but there are many other items on the menu, including pici, the hand-rolled pasta from the region, and buglione, a rich stew. Moderate.

GAIOLE: *Trattoria della Badia a Coltibuono,* tel. 0577/749-031. Badia a Coltibuono is a thirteenth-century abbey that is now home to the Stucchi Prinetti family whose best-known member is Lorenza de' Medici, noted Tuscan food authority (see the cooking schools that follow). The trattoria, on the grounds of the abbey, is a fine place to sample Tuscan country cuisine, though chef Maurizio Fenino is actually from Milano. Boned stuffed rabbit is one of many specialties. The exemplary wines, olive oil, honey, and other products of the estate are also sold here. Moderate.

MONTALCINO: *Trattoria Il Pozzo,* S. Angelo in Colle, tel. 0577/86-40-15. Montalcino is home to one of Italy's great wines, Brunello di Montalcino. At S. Angelo, a village in the midst of the vineyards, Laura Bindocci of Il Pozzo is a first-rate cook of regional fare, and her wine list includes many notable Brunellos as well as Vino Rosso di Montalcino, a lesser but nonetheless delicious local red. Moderate.

MONTALCINO: *Taverna dei Barbi,* Fattoria dei Barbi, loc. Podernone, tel. 0577/84-93-57. Fattoria dei Barbi is one of the important producers of Brunello di Montalcino and other fine wines. Taverna dei Barbi, on the winery estate, is a good place for simple, rustic food, including the cheeses and salumi (preserved pork products) made on the estate.

MONTALCINO: *Ristorante Poggio Antico,* tel. 0577/849-200. Roberto and Patrizia Minnetti, after many years at the helm of one of Rome's most interesting restaurants, moved up here a few years ago to bring Roberto's fine cooking closer to its country origins. The Minettis are rigorous in their devotion to local products, and the wine list includes Poggio Antico Brunello and many other fine wines from the region. Reservations recommended. Expensive.

MONTEFOLLONICO: *Fattoria La Chiusa,* tel. 0577/669-668. Dania Luccherini, chef and owner of this elegantly rustic restaurant in a handsomely vaulted old barn, was one of the first Tuscan chefs to adapt strictly local cooking to the disciplined exigencies of fine cuisine. The result is what many consider one of Tuscany's, if not

Italy's, finest restaurants. Warning: Lunch at La Chiusa can occupy most of an afternoon, but it will be time happily spent. The wine list is strong, with both Tuscan and international wines. La Chiusa also has beautifully restored rooms and suites, by the night or the week. Reservations recommended. Very expensive.

MONTEPULCIANO: *Ristorante Diva,* tel. 0578/716-951. Right on the main street leading up into this ancient city overlooking the Valdichiana, Ristorante Diva serves a traditional local cuisine to a devoted local clientele. It's always crowded at lunchtime but worth waiting for a table—the sense of being part of the local scene is almost as rewarding as the food itself. The wine list includes most of the great producers of Vino Nobile di Montepulciano, and you can buy wines, local sheep's milk cheeses, and other products in nearby shops. Moderate.

MONTEVARCHI: *Osteria di Rendola,* loc. Rendola, tel. 055-970-7491. In a restored stone barn on a small winery outside Montevarchi, Francesco Berardinelli brings an assured and gifted hand to traditional cuisine; his presentations, such as a richly filling zampe alla fiorentina, are as pleasurable to the eye as they are to the palate. There's a small but well thought out selection of wines, mostly from the region. Moderate.

MURLO: *La Befa,* loc. La Befa, tel. 0577/806-255. Call ahead for directions. This trattoria, located deep in the countryside on a *strada bianca,* a cart track, off the main road, is hard to find but worth the effort. La Befa is the epitome of a Tuscan country eating place, with a local bar and grocery shop in front. The cooking, prepared by various members of the Marchetti family, is robust and rigorously unrefined, with excellent pastas and grilled meats, especially game when it's in season. Inexpensive.

An excursion to La Befa might begin with a visit to the small but exquisite Etruscan museum in Murlo, of which La Befa is a hamlet. The museum's holdings all come from excavations at Poggio Civitate, a fascinating Etruscan site. Each year in early September, Murlo holds an open-air "Etruscan" banquet to benefit the museum in the main square of the little town.

SANTA FIORA: *Il Barilotto,* via Carolina 24; 0564/977-089. In the heart of Santa Fiora, a village perched on the slopes of Monte Amiata, Il Barilotto serves a rigorously local cuisine, including traditional acquacotta with a dollop of local sheep's milk ricotta, and ravioli 'gnudi or strozzapreti, soft, plump, airy dumplings of spinach and ricotta. Inexpensive.

IN FIRENZE PROVINCE:

ARTIMINO: *Ristorante da Delfina,* via della Chiesa 1, tel. 055/87-18-074. Carlo Cioni, chef and owner of this charming restaurant on a bluff overlooking the Arno below Florence, is an engaging authority on Tuscan country traditions. Cioni's grandmother Delfina, now in her nineties and apt to be shelling fava beans in a corner of the kitchen, is the honored source of much of his knowledge. It was she who founded the restaurant, with its surrounding vegetable gardens and handsome outdoor dining terrace, but her grandson is a worthy heir. Ribollita is a great specialty, as are many types of wild game grilled over wood embers. Reservations recommended. Moderate to expensive.

FIRENZE: *Cibrèo,* via dei Macci 118r, tel. 055/234-1100. With Fabbio Picchi in charge of the kitchen and his wife Benedetta overseeing the restaurant and making desserts, this small but elegant restaurant has achieved a well-deserved international reputation for strict adherence to Florentine traditions. No pasta is served, but you won't miss it when you taste the satiny richness of the chef's passato di peperoni gialli, a cream of yellow peppers that is as flavorful as a sunny garden. In the adjacent Bottega del Cibrèo, you can find a gamut of specialty food products, not just from Tuscany but from all over Italy. Reservations are a must. Moderate to expensive.

FIRENZE: *Trattoria La Baraonda,* via Ghibellina 67r, 055/234-1171. My personal favorite of perhaps half a dozen of these homey, rather old-fashioned Florentine trattorias where the food has all the honesty and direct simplicity that characterizes Tuscan cuisine. At the same time, the youthful owners of La Baraonda are not afraid of an occasional experiment with updated, modern ideas, and the results are delightful. Moderate.

VICCHIO DEL MUGELLO: *La Casa di Caccia,* loc. Roti Molezzano, tel. 055-840-7629. Telephone ahead for instructions or, better yet, persuade a local driver to lead you up to this wonderfully rustic hideaway on a hillside overlooking the Mugello. La Casa di Caccia is in the midst of a hunting reserve, and Mirella Settori is gifted at preparing the fruits of the chase. When she's not doing that, however, she turns out magnificent tortelli di patate, stuffed with potatoes and served with a rich meat ragù. Her panna cotta is an elegantly simple sweet to end the meal. (See recipes for tortelli, page 96, and panna cotta, page 241.) Reservations recommended. Moderate to expensive.

IN LIVORNO PROVINCE:

CECINA: *Trattoria Senese,* v. Diaz 34, 0586-68-0335. Cecina, bombed in World War II, is not much of a town architecturally speaking, though the Saturday market is vast and interesting and with a good fish section. The real reason to come to Cecina, however, is the Trattoria Senese, where Piero Falorno turns out one of the finest examples of cacciucco, the rich, tomato-y fish stew typical of the Tuscan coast, that I've ever tasted (see recipe, page 125). Call at least a day ahead to order. It's best to have at least four people, though the more the merrier, since more fish makes an even richer broth. Expensive—like all good fish restaurants.

CAMPORGIANO: *Mulin del Rancone,* 0583-61-86-70. On the banks of the Sérchio River, twelve kilometers from Castelnuovo Garfagnana, and incorporating parts of an old grist mill, Mulin del Rancone serves traditional cuisine of the Garfagnana—farro, dried mushrooms, river fish, chestnuts—and also has both an inn and a campground. Inexpensive.

LUCCA: *Buca di Sant'Antonio,* via della Cervia 1/3, 0583/55-881. In the heart of this delightful, rose-walled city, Buca di Sant'Antonio has been in existence for more than two hundred years. Often this indicates an eating establishment frequented only by tourists, where the waiters wear some version of local peasant costume. Here, at least in part because it is still a great local favorite, the cooking is genuine and delicious. Because of its popularity, reservations are a must, especially at lunch. Moderate to expensive.

LUCCA: *Locanda Buatino,* v. Borgo Giannotti 508, tel. 0583/343-207. Just outside the city walls, Locanda Buatino is an unprepossessing place with delicious food. It's very popular, and you'll see bankers and telephone linemen side by side scarfing up the offerings. Inexpensive.

LUCCA: *La Mora,* loc. Ponte a Moriano, tel. 0583/406-402. Just up the Sérchio River from Lucca, on the edge of the Garfagnana, La Mora is a stylish restaurant with a copious menu of regional specialties such as zuppa frantoiana, bean soup dressed with sweet local oil, and farro, the ancient strain of wheat that's still grown in the region. Service is elegant, and there's a first-rate wine list. Moderate to expensive.

IN THE PROVINCE OF MASSA CARRARA:

BAGNONE: da Lina, Piazza Marconi, 1, tel. 0187-42-90-69. The place to go for testaroli, the boiled pancakes that are a delicious regional specialty (see recipe, page 108).

CARRARA: Venanzio, Colonnata, tel. 0585/73617. Follow the narrow winding road up into the marble mountains that tower like alabaster cliffs above, carefully skirting huge trucks laden with blocks of pure white Carrara marble. At the end of the road is the marble-dusted village of Colonnata, renowned in Tuscany less for marble than for *lardo,* a type of pork back fat that's cured in marble boxes called *concie.* As an antipasta, you'll be served thin slices of lightly seasoned, faintly herbal lardo atop crisply toasted country bread so hot the lardo melts slightly and oozes over the surface. It's a unique and extraordinary experience, one no food lover should miss. Nor should you miss the *pecorino al fosso,* sheep's milk cheese that's been aged underground, served at the end of the meal. There are other good things on the menu here too, but it's for the lardo and Pecorino that one makes the pilgrimage to this strange and wonderful spot. Moderate.

In Prato province:

Quarrata: *Albergo La Bussola, Ristorante da Gino,* loc. Catena, tel. 0573-743-128. Though the official name is Da Gino, everyone calls this place La Bussola. The pasta is first rate and the grilled meats are excellent too. Moderate to expensive.

Cooking Schools

ANOTHER FINE way to experience a certain Tuscan style and get a good introduction to Tuscan foods and ways of cooking them is through one of the many cooking programs that proliferate in the region. Most offer week-long programs in spring and fall only. You'll find advertisements for cooking schools in many American cooking magazines. Varied programs may combine classes with visits to restaurants, wineries, food producers, and sites of artistic and historic interest. Four that are highly reputed are:

AVIGNONESI WINE AND FOOD WORKSHOPS. Sponsored by the Avignonesi winery, the week-long programs are held at Le Capezzine, the Avignonesi estate just below Montepulciano, while accommodations are in nearby Lucignano d'Asso, a restored village between Siena and Montepulciano. U.S. contact: Pamela Sheldon Johns, 1324 State Street, #J-157, Santa Barbara, CA 93101; tel. 805-963-7289; fax 805-963-0230; e-mail: CulinarArt@aol.com.

BADIA A COLTIBUONO, THE VILLA TABLE. Classes, under the direction of Lorenza de' Medici and her daughter Emanuela Stucchi, are held in a magnificent thirteenth-century Benedictine abbey in Gaiole, in the heart of the Chianti Classico region. Students are housed in monastic cells, splendidly appointed with modern conveniences. U.S. contact: Judith Ebrey, Dallas, TX; tel. 214-373-1161; fax 214-373-1162.

CAPEZZANA WINES CULINARY CENTER. Under the direction of Faith Willinger, classes are held and students are housed at the comfortable Capezzana winery estate, owned by the Contini-Bonacossi family in Carmignano just outside Florence. Telephone number at the winery is 011-39-55-870-6005; fax 870-6673. U.S. contact: Marlene Levinson, 55 Raycliff Terrace, San Francisco, CA 94115; tel. 415-928-7711; fax 415-928-7789.

COOKING IN FLORENCE. Under the direction of cookbook writer Giuliano Bugialli, the school is located in the Chianti Classico district, to which students are bused daily from a comfortable hotel in Florence. Mr. Bugialli also leads instructional trips to other parts of Italy. U.S. contact: P. O. Box 1650, Canal Street Station, New York, NY 10013; tel: 212-966-5325; fax 212-266-0601.

What to Bring Home

MANY FOOD products are legal to bring back to the United States, including anything that is sealed in a can (though I can't imagine anyone bringing home canned vegetables from Tuscany!). If you have any questions about any food product, be sure to declare it when you enter the United States; otherwise, you may be subject to a heavy fine for attempting to smuggle in prohibited goods. If you declare a food product that is not acceptable, you will lose the product but you will not be fined.

Don't, however, try to bring in prosciutto or any other type of meat product, even when it has been Cryovac-sealed. Italian prosciutto is sold legally in the United States, it's true, but only when the meat comes from slaughterhouses inspected by the U.S. Department of Agriculture. Since most Tuscans couldn't give a hoot about the USDA, the cured meat you buy there will have been slaughtered without benefit of American supervision. It's perfectly safe to consume, of course—the prohibitions are to protect U.S. herds, not U.S. consumers.

Even if you can't take meat home with you, it's worth paying a visit to a Tuscan butcher just to witness the quality and quantity of fresh and cured products that are available. Most towns of any size have two or three excellent butchers, but my personal favorite is Dario Cecchini in the town of Panzano, south of Greve (see pages 172–173). You'll recognize the shop by the strains of Mozart, Vivaldi, or Duke Ellington wafting out the door. Cecchini cures his own prosciutti and sausages; his lamb comes from his own flocks; and his Chianina beef is simply extraordinary. If you have access to a kitchen, or at least an outdoor grill, by all means buy bistecca chianina, a cut similar to T-bone or porterhouse, and try it for yourself.

Fresh mushrooms, like all fresh fruits and vegetables, are prohibited, but dried and packaged mushrooms are allowed and are far finer in quality than most of what's available in the United States. In fact, small packets of dried porcini mushrooms, available in markets and food shops, make excellent, lightweight gifts to bring back for food-lover friends. Dried beans (borlotti, cannellini, zolfini, and others) and farro, the emmer wheat that's still grown in the Garfagnana and elsewhere, are also fine take-aways. At Antica Bottega di Prospero, via Santa Lucia 13, in the heart of Lucca, you'll find a first-rate variety of beans, as well as farro, cornmeal in various mill sizes, and other dried grains and legumes. A more limited selection of similar products can be found in the weekly markets in most country towns.

Aged cheeses are also legal to bring home, although very young fresh cheeses are prohibited. I never come back to America without as many wheels of aged Pecorino as I can comfortably carry, since fine, aged Tuscan Pecorino is inexplicably hard to find in the United States. Every market has several cheese vendors, but Pienza, a handsome little hill town between Siena and Montepulciano, is a great place to shop for a variety of Pecorino cheeses, many of which are produced in the surrounding territory. Pienza's main street, leading up to the stunning small cathedral erected for Pope Pius II, Pienza's founder, is lined with small shops selling cheeses and other local food products.

Wine is legal to bring in, although there is an import quota, which simply means that you'll pay a small duty on any excess over the quota. For extraordinary wines of unattainable vintages, it's sometimes worth the effort—although the best way to enjoy the many varieties of Tuscan wine is right here on their home ground where the prices will astound you even while you listen to Tuscans complain about how steep they are.

To sample Tuscan wines, there are a number of *enoteche,* as wine shops are called. Often the wines will be strictly local, that is, produced only in the little miniregion surrounding the shop itself but there are a number of enoteche in wine centers like Gaiole, Greve, Montalcino, and Montepulciano that offer greater variety. The most important of these is the Enoteca Italiana, prominently located in the Medici fortress in Siena. To describe the Enoteca Italiana, I can only quote my friend Fred Plotkin, who says in his book *Italy for the Gourmet Traveler* (Little, Brown, 1996): "To call the Enoteca Italiana a place to taste wine is like calling the Vatican a place to pray." Prayerful or not, this national wine center is the site each June of a Settimana dei Vini, or wine week, at which the new DOC and DOCG wines are presented. A selection of wines from all over Italy is available for daily tastings, and the Enoteca is also a first-rate resource for information about wineries that welcome visits—not just in Tuscany but all over this great wine-producing country.

Perhaps the best food product to bring back from Tuscany is fine extra virgin olive oil, especially in late autumn when the oil is being pressed and you can buy it directly from a frantoio. I buy five- or ten-liter plastic jugs called bidone from a hardware store, rinse them out, then take them to a frantoio to be filled on the spot. Once home, I transfer the oil to rinsed-out glass wine bottles for storage. You can also purchase oil in glass bottles directly from the many wine estates that also produce olive oil, or in many shops and markets. Olive oil is awkward and it must be hand-carried (believe me, I speak from bitter experience; you'll regret it if you try to pack oil in your suitcase). Because the oil is heavy, make sure that what you buy is unusual enough and high enough in quality to offset the difficulty of transporting it.

Most towns of any size have a weekly market that is almost always a thrilling spectacle of foods, agricultural and household goods, clothing, linens, and hardware. My favorites are the Thursday market in Camucia, south of Arezzo, and the smaller Saturday market in Cortona, on the hill above Camucia. In Florence, don't miss the daily (except Sundays) San Lorenzo market or Mercato Centrale, one of the few covered markets in Tuscany, in a handsome late-nineteenth-century building with purveyors on many floors, and the open-air Sant'Ambrogio market near the Piazza Santa Croce.

There's one infallible way to find a market: When you see flocks of women coming toward you bearing plastic bags laden with produce, head in the direction from which they are coming. You'll almost always find a market.

ACKNOWLEDGMENTS

IT'S OBVIOUS to the most casual reader that this book could not possibly have been written without the help, guidance, and friendship over the years of many past and present members of the Antolini family, including Agostino, Diamante, and Clorinda, may they rest in peace, as well as Bruno, Beppa, Arnaldo, Maura, and baby Pamela—and of course Mita, always a dear friend.

I'd also like to thank others, Cortonesi and Tuscans, both native-born and naturalized, who have helped to steer me in the right directions: Nancy and Gaia Anderson, Martin Attwood, Emilio and Maria Banchelli, Rolando Beramendi, Maurizio Castelli, Dario Cecchini, Fabrizia Fabbroni, Marta Goretti, Pier Francesco Gregi, Andrea Grifoni, Diana Magi, Lorenza de' Medici and Emanuela Stucchi, Piermario and Paula Meletti Cavallari, Anna Mignani and Mario Rocchi, Mirella Settori, Maria Luisa Valeri, and Faith Willinger. Thanks for their generosity to other members of La Banda along with Faith—Carol, Corby, Fred, and Ed—and to my great helpers in the kitchen, Nelda McClellan, Frances Holdgate, and my daughter Sara. And a very special *grazie* to my Italian grammar and spelling coach, Anna Teresa Callen.

BIBLIOGRAPHY

BOOKS IN ENGLISH

Anderson, Burton, *Vino: The Wines and Winemakers of Italy,* Boston: Little, Brown, 1980. Nearly twenty years old, this is still one of the best books about Italian wines and wine-making, with lots of information about Tuscany and Tuscan wines. Much of the information may be dated, but the spirit of the book is as up-to-date as when it was first written.

————, *Pleasures of the Italian Table,* New York: Morrow, 1994. A discussion of the many disappearing treasures of Italian food, from cheeses to oils to wines to bread. Much of the discussion focuses on Tuscany, where Anderson has lived for the past twenty-five years.

Bianchi, Anne, *From the Tables of Tuscan Women,* New York: Ecco Press, 1995. This book really should be called "from the tables of Lucchese women," since it is very much focused on the region around Lucca, where the author lives. Part cookbook and part oral history, it gives an astute portrait of Lucchese women's lives as described in the food they cook and share.

Falassi, Alessandro, *Folklore by the Fireside: Text and Context of the Tuscan Veglia,* Austin: Univ. of Texas Press, 1980. A Tuscan anthropologist looks at Tuscan country customs through the veil of the *veglia,* the winter evening spent around the fire telling tales and making music.

Field, Carol, *In Nonna's Kitchen,* New York: HarperCollins, 1997. With its descriptions of the cooking of Italian grandmothers, the book ranges widely throughout Italy but many of these *nonne* are Tuscan, and their words of wisdom, along with their recipes, are well worth attending to.

Machlin, Edda Servi, *The Classic Cuisine of the Italian Jews,* New York: Dodd, Mead, 1981. The author was raised in the Jewish community of tiny Pitigliano in the south of Tuscany; she describes a cuisine and a way of life that, while observing Jewish dietary laws, is nonetheless Tuscan to the core.

Pezzini, Wilma, *The Tuscan Cookbook,* New York: Atheneum, 1978. One of the first, and still one of the best, collections of Tuscan recipes in English, with a focus on the cooking of the coastal regions north of Lucca and Pisa, where the author lived.

Romer, Elizabeth, *The Tuscan Year,* New York: Atheneum, 1985. A month-by-month description, with recipes, of the life and food of a Tuscan farming family in a remote valley on the eastern border with Umbria.

Books in Italian

Artusi, Pellegrino, *La Scienza in cucina e l'Arte di mangiar bene,* introd. and note of Piero Camporesi, Torino: Einaudi Tascabili, 1995.

Bezzini, Luciano, *Castagneto a tavola,* Pontedera: Bandecchi & Vivaldi Ed., 1994.

Codacci, Leo, *Civiltà della tavola contadina in Toscana,* Milano: Idealibri, 1990.

Colutta, Flavio, *Cucina e vini della Toscana,* Milano: Mursia Ed., 1974.

Fabbroni, Fabrizia, *Mangiare sotto la pergola,* Arezzo: Gente d'Arte Ed., 1991.

———, *Volti della terra in Casentino,* photographs by Gianni Ronconi, Firenze: Arnaud Ed., 1993.

Greci, Pier Francesco, *Cucina rustica nell'Aretino,* Arezzo: Gente d'Arte Ed., 1992.

Marchese, Salvatore, *La Cucina di Lunigiana,* Padova: Franco Muzzio Ed., 1989.

Da Monte, Mario, *A Tavola in Casentino,* Stia (AR): Ed. Fruska, 1995.

Noferi, Marco, *Pane e companatico,* Montevarchi (AR): Ed. Cartaverde, 1996.

Norcini, Franca Loretta, *Il Vello d'oro* (about cooking and folk traditions of the Casentino), Cortona: Ed. Grafiche Calosci, 1996.

Petroni, Paolo, *Il Libro della vera cucina fiorentina,* Firenze: Casa Ed. Bonechi, 1974.

Righi Parenti, Giovanni, *Dolci di Siena e della Toscana,* Padova: Franco Muzzio Ed., 1991.

———, *La Cucina toscana,* Roma: Newton Compton Ed., 1995.

Roghi, Bianca, and Maria Luisa Valeri, *Pane olio e sale: Uno sguardo al passato della Valdichiana,* Montepulciano: Ed. del Grifo, 1988.

Santini, Aldo, *La Cucina maremmana,* Padova: Franco Muzzio Ed., 1991.

Venturelli, Gastone, *Leggende e racconti popolari della Toscana,* Roma: Newton Compton Ed., 1983.

Source Guide

Many fine Tuscan and Tuscan-style ingredients are available from Italian and other specialty food shops in the United States. Among those that will ship orders to other parts of the country are:

Balducci's, 42–46 12th Street, Long Island City, NY 11101; tel. 718-786-9690, 800-225-3833; shop located at 424 Avenue of the Americas (Greenwich Village), New York, NY 10011.

King Arthur flours are available in markets in the Northeast or by mail order from The Baker's Catalogue, P. O. Box 876, Norwich, VT 05055-0876; tel. 1-800-827-6836.

The Mozzarella Company will ship goat's milk ricotta, as well as mozzarella and other Italian-style cheeses; 2944 Elm Street, Dallas, TX 75226; tel. 800-798-2954.

Todaro Brothers, 557 Second Avenue, New York, NY 10016; tel. 212-679-7766.

Vivande, 2125 Fillmore Street, San Francisco, CA 94115; tel. 415-346-4430.

Zingerman's Delicatessen, 422 Detroit Street, Ann Arbor, MI 48104-3400; tel. 313-663-3400.

INDEX